Agricultural Prices and Production in Post-reform India

Agricultural Prices and Production in Post-reform India

ASHUTOSH KUMAR TRIPATHI

Routledge
Taylor & Francis Group

LONDON AND NEW YORK

First published 2014
by Routledge

2 Park Square, Milton Park, Abingdon, Oxfordshire OX14 4RN
52 Vanderbilt Avenue, New York, NY 10017

Routledge is an imprint of the Taylor & Francis Group, an informa business

First issued in paperback 2019

Typeset by
Solution Graphics
A–14, Indira Puri, Loni Road
Ghaziabad, Uttar Pradesh 201 102

British Library Cataloguing-in-Publication Data
A catalogue record of this book is available from the British Library

ISBN: 978-1-138-02019-1 (hbk)
ISBN: 978-0-367-17676-1 (pbk)

To my daughter Aadya

Contents

List of Tables   viii
List of Figures   xii
Abbreviations   xviii
Foreword by C. P. Chandrasekhar   xx
Acknowledgements   xxiii

1. Introduction   1

2. Indian Agriculture under Economic Reforms:
   A Preliminary Review   21

3. Agricultural Price Policy and Farm Profitability:
   Examining Linkages   56

4. International Price Trends and Volatility   100

5. Agricultural Trade: Policies and Patterns   140

6. Trade Competitiveness of Indian Agriculture:
   A Comparison of Domestic and World Prices   177

7. Decomposing Variability in Agricultural Prices   208

8. Evaluation and Conclusion   224

   Appendix I: Methodology for Measuring Price Volatility   233
   Appendix II: The Decomposition Model   236
   Appendix III: Tables   239
   Appendix IV: Figures   287

Bibliography   294
About the Author   303
Index   304

List of Tables

2.1 Level and growth of value of output of crops:
TE 1980–81 to TE 2005–06 (at 1999–2000 prices)   26
2.2 Level and growth of crops yield: TE 1980–81 to
TE 2005–06 (at 1999–2000 prices)   28
2.3 Change in area of various crops: All India
(TE 1989–90 over TE 1980–81)   31
2.4 Change in area of various crops: All India
(TE 1996–97 over TE 1990–91)   33
2.5 Change in area of various crops: All India
(TE 2005–06 over TE 1997–98)   34
2.6 Estimates of effect of different factors on output
of agriculture: 1980–81 to 2005–06   39
2.7 Index of TOT between agriculture and non-agriculture
sector   40
2.8 The expansion of irrigation (irrigated area)   48
2.9 The growth in area under irrigation   48
2.10 Relative share of borrowing of cultivator households
from different sources   49
2.11 Institutional credit to agriculture   51

3.1 Minimum support/procurement price for wheat and
paddy (in terms of rice equivalent): 1981–82 to 2006–07   65
3.2 Common variety MSP in terms of rice equivalent and
state levy prices in select states: 1981–82 to 2005–06   69
3.3 Trend in different components of cost in production
of rice and wheat at the all-India level: 1981–82 to
2006–07   72
3.4 Average cost of production of different states and
all India for wheat and rice: 1981–82 to 2006–07   74
3.5 Price realised relative to MSP in wheat and rice
in different states   75
3.6 Determinants of procurement prices in case of paddy
and wheat: 1982–2006   81
3.7 Production and procurement of rice and wheat
by public agencies: 1981–82 to 2006–07   83

3.8   Percentage share of different states in total rice and
      wheat procurement   86
3.9   Market arrivals of rice and wheat as percentage
      of production in select states   87
3.10 Wheat procurement equations   89
3.11 Paddy procurement equations   91
3.12 Cost and returns in wheat per hectare: All India
      1981–82 to 2006–07   93
3.13 Cost and returns in paddy per hectare: All India
      1981–82 to 2006–07   96

4.1   Inter-year variability in annual prices   115
4.2   Intra-year variability in annual prices   116
4.3   Estimates of price volatility for wheat markets   122
4.4   Estimates of price volatility for rice markets   125
4.5   Estimates of price volatility for groundnut seed/
      oil markets   126
4.6   Estimates of price volatility for rapeseed/oil markets   130
4.7   Estimates of price volatility for soybean seed/
      oil markets   134
4.8   Estimates of price volatility for sugar markets   136

5.1   Wheat export quantities and amount of subsidy
      provided by the FCI: 2000–01 to 2004–05   145
5.2   Rice quantities exported and subsidy provided
      by the FCI: 2000–01 to 2004–05   147
5.3   Summary of import policy for edible oil: 1994–2007   150
5.4   Indian sugar tariffs and QRs status: 1991–2008   154
5.5   Agricultural trade and its share in GDP agriculture
      and total trade   156
5.6   India's export of select agricultural commodities:
      1991–2006   158
5.7   India's import of select agricultural commodities:
      1991–2006   159

7.1   Decomposing change in Indian wheat price, 2001–2004   213
7.2   Decomposing change in Indian rice price, 2001–2003   216
7.3   Decomposition result for changes in Indian edible
      oil prices   219
7.4   Decomposition result for changes in Indian sugar
      price, 1998–2000   222

APPENDIX

A-2.1   GDP of agriculture and allied sector and its
         percentage share in total GDP: 1980–81 to 2005–06   239
A-2.2   Index of TOT between agriculture and non-agriculture
         sector: 1982–83 to 2005–06   240

A-3.1   Levy rates for procurement of rice in India   242

A-5.1   Total supply and use of wheat in India: 1984–85 to
         2007–08   243
A-5.2   India and world rice trade: 1982–83 to 2006–07   245
A-5.3   Total supply and use of rice in India: 1992–93 to
         2007–08   247
A-5.4   Availability of edible oil for human consumption:
         1971–72 to 2004–05   248
A-5.5   Production, consumption and trade of sugar in India:
         1982–2006   249

A-6.1   Comparison of world reference price and domestic
         prices for wheat under importable hypothesis:
         1981–2005   251
A-6.2   Comparison of world reference price and domestic
         prices for wheat under exportable hypothesis:
         1981–2005   256
A-6.3   Comparison of world reference price and domestic
         prices for rice under exportable hypothesis:
         1981–2005   258
A-6.4   Comparison of world reference price and domestic
         price for groundnut under importable hypothesis:
         1981–2004   262
A-6.5   Comparison of world reference price and domestic
         price for groundnut oil under importable hypothesis:
         1981–2005   267
A-6.6   Comparison of world reference price and domestic
         price for rapeseed/mustard seed under importable
         hypothesis: 1981–2005   269
A-6.7   Comparison of world reference price and domestic
         price for rapeseed/mustard oil under importable
         hypothesis: 1981–2005   271

A-6.8 Comparison of world reference price and domestic price for soybean seed under importable hypothesis: 1981–2005   273

A-6.9 Comparison of world reference price and domestic price for soybean oil under importable hypothesis: 1981–2005   275

A-6.10 Comparison of world reference price and domestic price for sugar under importable hypothesis: 1981–2005   277

A-6.11 Comparison of world reference price and domestic price for sugar under exportable hypothesis: 1981–2005   282

List of Figures

2.1 Growth rate in GDP agriculture and allied sector
before and after reform at 1999–2000 prices   24
2.2 Movement of gross terms of trade and input–output
price ratio: 1981–82 to 2005–06   43
2.3 Gross capital formation in agriculture at 1999–2000
prices: 1980–81 to 2005–06   45
2.4 Percentage share in agricultural GDP of gross capital
formation in agriculture at 1999–2000 prices: 1980–81
to 2005–06   47
2.5 Consumption of total fertilisers and in terms of
per hectare gross cropped area   53

3.1 Rice common variety — Official milling margin as
percentage of state levy price in select states: 1980–81
to 2005–06   70
3.2 Trend in price realised by wheat and rice farmers:
1981–82 to 2006–07   74
3.3 Ratio of price realised to MSPs: 1981–82 to 2006–07   75
3.4 Price realised and cost of production in case of rice:
1981–82 to 2005–06   76
3.5 Price realised and cost of production in case of wheat:
1981–82 to 2006–07   77
3.6 Indices of costs and prices in case of rice: 1981–82 to
2006–07 (base 1981–82 = 100)   78
3.7 Indices of costs and prices in case of wheat: 1981–82 to
2006–07 (base 1981–82 = 100)   78
3.8 Paddy prices and production cost: 1981–82 to 2006–07   80
3.9 Wheat prices and production cost: 1981–82 to 2006–07   80
3.10 Percentage share of government agencies in marketed
surplus of wheat and rice: 1981–82 to 1999–2000   85

4.1 Trend in nominal world price for wheat: 1981–82 to
2004–05   104
4.2 Trend in nominal world price for rice: 1980–81 to
2005–06   106

4.3 Trend in nominal world price for groundnut (shelled),
CIF Europe: 1980–81 to 2003–04   107

4.4 Trend in nominal world price for rapeseed,
CIF Europe: 1980–81 to 2004–05   108

4.5 Trend in nominal world price for soybean, CIF
Rotterdam: 1980–81 to 2004–05   108

4.6 Trend in nominal world price for groundnut oil, CIF
Rotterdam: 1980–81 to 2004–05   108

4.7 Trend in nominal world price for rapeseed oil,
FoB ex-mill, Dutch: 1980–81 to 2004–05   109

4.8 Trend in nominal world price for soybean oil,
FoB ex-mill, Dutch: 1980–81 to 2004–05   109

4.9 Trend in nominal world price for raw sugar:
1980–81 to 2005–06   111

4.10 Medians of the conditional standard deviation in
wheat market prices: 1982–83 to 2004–05   123

4.11 Medians of the conditional standard deviation
in groundnut seed market prices: 1980–81 to 2002–03   128

4.12 Medians of the conditional standard deviation
in groundnut oil market prices: 1980–81 to 2002–03   129

4.13 Medians of the conditional standard deviation in rape/
mustard seed market prices: 1980–81 to 2004–05   132

4.14 Medians of the conditional standard deviation in
rapeseed/mustard oil market prices: 1980–81 to
2004–05   133

4.15 Medians of the conditional standard deviation in
international market prices of soybean seed and oil:
1991–92 to 2004–05   135

4.16 Medians of the conditional standard deviation in
international and domestic market prices of sugar:
1981–82 to 2005–06   137

5.1 India's import tariff on crude oil: 1991–2005   149

5.2 India's import tariff on refined oil: 1991–2005   149

5.3 India's export and import volume of wheat: 1980–81
to 2007–08   162

5.4 India's wheat export volume and percentage share in
the world's total export of wheat: 1980–81 to 2007–08   163

5.5 India's rice export volume and its share in the world's
total rice export: 1980–81 to 2006–07   164

5.6 India's total rice export and share of Basmati rice
in total rice export: 1980–81 to 2006–07   166
5.7 India's rice import volume and its share in the world's
total rice import: 1980–81 to 2006–07   166
5.8 Production, consumption and imports of edible oil
in India   167
5.9 Composition of India's vegetable oil imports:
1979–2006   168
5.10 India's export of oilseed cake meal and its percentage
share in the world's total export of oil meal: 1979–2006   169
5.11 Composition of India's oilseed cake meal exports:
1979–2006   169
5.12 India's export volume of oilseeds and its percentage
share in the world's total export of oilseeds: 1979–2006   171
5.13 Composition of India's oilseed exports: 1979–2006   171
5.14 India's import volume of raw and refined sugar:
1980–2006   172
5.15 India's export volume of raw and refined sugar and
its share in the world's total sugar export: 1980–2006   173

6.1 Domestic and world reference price for wheat under
importable hypothesis: 1981–2005   181
6.2 Trend in ratio of domestic price to world reference
price for wheat under importable scenario: 1981–2005   182
6.3 Domestic and world reference price for wheat under
exportable hypothesis: 1981–2005   183
6.4 Domestic and world reference price for rice under
exportable hypothesis: 1981–2005   184
6.5 Trend in ratio of domestic price to world reference
price for rice under exportable scenario: 1981–2005   184
6.6 Domestic and world reference price for groundnut
under importable hypothesis: 1981–2004   185
6.7 Trend in ratio of domestic to world reference price for
groundnut under Importable scenario: 1981–2004   186
6.8 Domestic and world reference price for groundnut oil
under importable hypothesis: 1981–2005   187
6.9 Trend in ratio of domestic to world reference price for
groundnut oil under importable scenario: 1981–2005   187
6.10 Domestic and world reference price for rapeseed/
mustard under importable hypothesis: 1980–2005   188

6.11 Trend in ratio of domestic to world reference price
for rapeseed under importable scenario: 1981–2005   189
6.12 Domestic and world reference price for rapeseed oil
under importable hypothesis: 1981–2005   190
6.13 Trend in ratio of domestic to world reference price for
rapeseed oil under importable scenario   190
6.14 Domestic and world reference price for soybean under
importable hypothesis: 1981–2005   191
6.15 Trend in ratio of domestic to world reference price for
soybean under importable scenario   191
6.16 Domestic and world reference price for soybean oil
under importable hypothesis: 1981–2005   192
6.17 Trend in ratio of domestic to world reference price for
soybean oil under importable scenario   193
6.18 Ratio of domestic to international price of groundnut
seed and oil   193
6.19 Ratio of domestic to international price of rapeseed/
mustard seed and oil   194
6.20 Ratio of domestic to international price of soybean
seed and oil   194
6.21 Domestic and world reference price for plantation
white sugar under importable hypothesis: 1981–2005   195
6.22 Trend in ratio of domestic to world reference price for
plantation white sugar under importable scenario:
1981–2005   196
6.23 Domestic and world reference price for plantation
white sugar under exportable hypothesis: 1981–2005   197
6.24 Trend in ratio of domestic to world reference price
for plantation white sugar under exportable scenario:
1981–2005   197
6.25 Divergence between domestic and world reference
price for wheat under exportable hypothesis: 1981–2005   199
6.26 A comparison between price wedge and wheat export
subsidy rate: 1991–2005   200
6.27 Divergence between domestic and world reference
price for rice under exportable hypothesis: 1981–2005   201
6.28 A comparison between price wedge and rice export
subsidy rate: 1991–2005   201
6.29 Divergence between domestic and world reference
price for groundnut oil under importable hypothesis:
1981–2005   202

6.30 Divergence between domestic and world reference
      price for rapeseed/mustard oil under importable
      hypothesis: 1981–2005   202
6.31 Divergence between domestic and world reference
      price for soybean oil under importable hypothesis:
      1992–2005   203
6.32 A comparison between price wedge and applied tariff
      rate for groundnut oil: 1991–2005   203
6.33 A comparison between price wedge and applied tariff
      rate for rapeseed/mustard oil: 1992–2005   204
6.34 A comparison between price wedge and applied tariff
      rate for soybean oil: 1992–2005   204
6.35 Divergence between domestic and world reference
      price for Indian plantation white sugar under
      importable hypothesis: 1981–2005   205
6.36 A comparison between price wedge and applied tariff
      rate for Indian plantation white sugar: 1992–2005   205

Appendix

A-1   Flowchart of methodology to compute conditional
          volatility   233

A-4.1(a) Conditional standard deviation of wheat market
          price at Karnal market   287
A-4.1(b) Conditional standard deviation of wheat market
          price at Ludhiana market   287
A-4.2(a) Conditional standard deviation of groundnut seed
          market price at Madras market   288
A-4.2(b) Conditional standard deviation of groundnut seed
          market price at Nandyal market   288
A-4.2(c) Conditional standard deviation of groundnut seed
          market price at Rotterdam market   288
A-4.3(a) Conditional standard deviation of groundnut oil
          market price at Madras market   289
A-4.3(b) Conditional standard deviation of groundnut oil
          market price at Hyderabad market   289
A-4.3(c) Conditional standard deviation of groundnut oil
          market price at Rotterdam market   289
A-4.4(a) Conditional standard deviation of rapeseed/
          mustard seed market price at Calcutta market   290

A-4.4(b) Conditional standard deviation of rapeseed/
mustard seed market price at Hapur market   290
A-4.4(c) Conditional standard deviation of rapeseed/
mustard seed market price at Kanpur market   290
A-4.5(a) Conditional standard deviation of rapeseed/
mustard oil market price at Calcutta market   291
A-4.5(b) Conditional standard deviation of rapeseed/
mustard oil market price at Delhi market   291
A-4.5(c) Conditional standard deviation of rapeseed/
mustard oil market price at Dutch market   291
A-4.6(a) Conditional standard deviation of soybean seed
market price at Rotterdam   292
A-4.6(b) Conditional standard deviation of soybean oil
market price at the Netherlands   292
A-4.7(a) Conditional standard deviation of sugar market
price at Bombay market   292
A-4.7(b) Conditional standard deviation of sugar market
price at Kanpur market   293
A-4.7(c) Conditional standard deviation of sugar market
price at Caribbean port (raw sugar)   293

Abbreviations

AoA	Agreement on Agriculture
APC	Agricultural Prices Commission
APEDA	Agricultural and Processed Food Products Export Development Authority
BoP	balance of payments
CACP	Commission for Agricultural Costs and Prices
CIF	Cost, Insurance and Freight
CoC	cost of cultivation
CoP	cost of production
CPO	crude palm oil
CSO	Central Statistical Organisation
CVD	countervailing duty
DAP	Di-Ammonium Phosphate
DGCI&S	Directorate General of Commercial Intelligence and Statistics
DGFT	Directorate General of Foreign Trade
DSB	Dispute Settlement Body
ECA	Essential Commodities Act
ERS	Economic Research Service
FAO	Food and Agriculture Organization (of the United Nations)
FCI	Food Corporation of India
FoB	Free on Board
GARCH	Generalised Autoregressive Conditional Heteroscedasticity
GCA	gross cultivated area
GDP	gross domestic product
GEAC	Genetic Engineering Approvals Committee
GoI	Government of India
GPS	Group Pricing Scheme
GVO	gross value of output
HPS	hand-picked select
HFCS	high fructose corn syrups
HVOC	Hindustan Vegetable Oils Corporation
IFS	International Financial Statistics

IMF	International Monetary Fund
IPP	Index of Prices Paid
ISEC	Indian Sugar Exim Corporation Ltd.
ISGIEIC	Indian Sugar and General Industry Export Import Corporation
ITT	Index to Terms of Trade
JNU	Jawaharlal Nehru University
MEP	Minimum Export Price
MMTC	Mineral and Metals Trading Corporation
MoA	Ministry of Agriculture
MOP	Muriate of Potash
MSP	Minimum Support Price
NDDB	National Dairy Development Board
NPK	nitrogen, phosphorous, and potassium
NSSO	National Sample Survey Organisation
OECD	Organisation for Economic Co-operation and Development
OGL	Open General License
PDS	public distribution system
PEC	Project Equipment Corporation
PTE	price transmission elasticity
QR	quantitative restriction
RBI	Reserve Bank of India
RRB	Regional Rural Bank
RP	reference price
RPS	Retention Pricing Scheme
SOPA	Soybean Processors Association of India
SPS	Sanitary and Phytosanitary
STC	State Trading Corporation
STE	State Trading Enterprise
TC	transportation cost
TE	Triennium Ending
TOT	Terms of Trade
TRV	tariff rate value
UNCTAD	United Nations Conference on Trade and Development
URAA	Uruguay Round Agreement on Agriculture
USDA	United State Department of Agriculture
WPI	Wholesale Price Index
WTO	World Trade Organization

Foreword

Globally, food crises, epitomised by periodic spikes in the global prices of food, have moved to centre stage. In 2012, the world experienced its third food crisis in five years. While, demand has indeed grown as population expands and countries move up the income ladder, the fundamental factors explaining these periodic crises seem to lie elsewhere. One is a long-term crisis affecting agriculture in many countries as a result of inadequate investment in essential infrastructure (such as irrigation and drainage, for example) and poor extension of the benefits of technical knowledge to the farming community. This not only directly affects the level and elasticity of supply, but also limits productivity increase. Combined with cost increases that are not easily passed on, these inadequacies are challenging the viability of crop production in many contexts. In the event when bad weather, for example, adversely affects food production at some source, the demand–supply imbalance provides cause for strain.

Second, with geopolitical and other factors keeping oil prices high and near their oil crisis levels in real Dollars, the world is turning to bio-fuels as a source of energy. The result is the diversion of food output to non-food uses and the shift of land away from the production of food to the production of 'feedstock' for fuel. FAO Director General Jose Graziano da Silva had in an article in the *Financial Times* of 9 August 2012 called on the US to substantially reduce the diversion of maize to ethanol production. 'With world prices of cereals rising, the competition between the food, feed and fuel sectors for crops such as maize, sugar and oilseeds is likely to intensify. One way to alleviate some of the tension would be to lower or temporarily suspend the mandates on biofuels. At the moment, the renewable energy production in the US is reported to have reached 15.2 billion gallons in 2012, for which it used the equivalent of some 121.9 million tonnes or about 40 per cent of US maize production. An immediate, temporary suspension of that mandate would give some respite to the market and allow more of the crop to be channelled towards food and feed uses,' he argued. The result is that food prices tend to move with fuel prices and remain high so long as the latter are buoyant. This, unfortunately, has been the case for more than a decade now, with few and very short signs of reprieve.

Third, the tendency to food price inflation that these developments generate is being strengthened by the discovery of commodities, including food products, as an 'alternative investment class'. The resulting financialisation of commodity markets and the rapid growth in commodity futures trading is, according to analysts, influencing spot prices, largely in the upward direction.

The continuous play of these factors means that any temporary shortfall in supply paves the way for sharp price increases, resulting in consecutive spikes of crisis dimensions. The result is that the number of the world's citizens deprived of adequate access to food and experiencing an intensification of chronic hunger has increased. The previous two crises, in 2007–08 and 2011, had also led to high food prices, resulting in increased hunger, localised famines and widespread increase in deprivation. These 21st-century crises confirmed that the world still remained prone to food price inflation (and volatility), with unacceptably adverse implications for nutrition, health and survival. Such inflation was even more unacceptable in developing countries such as India with a higher proportion of their populations living at the margins of subsistence.

For developing countries, the message is clear. Governments must intervene to drive a wedge between international and domestic prices to at least partially insulate their populations against these global shocks. India has had a long record in doing this. But there are growing concerns that this policy involving the use of multiple instruments is being diluted by liberalisation. In that context, this book is both timely and of immense significance.

Through a detailed and rigorous study of the Indian experience just before and after liberalisation, Ashutosh Kumar Tripathi attempts to assess how far international influences have determined the level and volatility of food prices in India. The study finds that while the *trend* unleashed by liberalisation of agricultural and food policy and markets elsewhere in the world is visible in India as well, the *moment* is still such that food price determination in India has a logic of their own. With India's Minimum Support Price (MSP) policy (which involves procuring a range of commodities at a cost plus price for provision to the consumer through the public distribution system) still in place, food prices in India are still relatively insulated from the worst of the tendencies in the global system.

This reliance on the MSP is clearly predicated on the use of trade policy in the form of calibrated changes in tariffs (depending on global price movements), import restrictions, and controls on exports to shield the domestic market from the full force of global trends. Tripathi's study surveys India's agricultural trade and trade policies in recent decades and empirically analyses the means by and degree to which they have been insulated from international price trends.

The conclusion is that it is because liberalisation has not been allowed to take its course in full, rather than because it has been substantially implemented, as some argue, that food crises originating in the global system have not overwhelmed India. The evidence gathered here to support these broad arguments and their many detailed components can be usefully referred to not just by academics and those engaged in development, but by policy makers concerned with food and agricultural price policy. This is of particular significance because indications are that policy is moving in directions that this book implicitly warns against. Hopefully, lessons learnt from here would help rein in not just that tendency, but serve as a warning against unthinking liberalisation backed by inadequate evidence and poor argumentation in other areas of policy as well.

New Delhi   **C. P. Chandrasekhar**
2014

Acknowledgements

This book is largely based on my doctoral dissertation in Economics, written for Jawaharlal Nehru University (JNU), New Delhi and completed in November 2011. The study was carried out under the supervision of Professor C. P. Chandrasekhar of JNU. I am highly indebted to him for his valuable guidance and supervision and the unfailing interest he has displayed at every stage of my work. I am grateful to Professor Ramesh Chand and Professor Surjit Singh for their extensive comments on and valuable suggestions of certain chapters.

I would like to pay my sincere gratitude to my un-official supervisor of PhD thesis, Professor William Liefert of the United States Department of Agriculture (USDA), Washington, DC, not only for his excellent guidance on decomposition method, but also for his advice, supervision and crucial contribution, which made him a backbone of this research and so to this book. His involvement with his originality has triggered and nourished my intellectual maturity that I will benefit from for a long time to come.

I gained many valuable insights from my discussions, on specific aspects of my work, with Professors Anjan Mukherji, Prabhat Patnaik, Jayati Ghosh, K. P. Kannan, and Dr C. S. C. Sekhar and Sachin Chaturvedi. I am indebted to all of them for their time and keeping my academic spirit high. Parts of this work were presented to the faculty of Economic Research Service, USDA, and to the MacMillan Centre for International and Area Studies, Yale University, during March and April 2009. I found the response of the audience at the presentation stimulating and very useful. I am most thankful to them for their helpful comments and suggestions. The company of friends played an instrumental role in the completion of this work. The warmth in their friendship and the countless light moments we shared have been of immense comfort throughout my stay in JNU.

I want also to acknowledge the support of the Fox International Fellowship granted by the MacMillan Center for International and Area Studies, Yale University, without which producing this work might not be possible. I am very much honoured to be a Fox International Fellow because of its great prestige. The fellowship gave me ample opportunities not only to interact with the faculty and students at Yale University but also to visit the USDA and work with Dr William Liefert. It was certainly, hands down, one of those chapters in my life that I will never forget.

I would also like to express my gratitude to an anonymous referee of the publisher whose comments were very useful in bringing about improvements in the manuscript, as well as to Professor C. P. Chandrasekhar for writing a Foreword for this book.

The help provided by the staff at the JNU Central Library, the Exim Bank Library, the Krishi Bhavan Library, the Ratan Tata Library, and the Central Secretariat Library has been immensely useful. I would like to thank the staff of Centre for Economic Studies and Planning, JNU, for their kind help.

Last, but not least, I would like to thank my wife Saumya for her understanding and love during the past few years. Her support and encouragement was in the end what made this work possible. My parents receive my deepest gratitude and love for their dedication and the many years of support during my PhD studies that provided the foundation for this work.

Finally, I bow before the Revered Master for giving me courage and resolve for accomplishing this challenging task.

1

Introduction

It is in the agriculture sector that the battle for long-term economic development will be won or lost.

Gunnar Myrdal (1968)

This statement, made by Myrdal more than three decades ago, is very pertinent for India even today. Despite its declining share in GDP, agriculture still remains the backbone of the Indian economy. Agriculture is still a major source of wage goods like food, fibre and fuel and also provides raw material for a large number of industries. Agriculture boosts the economy through backward and forward linkages. It provides livelihood to over 60 per cent of the population and a cushion for the ratio between the urban and rural income. Apart from its importance for the balanced and accelerated development of the overall economy, the basic characteristic of the agricultural production process which distinguishes it from industry explains why the agricultural sector cannot be entirely left to market forces. To elaborate, first, unlike industry, where the presence of excess capacity makes production more elastic, agricultural production in any given period is fixed by production conditions from the supply side. Second, the scale of operation in agriculture tends to be much smaller as compared to the industry. The ability of farmers to hold stocks is also limited. Therefore, taking these two together, one can argue that agricultural supply cannot be adjusted rapidly. Third, along with slow supply adjustment, output is also subject to large fluctuations induced by weather and other natural forces. And fourth, while supply adjustment is slow and tends to fluctuate a good deal, the demand for agricultural commodities tends to be price-inelastic, resulting, thereby, in a great deal of fluctuations in agricultural prices and income (Patnaik 2003).

On the other hand, looking at it from the demand side, large fluctuations in agricultural prices have profound influence on the inter-sectoral distribution of income and the levels of consumption because a majority of the poor in India do not have incomes that are index-linked. Government intervention in agriculture can also be justified from within the framework of neoclassical economics on three grounds — the 'public goods' argument, the equity or 'merit good' argument and the 'market failure' argument. First, some goods and services do not lend themselves to individual pricing because of collective use. In this case, the State as the collective interest holder is the best provider. Second, some goods and services are for all community members regardless of their ability and willingness to pay the market price. Lastly, market failures tend to result from structural rigidities due to the lack of responsiveness to price signals (Smith and Thomson 1991; Batley 1994; Dedehouanou and Ufford 2000). Thus, agricultural markets have remained under constant scrutiny, and governments in both the developed and the developing countries have been required to intervene in agricultural marketing.

In agriculture, although the government has no direct role in the production and investment decisions of farmers, it did and still does influence the legal and economic environment in which farmers and other economic agents operate. Indirectly, government policies have unintended effects. The policies concerning industrial protection, exchange rates and interest rates, and other fiscal and monetary policies can strongly influence the incentives for agriculture vis-à-vis other sectors. Directly, the government affects agriculture through sector-specific measures. For example, it subsidises farmers (mostly in developed countries); tries to stabilise prices; imposes import tariffs and quotas; provides food subsidies for urban areas; supports the use of fertiliser; builds irrigation systems; offers extension services; controls marketing; and provides credit, often at below market rates. On the basis of the impact on output, the way in which governments can intervene to alter market incentives in agriculture can be put under three categories (Schultz 1978). First, there are economic policies that are neutral with respect to the opportunity cost of agricultural production. Second, there are those where agricultural production is overvalued. Third, there are policies through which agricultural production is undervalued.

Typically, the high income developed countries fall into the second category. Product price support in these countries maintains high farm incomes and leads to surplus generation. On the other hand, with respect to consumption, setting high support prices discourages consumers, thereby expanding excess supply. The excess supply can be stored or dumped on the world market using export subsidies.

If the exporting country does not store the excess supply, its excess supply becomes perfectly inelastic for prices below its internal support price. The export subsidy becomes the difference between the domestic and world price that is required to sell the excess supply (Philip 1988).

1.1 AGRICULTURAL POLICY IN INDIA PRIOR TO THE ECONOMIC REFORM OF 1991

In India, the history of government intervention in agriculture dates back to the early 1940s when the country faced famine and consequent food shortages. Many committees were set up to frame and recommend market intervention policies. The strongest intervention began in the mid-1960s which has been closely associated with the adoption and spread of the new agricultural technology. The massive food shortages and the near famine-like conditions in some parts of the country due to the successive poor harvests resulted in the dependence on food aid and costly food imports. It compelled the government to follow the policy of self-sufficiency in food production. This coincided with the advent of high-yielding varieties of wheat and rice, which later came to be known as the 'Green Revolution'.

The adoption of these new varieties involved the use of modern inputs and investments on the part of the farmers. For this, it was necessary to create adequate incentives through a favourable price environment for the farmers. To achieve this objective, the strategy was built on three foundations. One of these foundations was to assure a remunerative price and market environment to the farmers, the other two being the provision of an improved package of farming technologies to the farmers and creating a system for the supply of critical modern inputs including credit for agriculture. As part of an agricultural development strategy, a package of market intervention policies was launched and developed over the years. The instruments for market intervention include, *inter alia*, (*i*) minimum support prices; (*ii*) buffer stocking; (*iii*) subsidised distribution of food grains through the public distribution system (PDS); (*iv*) levy on rice millers and sugar mills; (*v*) subsidies on fertiliser; (*vi*) lower user charges for canal water and electricity for irrigation; and (*vii*) regulation on domestic trade practices including, *inter alia*, stocking restrictions. Apart from these, another important component of the agricultural policy till the reform began in 1991 was the tightly controlled trade and exchange rate policies.

In the case of agriculture, except for a few traditional commercial crops, the rest of the agricultural sector was insulated from the world agricultural markets through almost total control of exports and imports. The estimated surplus over domestic consumption requirements determined the marginal quantities to be exported and vice versa for imports. More importantly, food grains, sugar and edible oils were imported in times of scarcity to prevent domestic prices of essential commodities from rising and to impart a measure of stability to the domestic prices in the interest of both the producers and the consumers.

The financial policy was also aimed to mobilise resources for public sector expenditures and for co-operative and institutional credit to the rural sector with a view to facilitating private investment in infrastructure and encouraging the adoption of the new technology. This policy was instrumental in accelerating agricultural growth and in raising the output and income level of a large number of cultivators particularly in the irrigated regions of the country. The rapid growth consequent to the adoption of the new seed-fertiliser technology resulted in rising food grain production, enabling the country to meet the demands of food grains.

1.2 THE CRITIQUE OF PLANNING FRAMEWORK

Until the beginning of economic reforms in the early-1990s, scholars have criticised the policy followed during the planned era on several grounds like increasing the regional inequality in productivity and income, high rural poverty, regional bias in government operations, poor performance of government operations in the procurement and distribution of the food grains, etc. But the general thrust of the agricultural policy within the framework of planning had not been seriously questioned. However, in the wake of the introduction of the new economic policy, all aspects of the planning framework and the associated macroeconomic policy have come under serious attack. The arguments are:

First, that the macro-economic policies under the planning framework were discriminatory against the agriculture. The inward-looking import substitution development strategy aimed at the rapid industrialisation is said to have shifted resources from tradable agriculture to industry by turning the terms of trade against the agriculture ... Second, that the overvalued exchange rate not only made the import and domestic production of the agricultural inputs more costly it also adversely affected all exports and specially hurt agricultural exports (Singh 1995).

Third, the sector specific policies at all stages of production, consumption and marketing of agricultural produce worked against agriculture. Such policies have restricted the role of competitive markets in India (Gulati 1998; Gulati and Kelly 1999; World Bank 1999). The stringent market regulation and restrictions and other commodity specific controls prescribed within institutional and price policy measures — insulation of domestic markets from external competition and import-export bans — debilitate markets. A proliferation of the impediments to the domestic agriculture trade leads to inefficient and non-competitive markets that often result in lesser market opportunities. All these factors suppress the effective incentives for cultivators/traders and further dissuade them from responding to market signals in the allocation of the resources, and divert resources away from agriculture sector, which is again detrimental to the growth in the output and productivity of crops.

It is further argued that the subsidies given on the agricultural inputs also led to resource misallocation. Some of the studies suggest that the volume of the subsidies on fertiliser is not entirely attributable to the farm sector (Gulati 1989; Tyagi 1993; Vidya Sagar 1993). According to one study, the various subsidies given to the agricultural sector on account of fertiliser, irrigation and electricity were estimated to be of the order of ₹90.9 billion per year during the 1980s (Gulati 1989). These subsidies placed an unsustainable burden on the state, reducing the capacity of the government to undertake large investments and benefitting the producers of a few crops and, that too, in a few of the states (Gulati and Sharma 1992, 1994). Such subsidies also failed to compensate the farmers for the negative impact of the lower administered price paid on the outputs; led to discrimination against agriculture due to the overvalued currency; and resulted in higher input prices due to the excessive protection given to industry. It is argued that the net effect has been that the agricultural sector was subject to negative protection and was discriminated against (Mody 1981).

1.3 Agriculture Policy in India in Post-reform Period

Since the beginning of the 1990s, the two biggest events in Indian economic history — the emergence of a market-based reform project and an incremental re-integration with the global economy — began to take shape. The process of stabilisation and adjustment initiated in 1991 has been associated with sweeping reform of the industrial licensing, pricing, and tax policies and the dismantling of the restrictions on the foreign trade in industrial goods. The economic reforms involved the devaluation of the Rupee by 18 per cent against the Dollar and the exchange rate was left to be determined by the market forces. The changes in the industrial and the trade policy were introduced to expose the industry to competition by reducing the protection hitherto enjoyed by the industrial sector. These changes were expected to improve the terms of the trade for the agricultural sector and to help attract more investible resources for this sector. Though the programme did not initially cover the agriculture sector, it was recognised that the economic reforms may not succeed in their objective of ensuring the broad-based growth in incomes and productive employment without the sustained development of the agricultural sector.

The package of reforms in agriculture is based on the diagnosis that while the sector remained net disprotected,[1] the subsidies arising out of the inappropriate pricing of the inputs and the outputs led to the inefficient use of resources and eroded the capacity of the government to finance public investment in the agricultural sector. For correcting these so-called distortions, several suggestions are made by scholars. These suggestions revolve around 'setting prices right' and include the withdrawal of subsidies on inputs, targeting the public distribution system to only the poor, abolition of the food management system and its attendant costs, and the liberalisation of the trade in agricultural commodities (Bhagwati and Srinivasan 1993; Pursell and Gulati 1993; Vyas 1994; Singh 1995).

As a result, the post-reform period witnessed a dilution of the supportive mechanisms that were built up, in stages, in the post-independence period to protect the farmers from the uncertainties of the market (Patnaik 2003). During the post-reform period, the government not only cut the subsidies on major inputs, but also absolved itself of the responsibility to produce or procure and distribute these inputs at the farm gates. The share of the input subsidies — on

---

[1] In spite of subsidies on inputs, as the output prices were maintained at below world levels, the agriculture sector has been net taxed (Gulati and Sharma 1994).

fertilisers, power and irrigation — in the , which was 0.6 per cent in 1980–81, rose to the level of 2.5 per cent in 1990–91 and then fell to 2.1 per cent in 1999–2000. The fall in the share of the input subsidies in GDP after 1991 was the result of a conscious official policy that aimed at restricting the subsidy provision, particularly for fertilisers (Gulati and Narayanan 2003).

The policy on agricultural credit also underwent significant changes as part of the larger programme of financial liberalisation. The RBI's Committee on the Financial System, the Narasimham Committee, made a sharp pitch for delinking monetary policy from the objective of redistribution, which was at the centre of social and development banking (RBI 1991). It argued that the banks should function on a commercial basis, and that profitability should be the prime concern in their activities. The banks were also to be permitted to close their rural branches, in the name of rationalisation of the branch networks. The recommendations of the Narasimham Committee, except for a few, were implemented to a large extent in the 1990s. As a result, the period of financial liberalisation witnessed the reversal of the achievements in rural banking that characterised the two decades after the nationalisation of banks. The flow of credit to the rural areas declined sharply in the 1990s (Shetty 1997; Ramachandran and Swaminathan 2001, 2005; Chavan 2002, 2005). The rate of growth of credit supply to the rural areas fell from 12.6 per cent between 1980 and 1990 to 3.2 per cent between 1990 and 2000.

As the existing laws on agricultural marketing were viewed as discriminatory for the farmers and the traders by not allowing them to maximise their gains, both in the domestic as well as in the international markets, following this, the government started reorienting the policies towards the agricultural sector. This resulted in a continuous reduction in controls on the internal and the external trade through relaxations in the zonal restrictions, removal of quantitative restrictions (QRs) on exports and imports, the de-canalisation measures in the output markets, and so on. The domestic policies relating to the production, supply and the distribution of the various agricultural commodities under the Essential Commodities Act (ECA), 1955 and the State Agricultural Produce Market Act, 1966 have been brought under review for appropriate modifications. In the case of cereals, the provision of fixing the procurement prices and the public agencies trying to procure the pre-decided quantities of the grains by imposing several formal and informal restrictions has been replaced by a system of Minimum Support Prices (MSPs).

India's external trade policy which was heavily controlled by government parastatals until the early-1990s through a web of QRs, licensing and the canalisation of exports and imports has undergone considerable change since then. Though agriculture was not covered in the trade liberalisation measures taken during the years of 1991–92, apart from the relaxation of some export controls, the pace of the reform of external policies in the agricultural sector picked up in 1993–94. Since then, significant measures have been taken to liberalise agricultural trade policy. Tariffs have been reduced, the quantitative restrictions on the agricultural trade have been removed, and the agricultural trade has been decanalised in the case of the most of the commodities. The provision of the Minimum Export Price (MEP) has been withdrawn. The move towards agricultural trade liberalisation was triggered both by internal policy assessments as well as external developments such as the World Trade Organization (WTO) agreements.

The signing of the Dunkel text in April 1994, which became effective since January 1995 onwards, has committed India to multilateralism. The provisions relating to agriculture are contained in the Agreement on Agriculture (AoA), also known as the Uruguay Round Agreement on Agriculture (URAA), and the Agreement on the Application of Sanitary and Phytosanitary (SPS) Measures, which form part of the WTO agreement. The URAA requires all non-tariff barriers to agricultural trade to be tariffed and converted into their tariff equivalents. The resulting tariffs were to be reduced by a simple average of 36 per cent over a period of 6 years in the case of the developed countries and 24 per cent over a period of 10 years for the developing countries. However, many of the developing countries including India were permitted to offer the ceiling bindings instead of the tariffication. These bindings were not subject to the reduction commitments. India bound 3,375 of its 6-digit commodity tariff lines including 683 commodity tariff lines relating to agricultural products. India was allowed to maintain QRs because of potential balance of payments (BoP) problems. However, India's QRs were later challenged in the Dispute Settlement Body (DSB) of the WTO and India lost its plea for their continued use.[2] Accordingly, India's QRs were

---

[2] The USA and some other countries in the dispute settlement body of WTO challenged India's continuation of QRs on the plea of BoP position.

removed during the period of 1999–2001. India took the opportunity under GATT Article XXVIII to renegotiate and raise the tariff bindings on 15 agricultural tariff lines for which it had very low or zero tariffs. These included skimmed milk powder, spelt wheat, corn, paddy, rice, maize, millet, sorghum, rapeseed, colza and mustard oil, and fresh grapes, among others.

1.4 ISSUES RELATED TO INDIAN AGRICULTURE AND REFORM PROCESS

The changes introduced in the agriculture policy during the 1990s as discussed, represent a fundamental departure from the past regime and indicates a greater reliance on market forces where price signals have assumed a more significant role, than before.

With the dilution of the government's supportive mechanisms during the post-reform period farmers were exposed to the working of the market. For example, the rationale for the provision of input subsidies has historically been to provide the farmers with (*a*) remunerative as well as stable prices to enable them to adopt the new technologies and raise yields, and (*b*) to compensate for the imperfections in the capital market and the risks associated with the adoption of the new and the high-cost technologies. Sen (1992) argues that the agricultural growth of the 1980s was primarily due to a more intensive use of fertilisers and pesticides; there was a perfect negative correlation between the yield of the food grains and the prices of the fertilisers relative to the food grains. There is also evidence that the marginal and the small farmers benefitted significantly from input subsidies.

In view of its improved position in the matter of foreign balance, India lost the plea for retention of QRs on account of BoP position both at the Dispute Settlement Body as well as at the Appellate body. According to the understanding arrived at between the parties regarding the reasonable period of time latest by March 2001, India removed the QRs on 714 items including 142 commodities belonging to the category of agricultural commodities during 1999–2000. On the occasion of the Export and Import policy announcement on 31 March 2001, the minister announced the removal of QRs on the remaining 715 items, thereby ending the 'License Permit Raj'. With the removal of the 715 items from the list, which include 142 groups belonging to agriculture, QRs on imports have been completely abolished and obligation to replace QRs by tariffs has been fulfilled. QRs are now maintained on imports of only about 5 per cent of tariff lines (538 items) under Articles XX and XXI of GATT on grounds of health, safety and moral conduct.

The estimates of Acharya and Jogi (2004) show that 36.4 per cent of the total input subsidies were availed of by the marginal and the small farmers while their corresponding share in the ownership of the operated area was 36 per cent. Therefore, given these benefits, the withdrawal of the input subsidies is certainly having short-term adverse effects on the levels of agricultural profitability even if it is assumed that all the reduced expenditure on the subsidy would be invested in agriculture.

The viability of agriculture depends critically on the ratio between the output price and the input price. If the profitability is to be maintained at the same level it would require a more than proportionate increase in the output price. According to an estimate (Sen 1992), maintenance of the relative prices resulting from one rupee cut in the fertiliser subsidy would require a transfer of ₹10 to the farmers either from the government or from the consumers. Both forms of transfer have significant fiscal and welfare implications. The proponents of the reform argue that in order to compensate for the input price rise, output prices (i.e., procurement prices) could be raised by the government (Parikh 1997). However, raising output prices involves two further issues (Sen 1992; Acharya 2000; Acharya and Jogi 2004). First, a large share of the farmers in India does not generate a marketable surplus; most of the production of the marginal and the small farmers go into household consumption and these groups would be adversely affected by the higher prices of the inputs. Second, the procurement operations of the government take place only in a few states and regions. As such, the geographical reach of a rise in the procurement price may be limited. The essence of these arguments is that the input subsidies and the output prices cannot be treated as substitutes.

The vast literature on the supply responsiveness of the farmers also shows that the relationship between the prices and the output is very weak (Rao 1988, 1989; Ghosh 1992; Sen 1992; Nayyar and Sen 1994; Hazell, Misra and Hojjati 1995; Vaidyanathan 2000). No doubt, there are major issues related to the accuracy of the economic models used to estimate the supply response in agriculture such as the measurement and the control of the different effects. Nonetheless, the range of the long-run supply elasticity of the aggregate agricultural output has historically been between 0.1 and 0.5 in the developing countries (Rao 1989). According to Rao, the resulting efficiency loss is quite small.[3] The studies also show that the responsiveness of the yield-raising inputs to the output prices is not significant. In fact, it is the other factors such as the inputs, technology, institutions, and the infrastructure that dominantly determine the growth in farm output. Chand (2004) argues that there was no significant relationship between the terms of trade and output growth in Indian agriculture. He observes three sets of patterns of output and price interaction in Indian agriculture in the 1990s: (*i*) the output growth of cereals slowed down while prices were rising; (*ii*) the output growth of fruits and vegetables improved when the extent of the price rise was small; and (*iii*) the output growth of oilseeds fell along with a fall in the prices. On the basis of these results, Chand argues that attempts to increase the production by raising prices alone do not produce the results if efforts on the technological fronts, input use and irrigation are ignored.

The changes introduced in the agriculture trade policy during the 1990s also represent a fundamental departure from the past regime and points to a greater degree of openness. The liberalisation of the agricultural trade which was put forward as an important step towards imparting efficiency to Indian agriculture; has generated intense debate among Indian academicians and policy makers because of its likely implications for national and household food security, the levels of poverty and the regional disparities in development. This debate is well warranted. There are several reasons for this. First, the domestic prices of essential commodities like staple cereals cannot be delinked from the levels of income of the masses. Second, the relative price structure that prevails in the world market is not based on the comparative advantage that different countries have in producing various commodities, but reflects only the residual market. Third, the world market price structure is highly distorted due to the support given by the developed countries to their farmers. Fourth, the increased alignment of the domestic and the world prices after trade liberalisation would import the volatility of international prices — formed in highly imperfect and monopolised market environments — into

---

[3] As Vaidyanathan (2000) argued, even a 15 per cent improvement in Terms of Trade (TOT) with a price elasticity of aggregate supply of 0.3, will raise output by about 5 per cent which is equal to less than the additional output in two years at present growth rates, hardly form any basis to project a sustained increase in the growth rate.

Indian agriculture. Fifth, the small country assumption does not hold for India. The experience suggests that India's entry into the world market immediately affects world prices and as a consequence the actual gain from free trade would be much smaller than what is anticipated. The recent evidence of this is in the case of sugar. World sugar prices ruled around $290 per tonne during the first quarter of 2009. When the market realised that there would be a sugar shortage in India, prices increased up to around $470 per tonne in the third quarter of 2009. By the end of the year, world sugar prices had doubled (Chand 2010).

One of the most important arguments put forward in support of trade liberalisation was that it would improve the prospects of an export-led growth process in agriculture. Though some scholars have warned against export orientation of Indian agriculture (Patnaik 1996), but their views were not paid attention to, as the pro-liberalisation lobby dominated the policy decisions at that time. Similarly, the fear concerning imports following the trade liberalisation were brushed aside because the domestic prices of most of the agricultural commodities, except edible oils, were then either lower than the international prices or were not cost-effective imports. However, the experience of the last 10 years since the implementation of WTO shows that there is quite a distance between the cup and the lip. Regarding India's share in the global agricultural trade, the initial years of the reform were quite favourable for agricultural exports. The domestic liberalisation and the devaluation of the exchange rate gave a boost to the agricultural export. In a short span of five years, the agricultural exports rose from $3.2 billion in 1991–92 to $6.87 billion during 1996–97. This also resulted in an increase in the share of the agricultural exports from below 18 per cent to more than 20 per cent in the total Indian export. It led to the view that Indian agriculture is highly competitive and that free trade would help the country harness its vast export potential (Gulati and Sharma 1994). Contrary to these expectations, the price situation changed dramatically after 1996 following the implementation of the URAA. The domestic supports in the developed countries negatively affected the market access of the developing countries in the third world country markets by distorting the prices in those markets. Due to the sharp decline in the global prices of agricultural commodities, the export earnings from the agricultural commodities started falling since 1997–98 and reached $5.8 billion in 1999–2000. Therefore, the momentum gained in agricultural exports with the start of the process of the economic reform got reversed in the post-WTO period. After this initial setback during the URAA implementation period (1995–2001), India's agricultural exports started recovering when the global prices started looking up since the early 2000s. However, the promise of an export-led growth process in the agricultural sector still remained unfulfilled till 2007–08.

On account of the huge subsidisation by developed countries, the prices in the world markets of many of the agricultural products were far below their production costs in India during the initial period of implementation of WTO. Hence, Indian farmers engaged in the production of some of these crops were denied their share in the world market and driven out of their domestic market. For instance, in August 1999, the soybean and soy oil import policy was liberalised in India. As a result, the subsidised imports of the soybeans were 'dumped' on the Indian market.[4] These imports amounted in total to three million tonnes in one year (a 60 per cent rise compared to earlier years) and the cost of it was nearly US$1 billion. Within one growing season, prices crashed by more than two-thirds and millions of the oilseed-producing farmers lost their market unable even to recover what they had spent on the cultivation (Mittal 2005). Similarly, in the background of the greater integration between the domestic and the international markets after the mid-1990s, domestic prices of cotton, tea, coffee, spices, and many fruits and vegetables fell following a sharp fall in the corresponding international prices. Due to the absence of quota controls as in the post-WTO period and the ineffectiveness of the low tariffs, the surge in the imports of various crops contributed in different degrees to the decline in their domestic prices (Bhalla 2004; Ghosh 2005).

As the data reveals, world prices of agricultural commodities are more volatile compared to domestic prices (Sekhar 2004). The increased alignment of the domestic and the world prices after the trade liberalisation can also effectively import the volatility in international prices to the domestic prices (Nayyar and Sen 1994). The volatility of the domestic prices creates different types of problems. On the one hand, it increases the uncertainties in cultivation, and on the other hand, it provides misleading price signals to the domestic producers of specific crops. Such misleading prices signals have the

---

[4] Dumping has been used in the economic sense of sales below cost and not in the legal sense as understood under the Anti-Dumping Agreement.

potential to affect shifts in the cropping pattern, which can be eco-logically unsound and economically unviable in the medium term.[5] The extreme volatility in the commodity prices, particularly of food commodities, adversely affects the poor agricultural labourers and those engaged in the unorganised sector because their wages are not index linked. For the exporters, price volatility increases cash-flow variability and reduces the collateral value of the inventories. Both these factors result in rising borrowing costs.

The empirical evidence provided by the stylised models also fails to provide clinching proof that the lesser players in the global economy would have much to gain from the dropping of the tariff walls in the ongoing negotiation under the Doha Round. In a series of papers published since 2004 onwards, World Bank economists have provided detailed projections by simulating the possible outcomes of the Doha Round negotiations.[6] The broad results from these studies lead to two varying interpretations. The first, regarding the effect of the ongoing trade liberalisation efforts on the real income up to 2015, shows that the results are significantly favourable for the developing countries since their expected real income gains are considerably larger than their existing share in the global production. Thus, while the developing countries as a whole account for a quarter of the global production at present, they would be able to enjoy one-third of the

---

[5] Examples of misleading price signals leading to cropping pattern shifts are the cases of vanilla in Kerala and soybean in Maharashtra. The most important reason for the rapid adoption of vanilla crop in upland Kerala was that while the prices of all the other major crops grown in the region were falling, vanilla prices were increasing. In 1995–96, the domestic price of processed vanilla was ₹2,000 per kg, which rose to ₹8,000 per kg in 2001–02. In 2002–03 and 2003–04, the domestic price shot up to ₹15,000 per kg. The rise in the price of processed vanilla was due to a cyclone-led fall in its production in Madagascar, which is the most important vanilla-exporting country. Production in Madagascar increased after June 2004, when the gestation period for the replanted crop ended. As a result, vanilla prices fell sharply to ₹1,618 in January 2005. Many farmers, who had replaced their coffee plantations with vanilla, were left helpless as a switch-back to coffee would have involved another gestation period of at least three years (see Nair and Ramakumar 2007).

[6] The most quoted of these papers are by Anderson, Martin and van der Mensbrugghe (2005 and 2006) and van der Mensbrugghe (2004).

global gains in the real income that is expected annually until 2015. An alternate view would be that the results are pointing to the increasing gulf between the relatively prosperous and the poorer regions and countries. In overall terms, it could be said that the disproportionately large gains for the developed countries would reinforce the status of the lesser share of the developing countries even after the so-called 'development round' has been implemented.

Several Indian scholars have also attempted to assess the implications of the trade liberalisation in agricultural commodities for growth, welfare and inter-regional inequalities (Bhagwati and Srivinasan 1993; Parikh, Srinivasan and Jha 1993; Pursell and Gulati 1993; Nayyar and Sen 1994; Bhalla 1995; Acharya 1997). While some of them suggested full liberalisation of the trade in the agricultural commodities, others favoured a gradual and cautious approach towards trade liberalisation which implies linking the price structure in the domestic market with that in the world market. Though the debate on the likely impact of the economic liberalisation in general and trade liberalisation in particular on domestic agriculture and, in turn, the farmers' income-cum-livelihood is still inconclusive, nonetheless, the above discussion on implementation experiences of WTO underscores the fact that the liberalisation of imports may have a negative effect on the Indian agrarian economy. In the changed economic scenario, the behaviour of international prices becomes all the more important as it has potential consequences that can damage domestic agriculture production by making it unprofitable as well as more risky. Analyses of the countries that have opened their markets significantly to trade and are price takers in the world commodity markets with limited fiscal resources also show that the behaviour of global commodity prices, both in terms of level and fluctuation, results in amplified pressures on the governments of these countries to counteract the transmission to internal markets of the perceived distortions in world prices caused by the subsidies and the high protection in the industrialised countries.

In the Indian context, contrary to the expectations and the anticipations with the changes in the macroeconomic policy framework and the trade liberalisation, the agricultural sector in India neither experienced any significant growth subsequent to the initiation of economic reforms in 1991 nor did it derive the expected benefits from the trade liberalisation. As a matter of fact, when compared with the immediate pre-liberalisation period (1980–83 to 1990–93), the agricultural growth in India recorded a visible deceleration during the post-liberalisation period (1990–93 to 2003–06). This happened at a time when the rest of the economy was growing at an unprecedented rate. The manufacturing output, seen as the bellwether for the policy stance since 1991, has even registered double digit growth in some of the recent years. The growth of the service economy has been less spectacular but more steady over a longer period. The slowdown in the agricultural growth not only affects agricultural income and the growth of the economy but also affects self-reliance and the self-sufficiency in agricultural products acquired after a hard struggle for the first four decades since independence.

The observed slowdown in Indian agricultural growth at the time of the emergence of a market-based reform project and the incremental re-introduction to the global economy give rise to a set of questions: what are the features of the observed slowdown in agricultural growth? Is this deceleration linked intrinsically to the reform process? What impact does change in the agriculture policy have on farm profitability /income? In other words, was state intervention in the agricultural output market sufficient enough to protect the farmers' income and provide enough incentives to them?

With the increasing influence of the global prices of agricultural commodities on domestic food prices and production under the more liberal and open trade regime, the question to be asked is: Does the long-run trend in the global prices of agricultural commodities pose any serious threat to domestic agriculture? Further, how have the global prices of agricultural commodities moved over time and what factors influence their movements? The other interrelated and important issue relates to whether the increased alignment of the domestic and the world prices after trade liberalisation led to any significant rise in domestic price volatility. And has domestic price volatility played a significant role in determining the trajectory of agricultural growth since 1991?

The trade policies that are designed to regulate the volume of trade flows are found to be an effective instrument in imparting stability to domestic prices. With the opening up of the economy to outside competition and with greater integration with the world economy, it is necessary to examine what role the changed trade policy plays in imparting stability to domestic prices and influencing the average level of prices. The liberalisation of the agricultural trade to impart efficiency to Indian agriculture through the export-led growth process also raises the question whether the agricultural trade liberalisation led to any significant change in the composition of the trade basket? Is there enough export demand for our products? Or can India manage to export its excess production at times of glut in the domestic production? Another important but a related question is: does India possess exportable surpluses?

The extent to which the international prices influence domestic prices depends upon government intervention in the form of policies, either at the border or as price support mechanisms which have the potential consequence of weakening the link or preventing the transmission of the movements in international prices. Along with the international prices, the government policies also affect the domestic prices both directly and indirectly. Typically, the indirect effects result from the impact of macroeconomic policies on the exchange rate, whereas the direct effects result from the impact of government intervention in agriculture in the pursuance of its objective of keeping the domestic prices at a reasonable level. In this context, the obvious question is whether the observed variability in domestic prices during the post-WTO period was due to government intervention in the agriculture market or whether government intervention helped in reducing the variability in the domestic prices.

1.5 OBJECTIVES OF THE STUDY

The overall objective of this book is to find answers for the above-mentioned set of questions with a view to examining the effect of the market-based reform project in addressing the observed slow growth of the agricultural sector since 1991. The specific objectives of our studies are as follows.

First, we try to analyse the agricultural growth performance and document the movement of the factors that have been recognised as being the determinants of agricultural growth with a view to identifying the proximate causes of the slowdown.

Second, we wish to seek answers to the question — what impact does changes in the agriculture policy have on farm profitability/income? In other words, was state intervention in the agricultural output market sufficient enough to protect the farmers' income and provide enough incentives to them? With a view to identifying the causes of the slowdown in agricultural production

Third, we examine the potential consequences of the behaviour of international prices in terms of their level and variability on domestic agriculture with a view to their possible role in determining the trajectory of agricultural growth since 1991.

Finally, an attempt is also made to analyse whether the observed variability in domestic prices was shaped by the incomplete transmission of the price signals to domestic prices due to government intervention in agriculture or whether government intervention helped in reducing variability in the domestic prices.

1.6 STRUCTURE OF THE BOOK

This book is organised in eight chapters. The following chapter (Chapter 2) deals with the trends in agricultural growth performance in terms of output, productivity and the area under the cultivation at the all-India level. The chapter also tries to identify the proximate causes of the slowdown in agricultural growth and documents the movement of the factors which have been recognised as being the determinants of the growth during the study period chosen for this research.

For analysing the impacts of the changes introduced in the agricultural price policy during the post-reform period on farm profitability/income and in turn production, it is important to examine the relationship of the prices with the cost and the income. The third chapter examines the relationship and documents the trend in farm profitability in order to assess the viability of farming. An attempt is also made here to critically examine the evolution of the foodgrain policy.

In addition to the impact of the change in the agricultural price policy on farm profitability/income in the post-reform period, another important issue that has gained greater significance during the post-reform period is the behaviour of the international prices due to the incremental re-integration of the domestic economy with the global economy. The behaviour of the international prices is analysed in Chapter 4. The analysis also documents the factors influencing the movement in global agricultural commodity prices as integration with the world economy also has a possible outcome that can damage the agricultural growth by increasing the volatility in domestic prices due to the highly volatile nature of the global prices of agricultural commodities. Hence, the variability of the world and domestic prices is also examined.

The trade policies that are designed to regulate the volume of trade flows are found to be an effective instrument in imparting stability to domestic prices along with influencing the average level of the prices. The fifth chapter analyses the trade policy regime in agriculture in the national context outlining its rationale and structure over the past quarter of a century. Since, the actual trade outcome is dependent on many factors and the trade policy at best gives an idea about the government's intentions, it also makes an attempt to analyse the export and import patterns of the selected agricultural commodities in the light of the domestic demand and supply situation along with the changes in international prices and the Indian agricultural trade policy.

The sixth chapter is an analysis of the impacts of the international prices on the domestic prices by making a comparison between the domestic and the international prices. In order to make a comparison, one requires knowing 'the price' at which the domestic producers compete with the traded commodities. To compute that price, adjustments were made in international prices to arrive at 'the price or reference price' for the domestic producers. This comparison also gives an idea of the price competitiveness of Indian producers. As a part of this comparison, the observed gap between the domestic and reference prices is then compared with the existed applied tariff duty/export subsidy rate in order to assess the adequacy of the same in order to fathom how far the trade policies were successful in maintaining the profitability/competitiveness of domestic production.

In the seventh chapter, a decomposition model is used in order to separate the factors responsible for changes in the domestic prices and quantify their effects on the domestic prices, with the key variables in the model being trade prices, the exchange rate and the agricultural trade policies. The model used in the decomposition allows one to measure the impacts of the different variables on the variability of the domestic prices under the scenario in which there is complete transmission of the price signals and also after cancelling out the effect of the incomplete transmission arising from government intervention as well as the poor infrastructure. The results obtained from the analysis can be used to draw inferences regarding the role of the government intervention in terms of imparting stability in the domestic prices.

The last chapter (Chapter 8) contains a summary of the main findings and overall evaluation of market-based reform project on agricultural growth. Some of the policy implications emerging from the study are also discussed.

1.7 APPROACH AND LIMITATION OF THE STUDY

To deal with the objectives of the study, the analysis is confined to six principal agricultural commodities. Two of these, rice and wheat, are from the group of cereal crops; the remaining four — of which groundnut, rape/mustard seed and soybean are important oilseeds and sugarcane a leading crop among the rest — belong to the group of cash crops. The selection of the agricultural commodities was largely dictated by three factors: the importance of the commodity in the trade basket; the current importance and the potential future impact of these commodities on food security and livelihoods; and the availability of data. The only exception regarding the selection of crops is while dealing with the second objective. In this case, the analysis is confined to only wheat and rice because of the highest level of protection offered to these crops by the State.

The specific approach and methodology adopted in achieving its broad objectives are described in the relevant chapters of the book. The study uses only secondary sources of information. The data were collected from various national and international sources, which are explained in the relevant chapters.

Though the study makes an attempt to address the observed slow growth of the agricultural sector since 1991, to examine the consequences of the market-based reform project, the analysis in different chapters goes back to 1980–81 to provide comparison between pre- and post-reform period and covers the past quarter of a century. The analysis in the book is subject to the limitation of extending the post-reform period beyond the agricultural marketing year (2005–06) due to difficulty in getting data on all the variables covered in the analysis for most recent periods.

2

Indian Agriculture under Economic Reforms

A Preliminary Review

Since the beginning of economic reforms in 1991, India has been through major changes in the macroeconomic policy framework of the planned economy that existed before the 1990s. However, no direct references were made to the agricultural sector in the reform package, though it was argued that the new macroeconomic policy framework would have profound implications for Indian agriculture for more reasons than one. First, it was expected that changes in exchange and trade policy, devaluation of the currency, gradual dismantling of the industrial licensing system, and reduction in industrial protection would benefit tradable agriculture by ending discrimination against it and by turning the Terms of Trade (TOT) in its favour.[1] Second, these policies together with globalisation would bring domestic farm prices in line with world market prices. This in turn would provide a justification to increase support prices, which will also turn the TOT in favour of agriculture. And third, with the signing of WTO agreements, some contended that India will record faster export growth in agricultural commodities and benefit from favourable prices for farm imports.

The first two of the above-mentioned implications of reform policies for Indian agriculture would, by altering relative prices in favour of agriculture, encourage private investment and technical change with consequent better agricultural growth (Gulati and Sharma 1991; Singh 1995; Ahluwalia 1996; Mishra, 1998). And, lastly, export growth in agricultural commodities was also expected to improve the barter Terms of Trade for primary commodities and shift the production possibility frontier through new export crops that would be like

---

[1] See Little, Scitovsky and Scott (1970) for the original statement, and Singh (1995) for an exposition.

product innovations (Anderson and Tyres 1990; Srinivasan 1993; Gulati and Sharma 1994).

At the theoretical level, the argument that 'with improvement in TOT, price incentives would generate a significant supply response' is much less general than it is made out to be. First, the analytical basis of the TOT argument is very weak, given its excessive concern with static allocative efficiency and neglect of inter-temporal considerations (Nayyar and Sen 1994). Also, it assumes that resources have perfect substitutability across uses and perfect mobility across sectors, both of which underestimate the structural rigidities in the economy. Second, it also missed the basic nature of the relation, i.e., substitution, income and wealth effects, of aggregate farm output and relative farm prices inherent to a decision-making unit/level at which consumption, saving, investment, labour supply, and production are all intertwined (Desai 2002). Third, even if the Terms of Trade are depressed by import substitution in industry, the resulting growth in non-agricultural employment can lead to a faster growth in per capita agricultural incomes than in the protected scenario (Sen 1992). Studies have also questioned the basic premise of the argument regarding the implications of aligning domestic prices to world prices. The current world prices, based on which simulations are run may be poor predictors of future world prices, particularly given that world prices are subject to significant volatility and that the world market is characterised by monopoly or monopsony.

The pattern of growth that Indian agriculture has experienced also highlights the fact that despite the changes in the macroeconomic policy framework and trade liberalisation, the agricultural sector in India neither experienced significantly higher growth subsequent to the initiation of economic reforms in 1991, nor did it derive the expected benefits from trade liberalisation. As a matter of fact, when compared with the immediate pre-liberalisation period (1980–83 to 1990–93), agricultural growth in India recorded a visible deceleration during the post-liberalisation period (1990–93 to 2003–06). The slow growth of agriculture has been explicitly noted as a matter of concern in the *Approach Paper to the Eleventh Plan* (GoI 2006) and accelerating the rate of growth of agricultural production is seen as central to more inclusive growth.

As the deceleration of agricultural growth occurred at a time when the economic policy regime has been undergoing reform, it has been suggested by some scholars that this deceleration is linked intrinsically to the reform process. It is in the light of this debate that this chapter addresses the observed slow growth of the agricultural sector. In order to identify the proximate causes for the slowdown, the analysis tries to explore the impact of the factors that have been recognised in various studies as determinant of agricultural growth. The chapter is structured as follows. Section 2.1 discusses the trends in agricultural growth performance in terms of output, productivity and area under cultivation at the all-India level. Section 2.2 tries to identify the proximate cause of the slowdown in agricultural growth. Section 2.3 documents the movement of the factors that have been recognised as being determinants of agricultural growth during the study period. Section 2.4 draws together some conclusions that emerge from the analysis.

2.1 AGRICULTURAL GROWTH PERFORMANCE

There has been a decline in the share of the agricultural and allied sectors in the overall gross domestic product (GDP). Agriculture, which accounted for more than 30 per cent of total GDP at the beginning of reforms, failed to maintain its pre-reform growth. On the contrary, it witnessed a sharp decline in its share in total GDP after the mid-1990s. The share of agriculture in total GDP which was around 27.46 per cent during 1994–95 to 1996–97 fell to 19.66 per cent during the period 2003–04 to 2005–06 (Appendix, Table A-2.1). The reason for the decline in agriculture's share in total GDP was sluggish growth in the agricultural sector in comparison to the overall growth of the Indian economy during the post-reform period.

The GDP contributed by the agricultural and allied sectors increased at an annual rate of more than three per cent[2] during the 1980s which was considered a reasonably satisfactory performance (Figure 2.1). The economic reform initiated during the 1990s aimed at far-reaching deregulation and involved significant changes in fiscal, trade and exchange rate policies. Though the agricultural sector was not targeted directly, it was affected indirectly by these changes. The impact of these and other changes was a small deceleration in the growth rate of GDP of agriculture (agriculture and allied sector together) during the first six years of reforms (TE 1990–91 to TE 1996–97), when it

---

[2] Growth was analysed by calculating the annual compound growth rate based on comparisons of triennial averages at terminal points of each period.

Figure 2.1: Growth rate in GDP agriculture and allied sector before and after reform at 1999–2000 prices

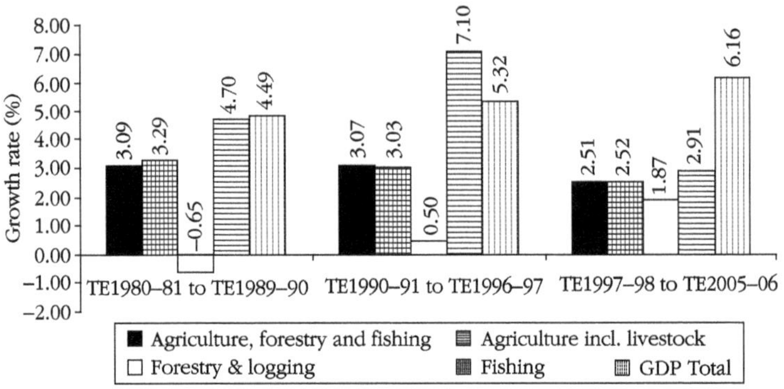

Source: *National Accounts Statistics,* various issues, Central Statistical Organisation (CSO), Government of India (GoI), New Delhi.

stood at 3.07 per cent, which was 0.02 of a percentage point lower than during the previous decade (Figure 2.1). However, during the subsequent eight to nine years the performance of the agricultural sector turned adverse and the sector registered only 2.51 per cent annual growth rate between TE 1997–98 and TE 2005–06. In sharp contrast to the agricultural sector, the overall GDP witnessed a higher growth during this period compared to initial years of reform.

Disaggregation of the GDP growth of the agriculture and allied sector (i.e., agriculture including livestock, fishery and forestry) shows that fishery was the main source for the acceleration of the growth rate in the initial years of reforms (Figure 2.1). However, the situation turned adverse beginning TE 1997–98 and this was true of all the sub-sectors of this sector. The growth rates in fisheries witnessed a decline from 7.10 per cent to 2.91 per cent whereas the growth of agriculture (including livestock) declined from 3.03 per cent to 2.52 per cent. The only sub-sector which recorded improvement in growth rates was forestry.

2.1.1 Level and Growth Rate of Crop Output

Besides the above overall trend in the GDP of agriculture including livestock, it is important to also look at the trends in the value of output of different agricultural crops within the agriculture sector. A disaggregation by agricultural crops shows that non-food grain crops experienced a high level of growth in comparison to food grain crops during the period TE 1980–81 and TE 2005–06 (Table 2.1). The period from TE 1980–81 to TE 1989–90 can be considered as a decade of reasonably satisfactory performance in India's agricultural development. At the all-India level, the value of total crop output grew at the rate of 2.86 per cent per annum. An interesting feature of the 1980s was that agricultural growth permeated to all agricultural commodity groups in India. In the case of food grains, cereals and millets grew at a rate of 3 per cent per annum while pulses witnessed an output growth of 2.12 per cent per annum. In case of non-food grain crops, oilseeds followed by condiments and spices were the main sources for the acceleration in the growth rate of agricultural output. Oilseeds and condiments and spices witnessed an unprecedented growth rate of 5.77 per cent and 4.14 per cent per annum in their respective value of total output during the 1980s. This quantum jump in the production of oilseeds in the 1980s was mainly due to a breakthrough in technology accompanied by public support on various fronts. The launch of the Technology Mission for Oilseeds in 1986 marked the beginning of a new phase in the production of oilseeds. The decade of the 1980s was also characterised by a similar growth pattern in the case of both food and non-food grain categories (Table 2.1).

Agricultural growth since 1990–91 reflects the impact of economic reforms on agricultural performance. Dividing the whole period further into pre- and post-WTO periods shows that the initial years of reform (i.e., TE 1990–91 to TE 1996–97) were characterised by a slight reduction in the growth rate of the value of total crop output in comparison to the decade of the 1980s. Disaggregation of the crop sector into food and non-food grains shows that, in sharp contrast to non-food grain crops, growth in output of food grains witnessed a sizeable reduction during the period (Table 2.1). In the category, food grains and pulses recorded negative growth, whereas, cereals and millets grew at a very slow pace during the period. As a result, growth in the value of total output of food grains declined from 2.87 per cent per annum during the 1980s to 1.55 per cent per annum during the period TE 1990–91 and TE 1996–97. In comparison to food grains, non-food grains showed a higher growth in value of output during the initial years of reform. The value of total output in case of non-food grains grew at 3.05 per cent per annum as compared to 2.86 per cent per annum during the 1980s. Horticultural crops and fibres, which accounted for 24 per cent and 4.30 per cent of the

Table 2.1: Level and growth of value of output of crops: TE 1980–81 to TE 2005–06 (at 1999–2000 prices)

Crops	Average value of output (₹ in crore)				Annual compound growth rates of VOP (% per annum)			
	TE 1980–81	TE 1990–91	TE 1997–98	TE 2005–06	TE 1980–81 to TE 1989–90	TE 1990–91 to TE 1996–97	TE 1997–98 to TE 2005–06	TE 1980–81 to TE 2005–06
Total cereals and millets	77,116	108,280	121,325	130,171	3.00	1.86	0.88	2.12
Paddy	39,584	57,420	63,427	68,615	3.27	1.59	0.99	2.22
Wheat	21,007	31,999	40,025	42,237	4.07	3.77	0.67	2.83
Total pulses	13,940	18,312	17,678	19,026	2.12	-0.35	0.92	1.25
Total food grain	91,056	126,592	139,003	149,197	2.87	1.55	0.89	1.99
Total oilseeds	14,027	25,920	32,168	35,664	5.77	3.74	1.30	3.80
Groundnut	6,974	10,820	10,266	9,962	4.17	-0.47	-0.38	1.44
Rape/mustard seed	2,400	5,422	6,835	8,838	7.73	5.07	3.27	5.35
Soybean	348	1,608	4,726	6,411	14.18	16.50	3.89	12.36
Sugar	9,113	13,262	16,071	20,863	3.42	3.16	3.32	3.37
Fibre	8,599	11,237	14,532	17,583	1.59	4.68	2.41	2.90
Drugs and narcotics	5,214	6,801	8,424	10,563	2.20	2.55	2.87	2.86
Condiments and spices	6,816	10,217	12,846	18,893	4.14	3.45	4.94	4.16
Fruits and vegetables	40,052	52,374	74,017	96,301	2.44	4.77	3.34	3.57
Total non-food grains	121,672	166,489	204,725	259,548	2.86	3.05	3.01	3.08
Grand total all crops	212,728	293,080	343,728	408,746	2.86	2.41	2.19	2.65

Source: National Accounts Statistics, various issues, Central Statistical Organisation (CSO), GoI.

value of output of total crops in the year TE 2005–06, were the main sources for the acceleration in growth rate of non-food grain output in the initial years of reforms (Table 2.1).

The most important feature of the post-WTO period was a sharp deceleration in the growth of the output of all major agricultural commodities. The growth in value of output of food grains came down from 1.55 per cent per annum during the initial years of reform to the level of 0.89 per cent per annum. While pulses experienced a positive growth in their value of output, output growth in case of cereals and millets declined from 1.86 per cent to 0.88 per cent per annum. Although during the post-WTO period, the growth in total value of non-food grains was almost stagnant at the level attained during the initial years of reform, growth in output of oilseed groups decelerated from 3.74 per cent to 1.30 per cent. Similarly, fibre crops, which were the major source of the acceleration in growth rate of non-food grains in the initial years of reforms, witnessed a decline from 4.68 per cent to 2.41 per cent. Condiments and spices along with plantation crops were the only commodity groups (in case of non-food grains) which experienced an improvement in their growth rates during the post-WTO period. To sum up, however, at the aggregate level the post-WTO period witnessed a slight reduction in growth of total output by value of the crop sector, while there was a significant decline in output growth in case of food grains along with oilseeds.

2.1.2 Changes in Yield of Agricultural Crops

Along with agricultural output, the growth rates of yields were also high during TE 1980–81 to TE 1989–90 not only at the aggregate level, but also in most of the crops/crop groups. In particular, food grains witnessed an unprecedented yield growth rate of 3.10 per cent per annum while cereal crops achieved a yield growth rate of 3.24 per cent per annum. Similarly, during TE 1980–81 to TE 1989–90, most of the non-food grain crops with the exception of fruits and vegetables recorded a moderate growth in their yield level (Table 2.2). It is clear from the analysis that during the period TE 1980–81 and TE 1989–90 food grain crops were the major source of growth in yield of total crops.

During the initial years of reform (i.e., TE 1990–91 to TE 1996–97), the growth rates of both agricultural output and of land yields slowed down as compared with the decade of the 1980s. At the all-India level, while the output growth rate decelerated to 2.41 per cent per

Table 2.2: Level and growth of crops yield: TE 1980–81 to TE 2005–06 (at 1999–2000 prices)

Crops	Yield (₹ per hectare of cultivated area)				Annual compound growth rates (% per annum)			
	TE 1980–81	TE 1990–91	TE 1997–98	TE 2005–06	TE 1980–81 to TE 1989–90	TE 1990–91 to TE 1996–97	TE 1997–98 to TE 2005–06	TE 1980–81 to TE 2005–06
Total cereals and millets	7,380	10,457	11,999	13,020	3.24	2.26	1.03	2.30
Paddy	9,872	13,598	14,623	15,930	3.03	1.22	1.08	1.93
Wheat	9,425	13,413	15,427	15,724	3.42	2.52	0.24	2.07
Total pulses	6,060	7,693	7,475	7,874	2.27	-0.31	0.65	1.05
Total food grain	7,142	9,941	11,142	12,019	3.10	1.89	0.95	2.10
Total oilseeds	9,039	10,960	11,503	12,352	1.62	1.03	0.89	1.26
Groundnut	9,759	12,772	13,673	15,179	2.82	0.92	1.31	1.78
Rape/mustard seed	12,513	11,843	11,068	13,847	-1.08	0.36	2.84	0.41
Sugar	28,192	34,175	35,373	30,858	1.83	0.40	-1.69	0.36
Fibre	9,146	13,038	14,214	18,293	3.09	2.33	3.20	2.81
Drugs and narcotics	47,861	57,963	67,792	76,819	1.69	2.03	1.57	1.91
Condiments and spices	32,244	42,104	45,402	62,188	2.41	1.47	4.01	2.66
Fruits and vegetables	83,937	80,067	97,365	99,980	-0.76	2.31	0.33	0.70
Total non-food grains	27,129	29,688	31,875	38,499	0.87	0.93	2.39	1.41
Grand total all crops	12,343	15,978	18,188	21,338	2.47	1.96	2.02	2.21

Source: National Accounts Statistics, various issues, Central Statistical Organisation (CSO), GoI; *Land Use Statistics at A Glance*, Directorate of Economics & Statistics, Ministry of Agriculture (MoA), GoI.

annum from 2.86 per cent per annum, the yield growth rate decelerated to 1.96 per cent per annum from 2.47 per cent per annum in the decade of the 1980s.

All crops/crop groups recorded a deceleration in their yield growth rates during TE 1990–91 to TE 1996–97 as compared with TE 1980–81 to TE 1989–90 (Table 2.2), the only exception being fruits and vegetables which recorded a high yield growth rate of 2.31 per cent per annum during TE 1990–91 to TE 1996–97 as compared with a negative yield growth recorded by it during the previous period. Due to high yield growth rates in horticultural crops, non-food grain crops at aggregate level showed a slight increase in their yield growth rate to 0.93 per cent per annum from 0.87 per cent per annum during the previous period. In sharp contrast to non-food grain crops, the yield growth rates in food grain crops decelerated to 1.89 per cent per annum from 3.10 per cent per annum during the previous period.

The post-WTO period (TE 1997–98 to TE 2005–06), witnessed a slight improvement in growth rates of land yields of agricultural crops at aggregate level. However, an interesting feature of the post-WTO period was the widening of the gap between food and non-food grain crops in terms of yield growth rates. In the case of food grain crops, following the pattern of output growth, the yield growth rate decelerated further to 0.95 per cent per annum from 1.89 per cent per annum during initial years of reform. In sharp contrast to food grains, the non-food grain crops witnessed a record improvement in yield growth rate. During the period TE 1997–98 to TE 2005–06, the yield growth rate of non-food grain crops accelerated to 2.39 per cent per annum from 0.93 per cent per annum in the initial years of reform. It is also clear from the analysis that since yield growth rates were the main source of output growth, yield growth rates in various crops/crop groups were highly associated with their output growth rates in all periods (Tables 2.1 and 2.2).

In summary, the growth of yields for food grains, non-food grains and total crops as a whole shows different patterns during the period TE 1980–81 and TE 2005–06. During the initial years of reform, while non-food grains experienced a stagnant growth rate, yield growth rates of food grains have come down significantly as compared to the decade of the 1980s with consequent impact on overall agricultural yields. However, during the post-WTO period though the food grains witnessed a further deceleration in yield growth rates, the yield growth rate for non-food grains improved significantly leading to a slight improvement in growth of overall agricultural yields.

2.1.3 Area under Agricultural Crops

There have been important changes in the cropping pattern in Indian agriculture during TE 1980–81 to TE 1989–90 when we had observed a notable growth in the yield levels and the growth rates of output of many crops. At the all-India level, the proportion of area under food grains registered a sharp decline from 73.98 per cent of total area in TE 1980–81 to 70.05 per cent of gross cultivated area (GCA) during TE 1989–90. It was for the first time since 1962 that area under food grains declined in absolute terms from 127.49 million hectares during TE 1980–81 to 124.99 million hectares during TE 1989–90. The shift away from food grains occurred mainly because of changes in the area under coarse cereals. During TE 1980–81 to TE 1989–90, the main area shift that took place was from coarse cereals towards oilseeds. At the all-India level, the share of area under coarse cereals in GCA declined significantly from 24.43 per cent during TE 1980–81 to 21.18 per cent of during TE 1989–90. On the other hand, the crop area under oilseeds increased by about seven million hectares and the share of oilseeds in GCA increased from 9 per cent in TE 1980–81 to 12.47 per cent in TE 1989–90 (Table 2.3).

The process of diversification in cropping pattern from food grains to non-food grains which began during the 1980s, continued over TE 1990–91 to TE 1996–97 and the share of food grains in GCA declined from 69.43 per cent in TE 1990–91 to 66.28 per cent by TE 1996–97. The economic reforms initiated during the early 1990s were expected to hasten the process of crop diversification from low value food grains to high value non-food grain crops. However, during the initial years of reform, the yield growth rates of most of the important crops including wheat and rice, oilseeds, and sugarcane decelerated considerably compared with the pre-reform period, i.e., TE 1980–81 to TE 1989–90 (Table 2.2). Consequently, during the initial years of reform, the pace of cropping pattern changes towards higher value crops slowed down as compared with the earlier phase. During TE 1990–91 to TE 1996–97, as during TE 1980–81 to TE 1989–90, the shift has occurred mainly from the area under coarse cereals and from some other crops like pulses. However, unlike the earlier period when oilseeds were the main gainers, during TE 1990–91 to TE 1996–97,

Table 2.3: Change in area of various crops: All India (TE 1989–90 over TE 1980–81)

Crops	TE 1980–81 Area (m ha)	TE 1980–81 As % of GCA	TE 1989–90 Area (m ha)	TE 1989–90 As % of GCA	Change in TE 1989–90 over TE 1980–81 Absolute change in area	Change in TE 1989–90 over TE 1980–81 % Change in area	Change in TE 1989–90 over TE 1980–81 % Change in share of crop area in GCA
Gross cropped area	172.34		178.43		6.09	3.53	3.53
Rice	40.10	23.27	40.93	22.94	0.84	2.09	-1.40
Wheat	22.29	12.93	23.58	13.22	1.29	5.80	2.19
Coarse cereals	42.10	24.43	37.78	21.18	-4.32	-10.26	-13.32
Total cereals	104.49	60.63	102.30	57.33	-2.19	-2.10	-5.44
Total pulses	23.00	13.35	22.69	12.72	-0.31	-1.34	-4.71
Total food grains	127.49	73.98	124.99	70.05	-2.50	-1.96	-5.31
Groundnut	7.15	4.15	8.03	4.50	0.89	12.44	8.60
Rape/mustard seed	1.92	1.11	4.13	2.32	2.22	115.52	108.17
Total oilseeds	15.52	9.00	22.25	12.47	6.73	43.38	38.49
Sugarcane	3.03	1.76	3.53	1.98	0.49	16.28	12.31
Total fibre	9.40	5.46	8.24	4.62	-1.16	-12.32	-15.32
Drugs and narcotics	1.09	0.63	1.14	0.64	0.05	4.59	1.02
Total condiments and spices	2.11	1.23	2.46	1.38	0.34	16.27	12.31
Total fruits and vegetables	4.77	2.77	6.35	3.56	1.58	33.07	28.53
Total non-food grains	44.85	26.02	53.44	29.95	8.59	19.15	15.08

Source: Land Use Statistics at a Glance, Directorate of Economics & Statistics, MoA, GoI.

although share of oilseeds has also increased, other crops like sugar-cane, fibres and horticultural crops also benefitted (Table 2.4). As compared with the initial years of reform, the post-WTO period (TE 1997–98 to TE 2006–07) witnessed a slower pace of process of diversification in cropping pattern. Area under food grains declined marginally by 0.62 million hectare during the post-WTO period, compared to an absolute decline of 2.51 million hectare during initial years of reform. The share of food grains in GCA also declined slightly from 66.02 per cent in TE 1997–98 to 64.81 per cent by TE 2005–06. During the post-WTO period, as during the initial years of reform, the shift has mainly been away from the area under coarse cereals and the main area shift that took place during the post-WTO period was in favour of horticultural crops. Area under horticultural crops recorded an absolute increase of 2 million hectares. The share of horticultural crops in GCA also increased from 4.02 per cent in TE 1997–98 to 5.03 per cent by TE 2005–06 (Table 2.5). In summary, during the 25 years from TE 1980–81 to TE 2005–06, the process of cropping pattern changes was pronounced. However, it was more prominent during the period TE 1980–81 to TE 1989–90 in comparison to TE 1990–91 to TE 2005–06 when a notable acceleration took place in the yield levels and the growth rates of output of many crops.

2.2 Factors Related to Agricultural Growth

In order to find out the reasons for the decline in the growth rate of agricultural output, the impact of various factors on agricultural output was estimated. Agricultural output is hypothesised to depend upon area; inputs like fertiliser; relative prices; technology (as proxied by irrigation); and infrastructure as measured by proxy indicators like investment in agriculture and institutional credit.

A number of studies for various countries have used different flexible forms of Cobb–Douglas production functions for agriculture. The most widely used among these forms is the Trans-log production function (Odhiambo 2004; Lezin and Long-bao 2005; Velazco 2006). The following general Trans-log equation was estimated in order to establish the effect of various factors on growth in agricultural output.

$$Ln(Y) = \alpha + \Sigma\beta_i Ln(X_i) + \mu$$

Table 2.4: Change in area of various crops: All India (TE 1996–97 over TE 1990–91)

Crops	TE 1990–91		TE 1996–97		Change in TE 1996–97 over TE 1990–91		
	Area (m ha)	As % of GCA	Area (m ha)	As % of GCA	Absolute change in area	% Change in area	% Change in share of crop area in GCA
Gross cropped area	183.43		188.34		4.91	2.68	
Rice	42.23	23.02	43.15	22.91	0.92	2.18	–0.49
Wheat	23.86	13.01	25.66	13.62	1.80	7.56	4.75
Coarse cereals	37.46	20.42	32.29	17.14	–5.18	–13.82	–16.07
Total cereals	103.55	56.45	101.09	53.67	–2.45	–2.37	–4.92
Total pulses	23.80	12.98	23.75	12.61	–0.06	–0.24	–2.85
Total food grains	127.35	69.43	124.84	66.28	–2.51	–1.97	–4.53
Groundnut	8.47	4.62	7.79	4.14	–0.68	–8.01	–10.41
Rape/mustard seed	4.58	2.50	6.03	3.20	1.45	31.74	28.31
Total oilseeds	23.65	12.89	27.72	14.72	4.07	17.21	14.15
Sugarcane	3.68	2.00	4.43	2.35	0.75	20.40	17.26
Total fibre	8.62	4.70	9.88	5.24	1.26	14.59	11.60
Drugs and narcotics	1.17	0.64	1.21	0.64	0.04	3.12	0.44
Total condiments and spices	2.43	1.32	2.72	1.45	0.30	12.28	9.35
Total fruits and vegetables	6.54	3.57	7.54	4.00	1.00	15.30	12.29
Total non-food grains	56.08	30.57	63.50	33.72	7.42	13.24	10.28

Source: Land Use Statistics at A Glance, Directorate of Economics & Statistics, MoA, GoI.

Table 2.5: Change in area of various crops: All India (TE 2005–06 over TE 1997–98)

Crops	TE 1997–98		TE 2005–06		Change in TE 2005–06 over TE 1997–98		
	Area (m ba)	As % of GCA	Area (m ba)	As % of GCA	Absolute change in area	% Change in area	% Change in share of crop area in GCA
Gross cropped area	188.99		191.56		2.57	1.36	
Rice	43.38	22.95	43.07	22.49	–0.30	–0.70	–2.03
Wheat	25.95	13.73	26.86	14.02	0.92	3.53	2.14
Coarse cereals	31.79	16.82	30.04	15.68	–1.75	–5.50	–6.77
Total cereals	101.11	53.50	99.98	52.19	–1.13	–1.12	–2.45
Total pulses	23.65	12.51	24.16	12.61	0.51	2.17	0.80
Total food grains	124.76	66.02	124.14	64.81	–0.62	–0.50	–1.83
Groundnut	7.51	3.97	6.56	3.43	–0.95	–12.59	–13.77
Rape/mustard seed	6.18	3.27	6.38	3.33	0.21	3.36	1.98
Total oilseeds	27.97	14.80	28.87	15.07	0.91	3.24	1.86
Sugarcane	4.42	2.34	4.46	2.33	0.04	0.98	–0.37
Total fibre	10.22	5.41	9.61	5.02	–0.61	–5.99	–7.25
Drugs and narcotics	1.24	0.66	1.38	0.72	0.13	10.65	9.16
Total condiments and spices	2.83	1.50	3.04	1.59	0.21	7.38	5.93
Total fruits and vegetables	7.60	4.02	9.63	5.03	2.03	26.70	25.00
Total non-food grains	64.23	33.98	67.42	35.19	3.19	4.97	3.56

Source: Land Use Statistics at A Glance, Directorate of Economics & Statistics, MoA, GoI.

where,

Y is the agricultural output,
X_is are different inputs,
β_i are their respective coefficients,
α is the intercept, and
μ is the error term.

Based on the above, the following Cobb–Douglas production function for the value of agricultural output at constant price (1999–2000 prices) in India has been framed.

$$Y = \alpha \cdot A^\beta \cdot I^\gamma \cdot P^\delta \cdot T^\lambda \cdot I_n^\phi \cdot Cr^\theta$$

Or

$$Ln(Y) = \alpha + \beta Ln(A) + \gamma Ln(I) + \delta Ln(P)$$
$$+ \lambda Ln(T) + \phi Ln(I_n) + \theta Ln(Cr)$$

where,

Y is the value of agricultural output at constant price,
A is net area sown,
I is consumption of fertiliser,
P is relative prices as measured by gross TOT between agriculture and non-agriculture,
T is irrigation as measured by percentage share of gross irrigated area in gross cropped area,
I_n is investment in agriculture, and
Cr is institutional credit.
β, γ, δ, λ, ϕ and θ are the respective elasticities.

The effect of these various factors on agricultural output was estimated for the period 1980–81 to 2005–06.

The rationale for inclusion and the expected relationships of the various explanatory variables with the independent variable, i.e., crop output, are stated in the following paragraphs.

Gross terms of trade

In this analysis, we have used gross Terms of Trade, measured as the ratio of agricultural GDP and non-agricultural GDP deflators. *A priori*, the impact of TOT on agricultural output is indeterminate in its direction (i.e., >0 = <0). This follows from two opposing effects of TOT. One of these is positive (i.e., >0), which follows from the reasoning that when Terms of Trade improve, farmers' incentives to save/invest improve, with consequent decline/increase in consumption/investment, which increases the aggregate agricultural supply. Another is that with the improvement in relative prices, returns to labour supply increases. which may also provide an incentive for increased effort with the resulting increase in aggregate output. But the negative impact (i.e., <0) of a change in Terms of Trade follows from the fact that when the relative prices improve, farmers' income also increases with consequent increase/decrease in consumption/investment, which eventually decreases aggregate output. Similarly, improved income encourages farmers to substitute leisure for labour supply and thereby lowers the aggregate output. Thus, depending on which of these positive and negative impacts is larger, the 'net' aggregate impact could be positive or negative (Desai and D'Souza 1999; Desai 2002).

Net area sown

Agricultural output should increase with net area sown. The reason behind using net rather than gross cropped area is to capture the effect of bringing the new land into production, and not the effect of changes in the gross cropped area that arise from increased multiple cropping on existing land as a result of new irrigation investment and quicker growing crop varieties.

Fertiliser consumption

Fertiliser consumption in terms of NPK (nitrogen, phosphorous, and potassium) has also been taken into account for explaining the changes in aggregate crop output for the reason that it is an important input for raising land productivity. Though one can expect a positive impact on agricultural output, it should also be borne in mind that beyond the optimum level, either overdose or sub-optimal input levels may also reduce returns.

Irrigation

Irrigation is expected to have a positive impact on production in its own right. Additionally, irrigation is used as a proxy for technological change. Irrigation may also increase the demand for capital goods arising from irrigation investment.

Public and private gross capital formation

Investment generates capital in the form of infrastructure, improvement in quality of natural resources and assets, and creation of productive assets, and it comes from two sources, viz., public and private. A high complementarity between these two types of investment was observed by many scholars. The public investment has been taken into account with a view to determine whether its declining trend since the mid-1980s has had an adverse impact on aggregate output. The reverse is expected in the case of private investment, because of its increasing trend over the period.

The TOT for agriculture was estimated by taking the ratio of implicit price deflators for agricultural and non-agricultural GDP at 1999–2000 prices. Institutional credit was taken as a sum of short-term and long-term direct agricultural loans advanced during the year by all institutional sources and were expressed at 1999–2000 prices by deflating the figures by the implicit price deflator for GDP from agriculture. Public and private investment in agriculture was taken as gross fixed capital formation (GFCF) in agriculture by the public and private sectors at 1999–2000 prices. Fertiliser was measured as the amount of nitrogen, phosphorous, and potassium (NPK) used during a year. Irrigation refers to the percentage share of gross irrigated area in gross cropped area.

2.2.1 Estimates from the Regression Analysis

Using all these variables in a single equation is not appropriate on econometric grounds and it also poses serious problems of multicollinearity. Therefore, the relationship between agricultural output and factors affecting it was estimated by using different sets of variables as explanatory variables.

The results of different formulations of econometric models are presented in (Table 2.6) along with their probabilities and other statistics. In Model 1, net area sown, consumption of total fertiliser, institutional credit, Terms of Trade and total investment in agriculture were used as explanatory variables. All these variables turned out to be statistically highly significant. Net sown area showed the most significant impact on output; 1 unit (i.e., 1,000 hectare) increase in net sown area resulted in 1.14 per cent increase in the value of agriculture output. Improvement in TOT for agriculture by 1.0 per cent led to a 0.68 per cent increase in value of output. Similarly, 1.0 per cent increase in existing level of total investment in agriculture institutional credit increased the value of agricultural output by 0.05 and 0.08 per cent, respectively.

It may further be noted that when the public and private investments are included as explanatory variables in Model 2, both the sources of investment in agriculture is found to play a positive role in influencing the aggregate crop output over the period. Elasticity of value of agricultural output with respect to public and private investment was estimated to be 0.08 and 0.07. As was the case with Model 1, the net sown area and irrigation have again emerged as the most significant influences on the value of agricultural output. Both the variables turned out to be statistically highly significant. In order to examine the relative role of price and non-price factors in effecting agricultural output, Model 3 captures only non-price and price variables (terms of trade). As shown in Table 2.6, price and non-price variables together explain 99 per cent of the variation in total agricultural output. However, in comparison to terms of trade (i.e., relative prices), it is the non-price factors (such as net area sown, irrigation) that dominantly determine growth in farm output.

Thus, what emerges from our analysis is that during the period 1980–81 to 2005–06, both price and non-price factors played a positive role in determining agricultural output. However, in comparison to price factors, non-price factors played a dominant role in determining output growth at the all-India level. We now proceed to an examination of changes in these factors to link these changes to output growth in various periods, classifying these into price and non-price elements.

2.3 Price and Non-price Factors and Recent Agricultural Growth

In seeking an explanation for slow growth we start out by looking at factors that played a positive role in determining agricultural growth in our analysis of the previous section.

2.3.1 Terms of Trade

Table 2.7 presents three kinds of sectoral terms of trade between the agricultural and non-agricultural sectors: first, the ratio of implicit price deflators for agriculture and non-agriculture sectors (i.e., gross terms of trade); second, indices reflecting the ratio of prices received to

Table 2.6: Estimates of effect of different factors on output of agriculture: 1980–81 to 2005–06 (Dependent variable: Value of agricultural output at 1999–2000 prices) (All variables in natural log)

Explanatory Variables	Model 1		Model 2		Model 3	
	Coefficient	Probability	Coefficient	Probability	Coefficient	Probability
Constant	(–) 8.15	0.04	(–) 13.55	0.00	(–) 10.46	0.02
Net Area Sown	1.14	0.00	1.71	0.00	1.43	0.00
Total Fertiliser in terms of NPK	0.29	0.00	0.09	0.15	0.15	0.08
Irrigation	–	–	1.01	0.00	0.55	0.08
Institutional Credit	0.08	0.00	–	–	0.09	0.00
Terms of Trade (–1)	0.68	0.00	–	–	0.38	0.14
Public Investment	–	–	0.08	0.01	–	–
Private Investment	–	–	0.07	0.00	–	–
Total Investment	0.05	0.18	–	–	–	–
Important Statistics						
R-squared	0.99		0.99		0.99	
Adjusted R-squared	0.98		0.98		0.98	
Log Likelihood	59.85		64.00		60.78	
D-W Stat.	2.20		1.85		2.12	

Source: Author's own calculation.

Table 2.7: Index of Terms of Trade (TOT) between agriculture and non-agriculture sector

	Combined index of prices paid	Index of prices received	Input-output price ratio	Agriculture's Terms of Trade Base 1990–91 = 100	Gross terms of trade Base 1999–2000 = 100
1981–82	61.9	54.9	1.61	88.7	87.08
1982–83	66.0	60.3	1.51	91.4	86.78
1983–84	70.1	64.2	1.42	91.6	86.54
1984–85	72.4	68.0	1.36	93.9	84.47
1985–86	75.2	70.4	1.34	93.6	84.24
1986–87	80.2	76.7	1.29	95.7	85.56
1987–88	88.3	86.0	1.19	97.4	89.80
1988–89	91.8	90.3	1.07	98.3	87.75
1989–90	98.1	97.5	1.02	99.4	88.77
1990–91	110.2	112.3	0.93	101.9	90.59
1991–92	123.8	130.8	0.91	105.6	96.85
1992–93	133.5	138.7	1.01	103.9	92.19
1993–94	146.1	151.4	1.01	103.6	94.95
1994–95	160.5	171.1	0.97	106.6	95.21
1995–96	173.7	182.9	0.95	105.3	95.78
1996–97	184.8	190.6	0.95	103.1	97.72

1997–98	194.9	205.9	0.93	105.6	100.61
1998–99	209.9	220.8	0.89	105.2	100.56
1999–00	214.0	219.8	0.93	102.7	100.00
2000–01	223.0	225.0	1.02	100.9	97.07
2001–02	229.0	235.3	1.00	102.8	95.69
2002–03	239.3	247.9	1.02	103.6	96.72
2003–04	248.7	251.2	1.03	101.0	95.68
2004–05	257.5	258.2	1.02	100.3	93.85
2005–06	270.6	275.8	1.00	101.9	95.23

Source: Report of CACP and National Account Statistics, CSO.

Note: Prices paid are for intermediate purchases and may be treated as variable inputs other than labour.

prices paid by the agriculture sector, i.e., agriculture's terms of trade (or barter terms of trade); and third, the ratio of index of prices paid out for intermediate consumption to prices received, or an index of input–output price ratios. This is only a version of the terms of trade itself, with the difference being that the former index (i.e., barter terms of trade) is more finely weighted.

For the purposes of our analysis in the previous section, we had taken the gross terms of trade measured as the ratio of the implicit deflators of agricultural and non-agricultural GDP. It does not, of course, represent the prices at which the commodities are traded among sectors. What it measures is the relative valuation of agricultural and non-agricultural products (Misra and Hazell 1996). Since it is based on the value added concept, one can argue that it is akin to income rather than barter terms of trade (Desai and D'Souza 1999). However, empirically, as one can see from Table 2.7, the gross terms of trade are moving along with barter terms of trade (agriculture's terms of trade), although there is no point-to-point correspondence between the two. It may be noted that the correlation coefficient (r) between gross terms of trade and barter terms of trade works out to be quite high, being 0.85 during the period 1981–82 to 2005–06. This reassures that gross terms of trade are quite akin to barter terms of trade. Despite some limitations of gross terms of trade, it has the following advantages: First, it is the simplest and the most economical in estimating terms of trade. The coverage of gross terms of trade is also quite comprehensive (Pandit 2000) and consistent with other estimates, like saving and investment, published by the Central Statistical Organisation (CSO). Second, the value added at factors cost does not take indirect taxes and subsidies into account. The GDP deflators are, therefore, free from the distortion caused by them. It, therefore, seems to provide a fairly accurate trend about the relative prices received by the two sectors involved in estimating terms of trade. And third, in principle, the gross terms of trade is better because it measures the relative returns to the investing resources in the two sectors, and it corrects for increases in productivity in both sectors.

The gross terms of trade and the input–output price ratio show dissimilar movements over the 15 years since 1990–91, the year immediately prior to the initiation of reforms (see Table 2.7 and Figure 2.2). The gross terms of trade had begun to move in favour of agriculture since early 1980s and continued to do so till around mid-1990s.

The rise in the 1990s was partly because of the falling levels of industrial protection and partly because of the rising administered (procurement) prices of food grains, particularly rice and wheat. However, the gross terms of trade began to fall sharply after 1997–98, owing to the sharp fall in international prices of primary commodities.

Figure 2.2: Movement of gross terms of trade and input–output price ratio: 1981–82 to 2005–06

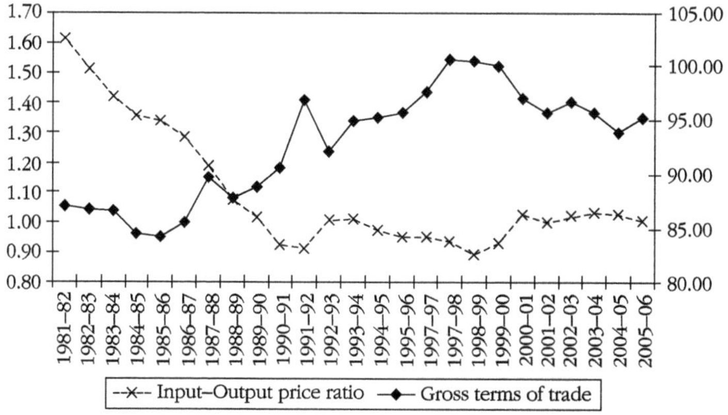

Source: Report of CACP and National Account Statistics, CSO.

On the other hand, the input–output price ratio was falling in the 1980s, denoting a shift in favour of agriculture. However, during the 1990s, the input–output price ratio, which fluctuated up to mid-1990s indicating no clear trend, began to rise since 1998–99 denoting a shift against agriculture. Therefore, the pattern of movement of the gross terms of trade and the input–output price ratio clearly indicates a favourable movement for agriculture during the 1980s. However, during the 1990s, although gross terms of trade showed trends that were favourable for agriculture up to mid-1990s, the input–output price ratio shows no clear trend since the early 1990s up to 1997–98 and then denotes a shift against agriculture as was the case with gross terms of trade. The observed dissimilar movement in the gross terms of trade and input–output price ratio since the early 1990s to mid-1990s requires explanation. It is, however, important to recognise this exercise for what it is. Here, we are calculating gross terms of trade as a ratio of the implicit deflators of agricultural and non-agricultural GDP. Unlike gross terms of trade, input–output price ratio is the ratio of index of prices paid for intermediate consumption to index of prices received. The relative movement of different indices of prices paid for during the period explains the observed difference in movement in gross terms of trade and input–output price ratio (Appendix, Table A-2.2). Taking the ratio of combined index of prices paid (instead of intermediate consumption) to index of prices received shows the similar trend as observed in gross terms of trade.

Comparing the growth in agricultural output with the movement in terms of trade shows that a high growth in agricultural output during the 1980s was accompanied by favourable movements in gross terms of trade and input–output price ratios. However, during the initial years of reform when output growth slightly decelerated, though gross terms of trade was moving in favour of agriculture the input–output price ratio exhibited no clear pattern. During the post-WTO period, say after 1997–98, when growth in agricultural output deteriorated further, both gross terms of trade and input–output price ratios showed a shift against agriculture. Therefore, the predicted impact of trade liberalisation on agriculture's terms of trade could not materialise. Second, analysis also reveals no unidirectional link between agricultural growth and relative prices during the entire post-reform period, thus indicating no significant or very marginal relationship between these two.

2.3.2 Investment in Agriculture

Capital formation in Indian agriculture is undertaken by both the public and the private sectors. While public investment is meant mainly for creation of infrastructure, private investment is used (mainly) for assets formation and for improvement of the quality of existing assets. The agricultural sector in developing economies, which accounts for a dominant share in overall GDP and also determines the growth of other sectors and the overall economy to a large extent, is generally characterised by lack of investment resources because private investment is deterred by the risk involved in agriculture (Schultz 1964) and institutional investment has also been meagre (Shonfield 1960). This highlights the requirement of special effort and the need to direct and induce public and private investments into the agricultural sector in these economies.

Beginning with the seminal work of Ragnar Nurkse (1953) in the early 1950s, a large number of studies have been conducted in all the countries on capital formation and investments in the agriculture sector. The foremost study in this area in India has been done by Tara Shukla (1965). This study prepared the estimates of value of durable physical assets, capital stock and capital formation for selective years during 1920–21 to 1960–61 at country level and for select states using data from the Agricultural Statistics of India, Livestock Censuses and various other reports. The estimates pertain to capital in the private sector. And subsequently, the work of estimation of capital formation in various sectors of the economy has been undertaken by the CSO, of the Government of India, and has been widely used by scholars to study capital formation in Indian agriculture.

A cursory look at the CSO series at constant prices (i.e., 1999–2000 prices) reveals that aggregate capital formation appears to collapse with the initiation of reforms and remains depressed throughout the 1990s. Capital formation rises over the level of 1990–91 only in 1999–2000, making the 1990s a period of low investment in agriculture (Figure 2.3). The figure for aggregate capital formation, however, masks a difference between the private and public sectors. The history of public capital formation in the 1990s is the continuation of a trend discernible since 1980–81. The consistent decline in public investment came to a halt only in 2000–01 when it reached the level of ₹7,156 crore or 40 per cent below its level in 1980–81. The behaviour

Figure 2.3: Gross capital formation in agriculture at 1999–2000 prices: 1980–81 to 2005–06

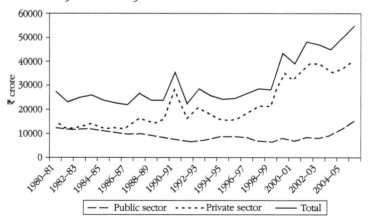

Source: National Accounts Statistics, various issues, Central Statistical Organisation (CSO), GoI.

of private capital formation is more volatile, unlike public capital formation, collapsing with the onset of the reforms and remaining depressed during the first half of the 1990s. However, unlike public capital formation it begins to rise from the mid-1990s and witnesses more than a twofold increase over the decade from the mid-1990s (Figure 2.3). Therefore, private investment since the early 1980s did not follow public investment, contrary to what has been asserted by some scholars (Krishnamurty 1985; Bhattacharya and Hanumantha Rao 1988; Shetty 1990; Hanumantha Rao 1994) that there is a high complementarity between the two types of investments.

Eyeballing the data, we find that the decline in public investment was much higher during the 1980s than during the decade of the 1990s. The volume of public investment in the agricultural sector declined by more than 35 per cent during 1980–81 and 1989–90 as compared with a marginal decline of 2 per cent during the 1990s. In sharp contrast to public investment, private investment in the agricultural sector witnessed an increase in its volume by 7 per cent and 30 per cent during the decade of the 1980s and 1990s, respectively.

The share of aggregate capital formation in agricultural GDP shows a declining trend until around the late 1990s and a reversal after that. A further disaggregation into public and private sector capital formation indicates that the share of public capital formation in agricultural GDP witnessed an uninterrupted decline until 2000–01 when it amounted to 1.76 per cent of agricultural GDP. The period after 2000–01 witnessed a reversal of this trend (Figure 2.4). The share of private capital formation in agricultural GDP was much higher and that share begins to rise from the mid-1990s. However, the decline in agricultural output growth since the initiation of reform is very much consistent with the decline in capital formation at the aggregate level. Nevertheless, the slowing of the rate of growth of output at a time of accelerating private investment since the mid-1990s requires explanation. The probable explanations could be the longer gestation period of infrastructure projects in the agricultural sector than elsewhere in the economy. Further, the impact of the depressed state of public capital formation may not have been fully offset by the rising capital formation in the private sector.

2.3.3 Irrigation

For agricultural production, irrigation is arguably the most important input (Vaidyanathan 2007) after seed, and the most important

Figure 2.4: Percentage share in agricultural GDP of gross capital formation in agriculture at 1999–2000 prices: 1980–81 to 2005–06

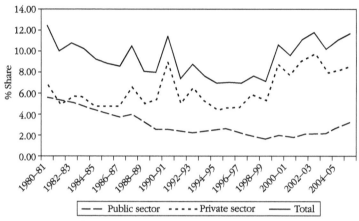

Source: *National Accounts Statistics*, various issues, Central Statistical Organisation (CSO), GoI.

element of public capital formation. However, the area under irrigation measures only the potential reach of an irrigation facility and not the actual delivery. However, it is the only indicator available which shows water made available via irrigation.

Note from the data in Tables 2.8 and 2.9 that growth in coverage of irrigated area in all the main crop categories has slowed in the 1990s. However, the initial years of reform has shown some improvement in the growth of area under irrigation, compared to the post-WTO period. For oilseeds and cotton, the growth in area under irrigation during the post-WTO period was negative. This information must be seen in light of the already very low levels of irrigated area in India by international standards. In the mid-1990s, the percentage of area irrigated in India was less than in Bangladesh and Nepal, lower than in China, and less than half that in Japan and Korea.

Decline in public investment during the 1990s is the main reason for the deceleration of the growth rate of area under irrigation. It is justified on the ground that more than 90 per cent of public investment in agriculture is used for development of medium, major and minor irrigation (Chand 2000). The other probable reasons could be decline in electric power to agriculture most of which is used for tubewells (Chand et al. 2007).

Table 2.8: The expansion of irrigation (irrigated area, percentage)

Crop/Year	1970–71	1980–81	1990–91	2000–01	2005–06
Rice	38.40	40.70	45.50	53.60	56.00
Wheat	54.30	76.50	81.10	88.10	89.60
Coarse cereals	8.30	9.20	9.00	12.50	13.00
Pulses	8.80	9.00	10.50	12.50	15.00
Food grains	24.10	29.70	35.10	43.40	45.50
Oilseeds	7.40	14.50	22.90	23.00	28.00
Cotton	17.30	27.30	32.90	34.30	36.10
Sugarcane	72.40	81.20	86.90	92.10	92.50

Source: Directorate of Economics & Statistics, Ministry of Agriculture, GoI.

Table 2.9: The growth in area under irrigation (percentage)

	1989–90 to 2006–07	1992–93 to 1996–97	1997–98 to 2001–02	2002–03 to 2004–05
Rice	1.33	1.97	1.26	–1.86
Wheat	1.42	2.18	0.34	1.03
Pulses	1.85	3.57	0.78	5.11
Food grains	1.25	1.74	0.91	–0.06
Cotton	0.88	5.24	–2.46	–4.34
Oilseeds	–0.28	2	–4.8	7.35
Sugarcane	1.94	2.73	2.38	–4.7

Source: Directorate of Economics & Statistics, Ministry of Agriculture, GoI.

2.3.4 Institutional Credit

Recognising the significance of the agricultural sector in India's economic development, the government since Independence has played a crucial role in creating a broad-based institutional framework for sufficient and timely supply of credit to the sector to cater its increasing credit requirements. In this context, a multi-agency approach involving co-operative banks, scheduled commercial banks and Regional Rural Banks (RRBs) has been followed for providing credit support to the sector. Thrust has been given on adequate and timely availability of credit at reasonable rates by expanding institutional framework, its outreach and scale. As a result, over a period of time, impressive progress has been achieved in terms of the scale and reach of agricultural credit. Some of the distinct trends can be listed as follows:

1. The public sector banks have made commendable progress, particularly in the aftermath of nationalisation of banks, in terms of setting up a wide banking network. The number of offices of scheduled commercial banks increased rapidly from 8,262 in June 1969 to 73,836 by March 2007.

2. Despite some setback in the trend observed particularly in the 1990s, one of the major achievements in India since Independence has been the widening of the institutional credit machinery and resulting decline in the role of non-institutional sources. For instance, the share of institutional credit, which was around 7 per cent in 1951, has increased to over 66 per cent in 1991, reflecting a parallel decline in the share of non-institutional credit from around 93 per cent to about 31 per cent (Table 2.10)

Table 2.10: Relative share of borrowing of cultivator households from different sources

Credit Sources	1951	1961	1971	1981	1991	2002
Non-Institutional	92.7	81.3	68.3	36.8	30.6	38.9
of which						
Money Lenders	69.7	49.2	36.1	16.1	17.5	26.8
Institutional	7.3	18.7	31.7	63.2	66.3	61.1
of which						
Cooperative Societies/ Banks	3.3	2.6	22	29.8	23.6	30.2
Commercial Banks	0.9	0.6	2.4	28.8	35.2	26.3
Unspecified	–	–	–	–	3.1	–
Total	100	100	100	100	100	100

Source: All India Debt and Investment Survey and National Sample Survey Organisation (NSSO).

Despite their wide network, co-operative banks, particularly since the 1990s, have lost their dominant position to commercial banks. The share of co-operative banks (22 per cent) during 2005–06 was less than half of what it was in 1992–93 (62 per cent), while the share of commercial banks (33 to 68 per cent) including RRBs (5 to 10 per cent) almost doubled during this period. The efforts to increase the flow of credit to agriculture seems to have yielded better results in the recent period as the total institutional credit to agriculture recorded a growth of around 21 per cent during 1995–96 to 2004–05 from little over 12 per cent during 1986–87 to 1994–95. In terms of total credit to agriculture, the commercial banks recorded a considerable growth (from around 13 per cent to about 21 per cent), while cooperative banks registered a fall (from over 14 per cent to over 10 per cent) during the above period (Table 2.11).

In order to investigate the role of credit in the slower growth of output since 1991, a comparative decadal analysis of direct credit to agriculture and disaggregation as per farm size was undertaken. The comparative analysis of direct credit to agriculture and allied activities during the 1980s and 1990s reveals that the average share of long-term credit in the total direct finance has not only been much lower but has also declined, which could have a dampening effect on agricultural investment. In Indian agriculture, the majority (more than 80 per cent) of farms are in the category referred to as small and marginal. Yet, the disaggregated picture of the size-wise distribution of credit also reveals the fact that the growth of direct finance to small and marginal farmers witnessed a marked deceleration from about 24 per cent in the 1980s to little over 13 per cent during the 1990s, which could have had a dampening effect on the productivity of small and marginal farms and, in turn, on the growth of output. The decline in growth of direct finance to small and marginal farms may be attributed, *inter alia*, to the 'risk aversion' of the bankers, which may lead to a focus on larger farmers who are better placed to offer collateral.

2.3.5 Fertiliser

The role of fertiliser use in increasing agricultural productivity and production during the last five and half decades has been well documented. A very close association is observed between the growth of fertiliser consumption and crop productivity in almost all the states of the country. No input in agriculture has seen as much growth as the use of fertiliser in the recent history of Indian agriculture. The trend in consumption of fertiliser in terms of total and per hectare of gross cropped area shows that there was a small deceleration in growth of fertiliser use after 1980–81, but the rate of growth was still quite high,

Table 2.11: Institutional credit to agriculture (₹ crore)

						Institutions				
Year	Cooperative Banks	Share (%)	RRBs	Share (%)	Commercial Banks	Share (%)	Grand Total	% change
1980–81	–	–	–	–	–	–	3,140	–
1981–82	–	–	–	–	–	–	3,607	15
1982–83	–	–	–	–	–	–	4,576	27
1983–84	–	–	–	–	–	–	5,066	11
1984–85	–	–	–	–	–	–	5,556	10
1985–86	3,874	55	–	–	3,131	45	7,005	26
1986–87	4,207	52	–	–	3,809	48	8,016	14
1987–88	4,420	52	–	–	4,009	48	8,429	5
1988–89	4,851	53	–	–	4,233	47	9,084	8
1989–90	5,082	52	–	–	4,719	48	9,801	8
1990–91	3,408	39	–	–	5,438	61	8,846	–10
1991–92	5,800	52	596	5	4,806	43	11,202	27
1992–93	9,378	62	831	5	4,960	33	15,169	35
1993–94	10,117	61	977	6	5,400	33	16,494	9
1994–95	9,406	50	1,083	6	8,255	44	18,744	14
1995–96	10,479	48	1,381	6	10,172	46	22,032	18

Table 2.11: (*Continued*)

Table 2.11: (*Continued*)

					Institutions				
Year	Cooperative Banks	Share (%)	RRBs	Share (%)	Commercial Banks	Share (%)	Grand Total	% change
1996–97	11,944	45	1,684	6	12,783	48	26,411	20
1997–98	14,085	44	2,040	6	15,831	50	31,956	21
1998–99	15,870	43	2,460	7	18,443	50	36,860	15
1999–00	18,260	39	3,172	7	24,733	53	46,268	26
2000–01	20,718	39	4,219	8	27,807	53	52,827	14
2001–02	23,524	38	4,854	8	33,587	54	62,045	17
2002–03	23,636	34	6,070	9	39,774	57	69,560	12
2003–04	26,875	31	7,581	9	52,441	60	86,981	25
2004–05	31,231	25	12,404	10	81,481	65	125,309	44
2005–06	39,404	22	15,223	8	125,477	70	180,486	44

Source: Economic Survey and NABARD, various issues.

Note: Commercial Banks and RRBs were clubbed together up to 1990–91.

being more than 8 per cent, resulting in a doubling of per hectare use of fertiliser by the year 1990–91. The serious slowdown started after 1991–92 which was further exacerbated after 1999–00. The rate of growth in fertiliser consumption declined to around 4 per cent or half the value of the 1980s during the period 1990–91 to 1999–2000. This can be seen from Figure 2.5 which presents total and per hectare use of NPK for the period 1980–81 to 2005–06.

Figure 2.5: Consumption of total fertilisers and in terms of per hectare gross cropped area

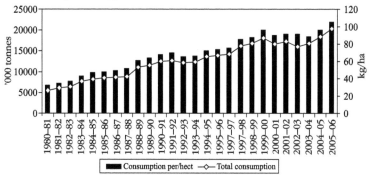

Source: *Agricultural Statistics at A Glance*, Directorate of Economics & Statistics, Ministry of Agriculture, GoI.

Total fertiliser consumption in the country reached a level of 18.069 million tonnes during 1999–00 and in the next four years it varied between 16.09 to 17.35 million tonnes. Similarly, per hectare use of NPK reached 95.4 kg during 1999–00 but remained below 92 kg during the next four years. The two years, 2004–05 and 2005–06, have seen some recovery in fertiliser use in the country. These trends suggest that the decline in crop productivity during the 1990s and onwards was closely associated with a decline in fertiliser consumption since the early 1990s.

The relative price shifts in case of fertilisers induced by economic reform have had a major impact on the final consumption of fertiliser and explains the decline in fertiliser consumption growth during the 1990s. Till 1992, fertiliser prices in India were controlled, and the maximum retail prices of various fertilisers were set by the government. A partial decontrol of fertiliser prices was undertaken in 1992, as part of the economic reform programme. The prices of phosphate

(P) and potash (K) fertilisers were decontrolled, while the prices of urea (N) continued to be under control. As a result, there were major increases in the prices of phosphate and potash fertilisers, while urea prices continued to be moderate. In 1990–91, the price per tonne of Urea, Di-Ammonium Phosphate (DAP) and Muriate of Potash (MOP) were ₹2,350, ₹3,600 and ₹1,300 respectively. The corresponding prices in 1995–96 were ₹3,320, ₹9,800 and ₹4,450 respectively. After 1997, there was an effort to restore parity in prices through a concession scheme, and in 2003 the Retention Pricing Scheme (RPS) on urea was replaced with a Group Pricing Scheme (GPS). Nevertheless, the relative price differences have persisted; in 2003–04, the prices of the three fertilisers were, respectively, ₹4,830, ₹9,350 and ₹4,455.

2.4 Conclusion

The analysis of this chapter may be summed up as follows:

First, the trend growth of agricultural output during the last 25 years shows that the decade of the 1980s witnessed an unprecedented annual growth rate of crop output with a significant change in the cropping pattern away from coarse cereals towards more valuable oilseed crops. An interesting feature of the 1980s was that agricultural growth permeated to all agricultural commodity groups in India. The post-reform period was characterised by a serious retrogression both in the matter of levels and growth rates of yield and output in almost all crops/crop groups and a slowdown in diversification towards oilseeds. The disquieting aspect of the post-reform growth process was that the agricultural and non-agricultural sectors were on a disparate growth path.

Second, the analysis of factors related to agricultural growth during the period 1980–81 to 2005–06 shows that both price and non-price factors played a positive role in determining agricultural output. However, in comparison to price factors, non-price factors played a dominant role in influencing output growth at the all-India level.

Third, the analysis of the factors that influence agricultural growth shows that a slowdown/stagnation or even decline in growth of fertiliser use, irrigation and net sown area, and a decline in the capital stock in agriculture have had an adverse impact on agricultural growth during the post-reform period. On the price front, the predicted positive impact of trade liberalisation on agriculture's terms of trade could not materialise. Also, no unidirectional link between agricultural growth and relative prices was observed, thereby indicating no significant relationship between these two. The evidence of price shifts is too marginal to account for the observed slowing of growth during the post-reform period.

3
Agricultural Price Policy and Farm Profitability
Examining Linkages

Agricultural price policy basically involves intervention in agricultural produce markets with a view to influencing the level of, and fluctuations in, prices and the price spread from farm gate to the retail level. The formulation of agricultural price policy is complicated by the multiplicity of functions that price performs. The objectives, thrust and instruments of agricultural price policy have undergone conspicuous shifts during the last 50 years. Upto the mid-1960s, the main instruments of policy were controls/restrictions on food grain sales, food imports and distribution of food grains at pre-specified prices that were normally below the market prices. After the mid-1960s, when new seed-fertiliser technology became available, price policy was assigned a positive role of augmenting the availability of food grains by increasing domestic production. The emphasis of the policy was on achieving the twin objectives of assuring remunerative prices to the farmers and providing food grains to the consumers and raw material to the industry at reasonable prices. The framework of the policy was modified in 1980 and its emphasis shifted from maximising the production of food grains to ensuring a diversified production pattern consistent with the overall needs of the economy. Again in 1986, the emphasis of policy shifted to building into the system factors, which in the long run would influence the prices of farm products and make the farm sector more vibrant, productive and cost effective. Further, in the wake of liberalisation, price policy assumed a significant role as a means of providing a safety net to farmers exposed to the workings of the market in the form of state intervention in the agricultural product markets as well as a component of the safeguard measures. In sum, the context of price policy has changed substantially over the years and so also has the role and effectiveness of price policy as a tool to influence the agricultural economy.

The post-reform period witnessed a dilution of the supportive mechanisms that were built up, in stages, in the post-Independence period to protect the farmers from the uncertainties of the market (Patnaik 2003). During the post-reform period, the government not only cut the subsidies on major inputs, but also absolved itself of the responsibility to produce or procure and distribute these inputs at farm gates. At the same time, greater reliance on free markets was expected to deliver higher incomes and greater efficiency to the farm sector while enabling subsidies to be reduced. A crucial part of the reforms strategy was, therefore, to increase agricultural prices and reduce subsidies. This was sought to be achieved both by allowing freer trade and by offering higher support prices. As a consequence, the earlier policy of 'low-input and low-output' prices shifted to 'high-input and high-output' prices (Acharya 1997).

Therefore, ironically, the post-reform period required higher emphasis and dependence on price policy as compared with previous decades, where price policy aimed only at maintaining a balance between the interests of consumers and producers. This has provoked many social scientists to have a fresh look at support/procurement prices as instruments for influencing important parameters of the agricultural economy. As discussed in Chapter 2, the post-reform period has been characterised by deceleration in the growth rate of crop yields as well as total agricultural output along with changes in growth patterns in favour of certain crops. As a matter of fact, returns to agriculture are crucial in determining the sustenance of the farm sector. State intervention in procurement of grains through fixing of procurement prices for various agricultural commodities acts as a means of protecting farmers' income and also providing incentives to the farmers. This warrants examining the effectiveness of procurement prices in getting sufficient income to the farmers. In more concrete terms, the specific questions that arise are: What is the relationship of procurement prices with other costs and prices? What determines the procurement volume? And what impact does price policy have on farm profitability/income? An in-depth analysis of costs and returns in the case of wheat and rice, which are the crops offered the highest protection by the State, gives some idea about the profitability of Indian agriculture and provides insights into the working of the price policy.

The present chapter examines these issues empirically. The chapter is organised into seven sections. Section 3.1 of the chapter deals with the phases of evolution of food policy in the Indian economy. Trends in procurement prices of wheat and rice are discussed in section 3.2. Section 3.3 examines the relationship between costs, prices received by farmers and procurement prices. Section 3.4 tries to identify the determinants of procurement prices. Trends and determinants of procurement volumes are investigated in section 3.5. Section 3.6 examines the trend in profitability in order to assess the viability of farming. Section 3.7 presents some concluding observations and identifies the causes for higher support prices in recent years. The data used in the analysis were taken from the cost of cultivation reports of the Directorate of Economics and Statistics, Ministry of Agriculture.[1] Using this data, the costs and returns are calculated at the all-India level to assess the emerging trends in profitability.[2] Weights based on area and production of the respective crops are used to aggregate the data from the different states. We have used area-based weights for all the variables except cost of production.

3.1 Evolution of the Food Grain Policy

The food grains market in India has a long history of institutional intervention and has passed through several phases. The government's action has evolved with the development of the economy. The history of evolution of government policy in this sphere is vital to the appreciation of the significance of government intervention in the food grain sector. Two elements may be distinguished in the government's food policy: the short-term concern with demand management, and the long-term objective of attaining national self-sufficiency in food grains. The short-term concern with demand management attempts to maintain adequate supply over the crop year and, thus, focusses on inflationary pressure within the economy. In contrast, the long-term concern is with the pattern and rate of growth of production of major food grains in the economy. The discussion

---

[1] Report of 'Cost of Cultivation of Principal Crops in India', published in 1991, 1996, 2000 and 2007 by the Directorate of Economics and Statistics, Ministry of Agriculture.

[2] States covered in the analysis of costs and returns for 'wheat' include Haryana, Madhya Pradesh, Punjab, Uttar Pradesh, Bihar, and Rajasthan; whereas for 'rice', the states of Andhra Pradesh, Haryana, Madhya Pradesh, Punjab, West Bengal, Odisha, and Uttar Pradesh were included.

that follows tracks the evolution of food policy in the Indian economy through its different phases:

The period 1939–46

Indian food policy has its origins during World War II,[3] when a series of food price control conferences were held by the colonial British administration in response to a sharp rise in food grain prices. These conferences held between 1939 and 1942 can be seen as a watershed in thinking about food policy. The first scheme for centralised purchase of food grains was discussed by the sixth price control conference in September 1942. During this conference, the basic principles of a public distribution system were laid down for the first time. In December 1942, a separate food department was set up, and in 1943 this department formulated an All-India Basic Plan that gave further form to the developing food policy. The Basic Plan included issues such as procurement, distribution of supplies received under the scheme, inspection, and storage. Price stabilisation was the first principal objective of the food distribution policy, dating from this period of war-induced scarcity (Chopra 1988). The period (1942–43) was characterised by high inflation in grain prices along with a deteriorating food supply situation not only in Bengal but also in other parts of country such as Bombay and Travancore-Cochin. In this background, the Foodgrains Policy Committee in 1943 recommended the introduction of rationing in urban centres of India, which continued for some time even after the end of the war.

The period 1947–57

During this period, food policy was marked by frequent shifts in emphasis on the different elements of policy. The economy swung from continuing war-time controls on food grain sales to complete 'de-control' and a return to controls. For instance, in the early 1950s, rationing and procurement programs were scaled down and by 1954 the government had fully withdrawn from grain marketing. But in 1955, food problems arose again. The weather was poor, and the earlier low food grain prices had an adverse effect on production.

---

[3] India had no experience with food rationing or with any other form of food control. Since 1861, when the Government of India had adopted a *laissez-faire* policy, it had refrained from interference with trade and prices of food grains (Bhatia 1991).

In 1957, the demand for food grains was outstripping supply. Distortions of the free market became increasingly evident. The same year, the Government of India again reversed food policy and reintroduced controls (Chopra 1988). The year 1957 can be seen as a second watershed in the history of Indian food policy. It appears that the government was responding in an ad-hoc manner to the overall supply position in each year.

The period 1957–63

The Foodgrains Enquiry Committee, 1957 observed that the total dismantling of controls during the early 1950s appears to have been a hasty step, particularly inasmuch as the government failed to take the opportunity to build up buffer stocks as prices fell. Similarly, full control, in the sense of complete rationing and procurement, was not seen as desirable as the government's responsibility would become too large to carry (GoI 1957). Accordingly, the committee argued in favour of controls of a flexible indirect nature and recommended the creation of a government organisation that would conduct the activities of the erstwhile Department of Food and act as a trader in the market, with an aim to stabilise prices and supplies and curb perceived speculative activities by traders. During the period, an important objective of food policy was distribution of food grains to the poorer sections of the population. The expansion of public distribution during the period was greatly facilitated by the large-scale imports under US Public Law-480 (PL-480). Over the period 1958–66, India imported nearly 50 million tonnes of food grains, most of it under PL-480.

The period 1964–67

A Foodgrains Prices Committee was set up in 1964 to suggest the required steps towards organising the agricultural price policy of the country. This marks a third watershed in the history of Indian food policy. Following the recommendation of the committee, a series of measures were taken and as a result the Agricultural Prices Commission (APC) and the Food Corporation of India (FCI) came into being in January 1965. The committee recommended: first, the setting up of the FCI in order to enable the government to undertake trading operations through which it can influence the market prices; and second, the creation of the APC to advise the government on a continuous basis, on agricultural price policy and price structure in the context of the need to raise agricultural production (Report of the Jha Committee on Foodgrains Prices for 1964–65, cited in Chopra 1988). In this period, Indian food policy acquired its third objective, i.e., to guarantee reasonable prices to the farmers and thereby increase production. This shift in food grain price policy had a lot to do with the desire to become self-sufficient in food grains. Due to various factors, such as a succession of bad harvests, massive food shortages and near famine-like conditions in some parts of the country,[4] challenges to national integrity due to dependence on food aid, and costly food imports, the then government decided to follow a policy of self-sufficiency in food which marked a watershed in the history of evolution of food policy. This coincided with the advent of new high-yielding seed varieties for wheat and rice. Adoption of these new seeds involved use of modern inputs and investments on the part of the farmers. This made it necessary to provide incentives and create a favourable price environment for the farmers who adopted the new seeds. To achieve this, the government adopted a policy package in which public procurement at support/procurement price was a major element (Krishnaji 1990).

In sum, the important features of the development of India's food policy during the last 25 years have been the following: up to 1957 there was no long-term food strategy and food policy was seen primarily as a means to tackle food emergency situations through price stabilisation. Public distribution was virtually abolished twice to be re-established a few years later. From 1957, a consistent price and import regime was introduced meant to keep food grain prices down along with distribution of food grains to the poorer sections of

---

[4] Two consecutive years of drought over this period mark a watershed in the evolution of food policy. The magnitude of crop loss was significant enough to stretch government operations. The food grain production during 1965–66 declined by over 17 million tonnes, which was 19 per cent less from the previous year's production. The food grains production improved marginally in 1966–67, but remained 10.90 per cent below the average figure for the three years prior to the first year of drought. Food grain prices recorded their highest rate of increase ever since 1950. This forced the government to step in with a massive public distribution programme which was greatly facilitated by the large scale imports of food grains under PL-480. In the peak year 1966, India imported more than 10 million tonnes of food grains, which was about 14 per cent of the total amount of available food grain in the country.

the population at reasonable prices. This policy changed in 1964–65. Imports gradually stopped; the government started to fix minimum prices in order to protect farmers' income and thereby stimulate agricultural production.

The overall objective of the food grain policy in India since the mid-1960s has been to (*i*) ensure a reasonable support price that will induce farmers to adopt improved methods of cultivation for increasing production; (*ii*) ensure that consumer prices do not rise unduly; (*iii*) avoid excessive price fluctuations and reduce the disparity of prices between states; and (*iv*) build up sizeable buffer stocks of food grains through imports and internal procurement (GoI 1965). The basic instruments through which these functions were to be operationalised included: (*i*) announcement of MSPs for major food grains; (*ii*) procurement prices for purchasing surplus from the cultivators; (*iii*) creation of a Public Distribution System (PDS) and buffer stocking facilities for the purchased grain; and (*iv*) imposing zonal restrictions on the movement of food grains to manage supply and demand.

It was not until 1965, when the Jha Committee on Foodgrain Prices gave its report, that cohesive and systematic thinking on fixation of support/procurement prices started (ibid.). The setting up of the Agricultural Prices Commission in 1965 was an outcome of the recommendation of the Jha Committee. While formulating the price policy, the Commission was required to keep in view (*a*) the need to provide incentives to the producers for adopting the new technology and maximising production, and (*b*) the likely effect of the price policy on the cost of living, the level of wages and the industrial cost structure.

In order to reconsider the prevailing structure of the APC and review its methodology, a committee under the Chairmanship of S. R. Sen was appointed in 1979. The Committee was to examine the methods for arriving at cost of cultivation, and suggest required modifications. The Sen Committee in its report gave a number of recommendations towards this (GoI 1980). The emphasis of the policy, as reflected in the revised terms of reference for APC, which was in 1985 renamed as the Commission for Agricultural Costs and Prices (CACP), shifted from maximising production to developing a production pattern consistent with the overall needs of the economy. Again, in 1986, the emphasis of policy shifted when a long-term policy perspective for agricultural price policy was presented in the parliament. It was emphasised that the policy should seek to build into the system the major factors, which, in the long run, influence the prices of farm products for making the farm sector more vibrant, productive and cost effective (GoI 1986: 32–33).

The policy was again subjected to a rigorous review after a programme of economic reform was launched in 1991 and India became a signatory to the new world trade arrangement, which, for the first time, included agriculture. The package of reforms in agriculture is based on the argument that subsidies arising out of inappropriate pricing of inputs and output led to inefficient resource use and eroded the capacity of the government to finance public investment in agriculture. The suggested agenda for the agricultural sector, therefore, revolves on setting the prices right and includes withdrawal of subsidies on inputs, targeting the PDS only to the poor, abolition of food management system and its attendant costs and liberalisation of trade in agricultural commodities. The essence of the package is that subsidies on farm inputs and food should be phased out and adjustment in agricultural prices be made for arresting the deterioration in the terms of trade for the agricultural sector. The agenda of setting the prices right essentially means moving from the 'low input low output price' regime to a regime of 'high input high output prices'. A crucial part of the strategy during the post-reform period was, therefore, to increase agricultural prices and reduce subsidies. This was sought to be achieved both by allowing freer trade and by offering higher support prices (Acharya 1997).

3.2 Trend in Support Price

Since the mid-1960s, the APC recommended Minimum Support Prices as well as procurement prices for agricultural commodities. The MSPs were announced before the beginning of the sowing season, whereas, towards the beginning of the harvesting season, procurement prices were announced. Support price is the minimum price below which the market price is not allowed to fall. Thus, it acts as a floor to the market and the government is committed to buy unlimited quantities that are offered at this price. Procurement price, on the other hand, is the price at which the government procures from the cultivators a desired quantity and thereafter may withdraw from the market. This quantity may be determined by the level of buffer stocks considered necessary and the needs of the public distribution system. However, when procurement is done by imposing some element of compulsion on farmers or sellers, the procurement price in effect becomes a levy price. In a regime where two sets of prices exist, the procurement prices were either greater than or equal to the support prices but lower than the market prices. In the latter years (i.e., the beginning of the 1970s), the distinction between support price and procurement price was abolished, with procurement price becoming the only relevant policy instrument.

Since its inception, the commission has been recommending prices for various crops the number of which has been increasing. Today, these recommendations cover 24 commodities,[5] which account for 75 per cent of the total value of crop output and 82 per cent of the gross cropped area (Acharya 2001). In case of paddy/rice, the price policy is implemented through a two-tiered structure managed by both central and state governments. Under this system, about two-thirds of total procurement is purchased in primary markets in the form of unmilled rice/paddy at the MSP and about one-third is purchased as milled/levy rice through a statutory, fixed-price levy imposed on rice millers. Under the levy, the state levy control orders issued by various states requires private rice mills to deliver a fixed percentage of their output to the FCI and state governments for the PDS and buffer stocks. For these deliveries, mills receive a state-prescribed pan-territorial and pan-seasonal levy price that is based on the MSP for paddy plus 'average' rice milling costs and a 'margin' of profit for the millers (CACP 1998).

3.2.1 Procurement Prices in Case of Wheat and Rice

The trends in procurement prices for wheat and rice show that support prices witnessed much higher increases during the 1990s than in the 1980s (Table 3.1). Till the beginning of economic reforms, procurement prices were based entirely on domestic factors, mainly on the cost of production of crops. Though the CACP was required to take into consideration the international price situation, this aspect was never given any weight while arriving at the level of MSPs. In general, the MSP was lower than international prices. The devaluation of the rupee in June 1991, as part of structural adjustment, further

---

[5] These commodities are paddy, wheat, jowar, bajra, maize, ragi, barley, gram, tur, moong, urad, groundnut, rapeseed/mustard, toria, soybean, sunflower seed, sesamum, nigerseed, copra, cotton, jute-mesta, VFC tobacco, and sugarcane.

Table 3.1: Minimum support/procurement price for wheat and paddy (in terms of rice equivalent) (₹/Qtl): 1981–82 to 2006–07

Mkt Year	Wheat		Rice		Excess of procurement price over recommended price (%)		Percentage change over previous year MSP	
	Recommended	Fixed	Recommended	Fixed	Wheat	Rice	Wheat	Rice
1981–82	127	130	172	172	2.36	0.00	11.11	9.52
1982–83	142	142	182	182	0.00	0.00	9.23	6.09
1983–84	151	151	197	197	0.00	0.00	6.34	8.20
1984–85	155	152	204	204	-1.94	0.00	0.66	3.79
1985–86	157	157	209	212	0.00	1.43	3.29	3.65
1986–87	162	162	218	218	0.00	0.00	3.18	2.82
1987–88	165	166	224	224	0.61	0.00	2.47	2.74
1988–89	173	173	239	239	0.00	0.00	4.22	6.67
1989–90	183	183	257	276	0.00	7.56	5.78	15.63
1990–91	200	215	306	306	7.50	0.00	17.49	10.81
1991–92	225	225	351	351	0.00	0.00	4.65	14.63
1992–93	245	275	388	403	12.24	3.85	22.22	14.89
1993–94	305	330	463	463	8.20	0.00	20.00	14.81
1994–95	350	350	507	507	0.00	0.00	6.06	9.68
1995–96	360	360	530	537	0.00	1.41	2.86	5.88

Table 3.1: (*Continued*)

Table 3.1: (*Continued*)

Mkt. Year	Wheat		Rice		Excess of procurement price over recommended price (%)		Percentage change over previous year MSP	
	Recommended	Fixed	Recommended	Fixed	Wheat	Rice	Wheat	Rice
1996–97	380	380	552	567	0.00	2.70	5.56	5.56
1997–98	405	475	619	619	17.28	0.00	25.00	9.21
1998–99	455	510	657	657	12.09	0.00	7.37	6.02
1999–00	490	550	694	731	12.24	5.38	7.84	11.36
2000–01	550	580	761	761	5.45	0.00	5.45	4.08
2001–02	580	610	776	791	5.17	1.92	5.17	3.92
2002–03	610	620	791	791	1.64	0.00	1.64	0.00
2003–04	620	620	821	821	0.00	0.00	0.00	3.77
2004–05	630	630	836	836	0.00	0.00	1.61	1.82
2005–06	640	640	836	851	0.00	1.79	1.59	1.79
2006–07	650	700	910	925	7.69	1.64	9.38	8.77

Source: Reports of the Commission on Agricultural Cost and Prices, various issues, Ministry of Agriculture, GoI.

raised the gap between MSP (domestic prices) and international prices. At the same time, the government had adopted the new economic policy, which aimed at the integration of the domestic economy with the global economy. All these factors led the government to implement a substantial hike in MSP to reduce the gap between domestic and international prices. The procurement price of wheat was raised by 80 per cent from ₹183/qtl to ₹330/qtl in a short span of four years from 1989–90 to 1993–94. Procurement price of wheat was raised by more than 20 per cent for two consecutive years — 1992–93 and 1993–94. The increase was almost double the highest recorded rise in procurement price during the 1980s. The procurement price of wheat was once again raised by 25 per cent in 1997–98. As has been the case with wheat, the procurement price of rice also witnessed much higher increases during the 1990s than in the 1980s. During the five years from 1989–90 to 1993–94, rice procurement price was raised by about 11 to 17 per cent. As a result, procurement price increased by around two times from the level of ₹239/qtl in 1988–89 to ₹463/qtl in 1993–94. Some studies have shown that these increases in MSPs completely ignored domestic demand-side factors and were much higher than was justified by the cost of production (GoI 2002). When world prices started falling since 1997–98, there was pressure by farmers' groups to protect them from low world prices by increasing MSPs. Consequently, the government continued increasing the MSP for wheat and rice even when international prices started declining after 1996–97.

However, following the accumulation of large surplus stocks due to excess supply, since 2002–03 there have been relatively small nominal annual increases in procurement prices (Table 3.1). The changes in MSP show that the increase in rice and wheat prices were the highest during the period 1991–92 to 2000–01 as compared to those of earlier decades. Rice prices for common variety increased from ₹351 to ₹761 while wheat prices rose from ₹225 to ₹580 during this period (Table 3.1). In the 1980s, the rate of increase in MSP of rice was higher than that of wheat.

Apart from increase in procurement prices over the time, it is evident from Table 3.1 that in case of wheat there were four years during the 1990s — 1992–93 and 1997–98 to 1999–2000 — when a significantly higher margin between the procurement prices fixed by the government and the recommended prices was observed. The level of the difference between the actual procurement prices announced by the government and those recommended by the commission was relatively small during the 1980s in comparison to the 1990s. This clearly shows that there has been an attempt to fix procurement prices of wheat higher than those recommended by the CACP particularly during 1990s which point to a desire to offer much higher incentives during the 1990s in comparison to the 1980s. A more or less similar trend is observed in the case of rice as well. There is one distinction, however. The level of the difference between the actual procurement prices announced by the government and those recommended by the commission is relatively small during the 1990s in comparison to the 1980s.

3.2.2 Rice Levy Price and Milling Margins

In addition to procuring paddy from farmers or from traders, the FCI also procures rice for the central pool through the levy route. This is done under the auspices of the Levy Control Orders issued by the state governments under the Essential Commodities Act, 1955, requiring millers to deliver a certain proportion of their total processed output (rice) at pre-determined procurement prices to the FCI or its designated agencies. The proportion of levy imposed on millers varied from 75 per cent in Andhra Pradesh, Haryana, Orissa, and Punjab to 30 per cent in Madhya Pradesh during 2005–06 to 2007–08 (Appendix, Table A-3.1). In states like Tamil Nadu and West Bengal, it was fixed at 50 per cent, while in Uttar Pradesh it varied from 60 per cent (eastern region) to 75 per cent (western region). Based on MSPs, and taking into account the other statutory and non-statutory charges for milling of paddy of the respective states, the Ministry of Food & Consumer Affairs announces the prices of levy rice. The levy price varies from state to state (Table 3.2), due to varying tax and fee structures obtaining in different states. However, the levy prices in each state have followed the trend in the MSP.

Milling margins[6] permitted under the rice levy system not only declined in some years but they also discriminated against some states (Figure 3.1). The levy, to the extent that they force mills to deliver rice to FCI at below market prices, discriminate against Andhra Pradesh, Haryana and Punjab, the states that supply about 75–80 per

---

[6] Milling margin = (State levy rice price – Rice equivalent of paddy MSP)/ State levy rice price × 100.

Table 3.2: Common variety MSP in terms of rice equivalent and state levy prices in select states: 1981–82 to 2005–06

Mkt year	Andhra Pradesh	Haryana	Madhya Pradesh	Orissa	Punjab	Uttar Pradesh	MSP Rice equivalent
1981–82	190.50	194.70	187.30	191.25	193.80	182.80	172
1982–83	201.55	205.85	198.10	202.30	204.85	193.20	182
1983–84	217.30	221.75	213.55	218.15	220.65	208.05	197
1984–85	227.40	233.90	223.55	228.30	230.75	217.65	204
1985–86	235.30	241.90	231.30	237.80	238.70	225.10	212
1986–87	241.60	248.30	237.50	244.20	245.00	231.05	218
1987–88	250.15	254.75	243.65	250.55	251.30	237.00	224
1988–89	266.05	270.85	259.15	266.50	269.50	251.85	239
1989–90	288.40	296.00	283.50	291.50	294.55	275.20	276
1990–91	336.00	348.00	335.00	345.00	347.00	331.00	306
1991–92	388.00	397.00	383.00	395.00	396.00	378.00	351
1992–93	454.00	463.00	449.00	463.00	463.00	441.00	403
1993–94	521.00	531.00	515.00	531.00	535.00	503.00	463
1994–95	567.00	582.00	548.00	578.00	585.00	558.00	507
1995–96	623.20	620.20	574.90	601.70	624.40	600.90	537
1996–97	625.90	671.70	625.90	634.20	678.30	651.40	567
1997–98	735.10	729.40	679.40	710.30	763.60	707.20	619
1998–99	783.40	780.70	724.30	757.20	788.40	757.20	657
1999–00	867.30	864.20	802.90	838.00	870.90	838.00	731
2000–01	899.80	904.20	839.70	869.00	903.60	868.90	761
2001–02	935.10	939.10	872.10	903.10	939.10	903.10	791
2002–03	970.30	974.30	907.90	938.30	974.30	938.30	791
2003–04	999.00	1,003.00	936.50	965.70	1,003.00	966.90	821
2004–05	999.00	1,003.00	936.50	965.70	1,003.00	988.00	836
2005–06	1,009.00	1,013.40	938.10	965.70	1,013.40	988.00	851

Source: Food Corporation of India (FCI), annual reports, various years.

cent of rice levied for the FCI. Apart from regional biases in terms of milling margins, the levy system also reduces the mills' profitability as indicated in a World Bank study report (1999a). The frequent peak-period bottlenecks in FCI receiving centres further prevents the timely lifting of the levy rice.

3.3 Relationship between Costs, Prices Realised and Procurement Prices

While fixing the procurement price of a particular commodity, the CACP claims to rely on various criteria ranging from its cost of

Figure 3.1: Rice common variety — Official milling margin as percentage of state levy price in select states: 1980–81 to 2005–06

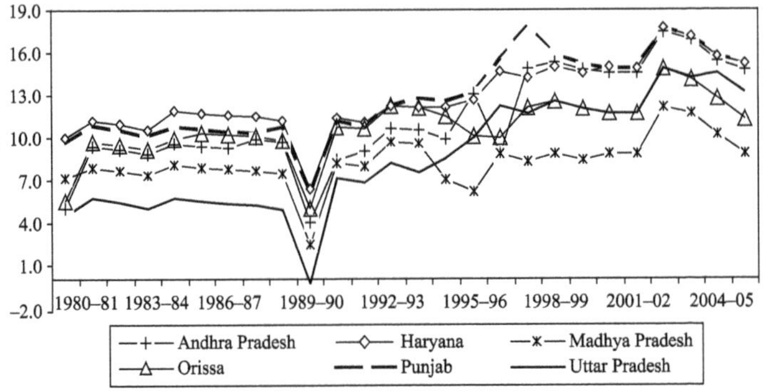

Source: Computed from Table 3.2.

production to the international price situation.[7] But the weight given to each of these criteria while fixing prices is not explicitly stated (Gulati 1987). With regard to production costs, the CACP takes into account the actual paid out costs on purchased inputs including purchased labour and some imputed value for land and family labour (the so-called C2 cost), and some value (at the rate of 10 per cent of the C2 cost) for the farmer's managerial input. The C2 plus the value for managerial input forms the so-called C3 cost, which forms the basis for the support price recommended by the CACP.

The trends in C2 cost of cultivation (CoC) per hectare and C2 cost of production (CoP)[8] per quintal, and A2 cost of cultivation[9] for the

---

[7] The CACP recommends support prices after considering the cost of production, changes in input prices, input–output price parity, trends in market prices, demand and supply, inter-crop price parity, effect on industrial cost structure, effect on general price level, effect on cost of living, international market price situation, and parity between prices paid and prices received (GoI 1986).

[8] The C2 costs include paid out costs plus imputed value of family labour, rental value of owned land, and interest on value of owned fixed capital assets.

[9] The A2 (paid out costs) include the value of hired labour (human, animal, machinery), value of seed (both farm produced and purchased), value of insecticides and pesticides, value of manure (owned and purchased), value of fertiliser, depreciation on implements and farm buildings, irrigation charges,

period 1981–82 to 2006–07 for rice and wheat crops are presented in Table 3.3. It may be observed that the total CoP in the case of both rice and wheat witnessed high growth during the 1990s when compared with the 1980s. In absolute terms, the nominal CoP per quintal, in the case of both rice and wheat, during the one and a half decades of the reform period, increased three times faster than in the 1980s. Taking the first half of the current decade alone (i.e., 2001–02 to 2006–07), the increase was around four times higher (Table 3.3). The role played by market forces, with the freeing of controls, in this unprecedented increase in input costs is clearly identifiable.

The average cost of production of wheat and paddy in all the major producing states of India for the years between 1981–82 and 2006–07 is provided in Table 3.4. The states of Rajasthan, Punjab and Haryana are the efficient producers of wheat in the triennium ending (TE) 2006–07 (Table 3.4). The farmers of Rajasthan and Punjab could produce a quintal of wheat at lower cost than the all-India average. In the case of paddy, farmers in Punjab turned out to be most efficient producers. The farmers of Punjab could produce a quintal of rice at 15 per cent lower costs than the all-India average and they have improved the efficiency of production by reducing the cost of production relative to the all-India average during the study period. Farmers from Madhya Pradesh incur the highest cost in rice production and produce paddy at 30 per cent higher costs.

Farmers are more concerned with the prices they realise rather than the MSP per se. For an individual commodity, the prices realised by the farmers (i.e., prices received by the farmers) are best represented by the implicit price received by the farmers, which is the ratio of the value of main product to the average yield. The trend in prices realised by wheat and rice farmers is presented in Figure 3.2. The nominal prices received by the farmers show an increasing trend throughout the period. As was the case with the MSPs, it may be observed that the price realised by farmers both in case of rice and wheat witnessed high growth during the 1990s when compared with the 1980s.

The ratio of price realised to MSPs was higher than 1.0 for rice and wheat almost during the entire period (Figure 3.3). Only in the case of rice, it was lower than 1.0 during 2000–01 to 2003–04. In the subsequent years, the ratio was closer to 1.0. On the other hand, the prices

---

land revenue, cesses and other taxes, interest on working capital, and also miscellaneous expenses (artisans, etc.) and rent for leased-in land.

Table 3.3: Trend in different components of cost in production of rice and wheat at the all-India level: 1981–82 to 2006–07

Years	Rice			Wheat		
	C2 cost of production ₹/Qtl	C2 cost of cultivation ₹/ba	A2 cost of cultivation ₹/ba	C2 cost of production ₹/Qtl	C2 cost of cultivation ₹/ba	A2 cost of cultivation ₹/ba
1981–82	112	2,856	1,618	129	3,273	1,905
1982–83	129	2,953	1,714	129	3,473	2,020
1983–84	122	3,546	1,996	137	3,439	1,990
1984–85	128	3,670	2,029	139	3,739	2,045
1985–86	121	3,561	1,932	132	3,948	2,331
1986–87	137	4,076	2,329	139	4,082	2,413
1987–88	161	4,938	2,792	157	4,874	2,809
1988–89	175	5,934	3,271	175	5,639	3,292
1989–90	180	5,880	3,246	179	5,770	3,362
1990–91	205	6,987	3,717	207	6,871	3,799
1991–92	231	7,680	4,115	222	7,676	4,291
1992–93	252	7,637	4,019	256	8,744	4,790
1993–94	NA	NA	NA	NA	NA	NA
1994–95	316	12,092	6,344	307	11,112	5,539
1995–96	339	12,059	6,318	330	11,753	6,150

1996–97	367	14,169	7,101	382	13,898	6,994
1997–98	394	14,832	7,646	400	13,328	6,895
1998–99	443	16,791	8,725	408	14,333	7,241
1999–00	465	17,469	8,745	436	16,553	8,106
2000–01	465	18,493	9,598	463	17,260	8,813
2001–02	479	19,892	10,591	477	17,402	9,117
2002–03	544	21,594	11,858	516	19,027	10,115
2003–04	493	21,858	11,759	509	19,091	10,271
2004–05	541	23,056	12,432	550	19,989	11,068
2005–06	552	23,566	12,357	617	22,194	11,733
2006–07	579	24,183	12,681	630	24,155	12,800
Averages						
1981–82 to 1990–91	147.0	4,440.1	2,464.4	152.4	4,510.7	2,596.7
1991–92 to 2000–01	363.6	13,469.2	6,956.9	356.0	12,739.7	6,535.5
2001–02 to 2006–07	531.3	22,358.4	11,946.3	549.8	20,309.5	10,850.7

Source: Computed from CACP data.

Table 3.4: Average cost of production of different states and all India for wheat and rice (₹/quintal): 1981–82 to 2006–07

Wheat	TE 1983–84	TE 1989–90	TE 1998–99	TE 2006–07
Haryana	133	134	365	563
Madhya Pradesh	135	211	483	678
Punjab	127	151	391	556
Rajasthan	125	170	400	526
Uttar Pradesh	135	184	371	629
Bihar	132	–	452	651
All India	132	170	397	599
Paddy	TE 1983–84	TE 1988–89	TE 1998–99	TE 2006–07
Andhra Pradesh	125	165	425	534
Haryana	–	147	480	644
Madhya Pradesh	107	175	450	723
Punjab	110	146	370	471
West Bengal	139	–	433	595
Uttar Pradesh	120	153	339	582
All India	121	158	401	557

Source: Computed from CACP data.

Figure 3.2: Trend in price realised by wheat and rice farmers (₹/quintal): 1981–82 to 2006–07

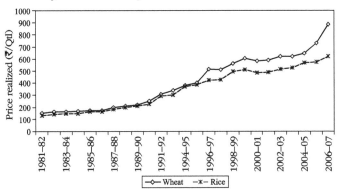

Source: Computed from CACP data.

realised by farmers were more than the MSP for wheat in all the years (except 2001–02) during the period 1981–82 to 2006–07.

There are significant regional disparities when we consider the ratio of price realised to MSP. There was a decline in the ratio in

Figure 3.3: Ratio of price realised to MSPs: 1981–82 to 2006–07

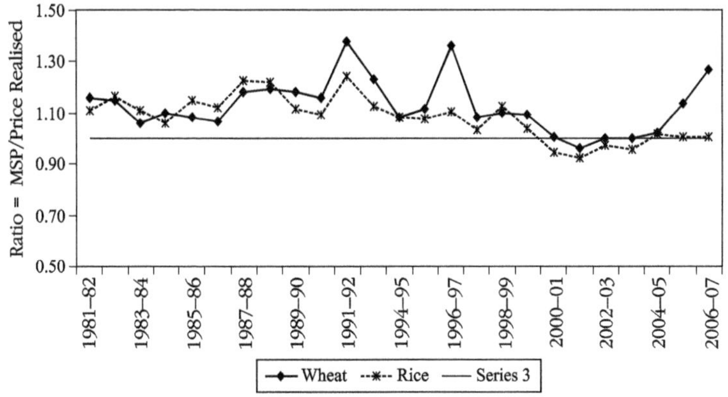

Source: Computed from CACP data.

the TE 2006–07 at the all-India level in both the crops. In rice, the ratio was much lower in states like West Bengal, Orissa and Uttar Pradesh (Table 3.5). In the case of Haryana, the ratio was higher by 32 per cent in the same triennium, which means that the realised price is 32 per cent higher than the respective support price. The ratio for wheat was higher than for rice in the post-reform period. For example, the realised price for wheat was 15 per cent higher as compared to the MSP at an all-India level in the TE 2005–06.

Table 3.5: Price realised relative to MSP in wheat and rice in different states (in percentage)

Wheat	TE 1983–84	TE 1989–90	TE 1998–99	TE 2006–07
Haryana	103	111	113	111
Madhya Pradesh	128	147	125	132
Punjab	105	109	113	111
Rajasthan	120	142	124	118
Uttar Pradesh	108	115	115	112
Bihar	138	–	119	118
All India	112	118	117	115
Rice	TE 1983–84	TE 1988–89	TE 1998–99	TE 2006–07
Andhra	110	118	109	104
Haryana	–	144	129	132

Table 3.5: (*Continued*)

Table 3.5: (*Continued*)

Rice	TE 1983–84	TE 1989–90	TE 1998–99	TE 2006–07
Madhya Pradesh	111	123	110	114
Punjab	106	118	107	107
West Bengal	128	–	117	95
Orissa	117	–	–	85
Uttar Pradesh	107	117	98	99
All India	113	119	109	101

Source: Computed from CACP data.

A comparison between rice cost of production and price realised by farmers is shown in Figure 3.4. The price realised by farmers moved faster than the cost of production till around 2000–01. Later, the prices realised were almost similar to the cost of production without any margin. In the case of wheat, the prices realised by farmers have always been higher than the cost of production (Figure 3.5). Since the mid-1990s, the margins have been higher particularly in the last year of the study, i.e., 2006–07.

Figures 3.6 and 3.7 enable a visual grasp of how the indices of procurement price, cost of production and wholesale prices have moved over 1981–82 to 2006–07, in the case of both rice and wheat. The Wholesale Price Index (WPI) for rice increased from 100 in 1981–82 to 492.3 in 2006–07. The index of cost of production shows

Figure 3.4: Price realised and cost of production in case of rice: 1981–82 to 2005–06

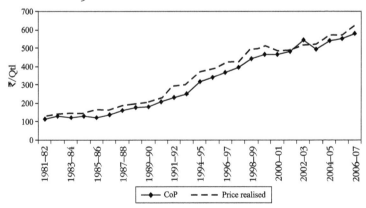

Source: Computed from CACP data.

Figure 3.5: Price realised and cost of production in case of wheat: 1981–82 to 2006–07

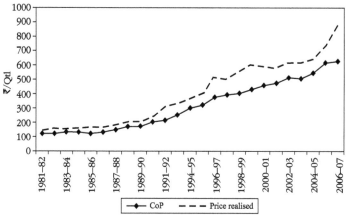

Source: Computed from CACP data.

that it was moving almost on par with the WPI till 2001–02. In the last five years of the study, i.e., 2002–03 to 2006–07, the cost of production has risen faster than WPI (Figure 3.6). Therefore, the rice farmers faced a difficult situation in terms of a higher cost of production relative to the WPI. The index of MSP of rice increased from 100 in 1981–82 to 539 in 2006–07. The growth in the MSP is almost similar to that in cost of production till 2001–02 after which fluctuations in the cost of production is higher relative to the procurement price (Figure 3.6).

In the case of wheat, procurement prices, cost of production and WPI were moving close to each other till the early 1990s. Thereafter, procurement price and WPI were always higher than production cost leaving a comfortable margin especially during the late-1990s (Figure 3.7). In other words, production costs were lower than output prices for wheat crop and the margins were higher for wheat as compared to rice.

3.4 Determination of Procurement Prices

An earlier study on determination of procurement price done by Krishna and Raychaudhuri (1980) showed that the procurement price fixed by the government was determined by the average of last two

Figure 3.6: Indices of costs and prices in case of rice: 1981–82 to 2006–07 (base 1981–82 = 100)

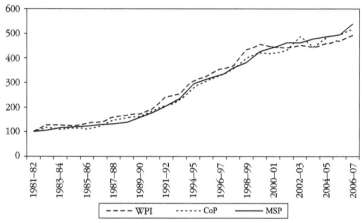

Source: Computed from CACP data.

Figure 3.7: Indices of costs and prices in case of wheat: 1981–82 to 2006–07 (base 1981–82 = 100)

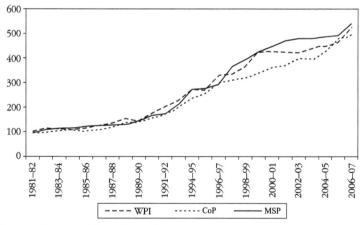

Source: Computed from CACP data.

years' wholesale prices of wheat. They fitted a log linear regression equation for the period 1965–66 to 1975–76 with procurement price as the dependent variable and average wholesale price for two years as the independent variable. A similar exercise was undertaken for rice, which came to the conclusion that regardless of the prescribed criteria for price fixation, the prices are actually based on the simple rule of thumb that if market price rises for one or two years, the procurement price should be raised by about half to two-thirds of the percentage increase in the market wholesale price. In a similar fashion, Gulati and Sharma (1990) also tried to identify the determinants of procurement prices. In their analysis, they fitted a linear regression equation with procurement price as dependent variable and cost of production along with past trend of wholesale prices as independent variables and reached the conclusion that, cost of production, which is essentially a medium-term concept, exerts its influence with a lag but the effect of wholesale prices is more immediate.

Based on this evidence, we first tried to analyse the pattern of co-movement of procurement prices with production cost and wholesale prices received by the farmers. The movement of wholesale prices received by the farmers in relation to that of procurement prices suggests a strong correlation between the two. However, it appears that far from being the reluctant follower, procurement price is the leader with a strong and instant effect on wholesale prices. Far from suggesting that past movements of wholesale prices do not guide the CACP in price fixation, we are of the opinion that the recommended prices cannot be totally divorced from past trends.

As a matter of fact, this is one of the criteria that the CACP itself admits as having an influence on procurement price fixation. However, procurement prices exert a much stronger influence on current year's wholesale prices as price setters than the other way around. That is why procurement prices are kept below the wholesale prices. Hierarchically, then the relationship goes as follows: cost of production < procurement prices < wholesale prices (Figures 3.8 and 3.9). Therefore, based on this relationship between procurement prices, cost of production and wholesale prices received by farmers, in our formulation we assume procurement price as being a function of lagged cost of production in the two preceding years and past trend in wholesale prices received by the farmers.

While the cost of production takes care of the trends in factor markets, the lagged wholesale prices reflect the market demand and supply situation. Since the cost of production is a medium-term concept, its effect on procurement price may not be immediate. Additionally, the information on cost of production is also available

Figure 3.8: Paddy prices and production cost: 1981–82 to 2006–07

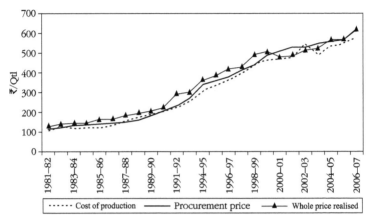

Source: Reports of the CACP, various issues.

Figure 3.9: Wheat prices and production cost: 1981–82 to 2006–07

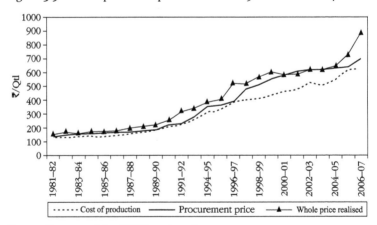

Source: Reports of the CACP, various issues.

only after a gap of two years; therefore, it is not possible to take into account the current season's cost of production as the basis for fixing procurement price. Therefore, in our formulation we have taken the cost of the production with two year lag. With these variables, we have estimated the equations on support price determination in the case of both wheat and paddy.

The results presented in Table 3.6 bring out the importance of the past trend in wholesale prices received by the farmers in determination of procurement prices. The past trend in wholesale prices turns out to be significant in both the equations with elasticities of 0.72 for wheat and 0.74 for rice, which is substantially higher than the cost of production elasticities of 0.33 and 0.32 in case of wheat and rice, respectively. The coefficient of the cost of production variable has the expected sign in both the equations. However, low elasticities suggest that the impact of cost of production on procurement prices is rather weak. Both the independent variables explain a major part of the variability in procurement prices in case of wheat and rice as shown by a very high value of the R squared. And all the elasticity coefficients in the estimated (log-linear) regressions have significantly high t-values. Therefore, the results indicate that the wholesale prices (with a time-lag) play a pivotal role in determining the procurement prices in India.

Table 3.6: Determinants of procurement prices in case of paddy and wheat: 1982–2006

Explanatory Variables	Coefficient	Probability
Wheat		
Constant	−14.58	0.15
Cost of production (−2)	0.46 (0.33)	0.01
Wholesale price received by farmers (−1)	0.67 (0.72)	0.00
Important statistics		
R-squared	0.99	
Adjusted R-squared	0.99	
Log likelihood	−99.99	
D-W statistics	1.32	
Paddy		
Constant	−9.47	0.35
Cost of production (−2)	0.39 (0.32)	0.00
Wholesale price received by farmers (−1)	0.73 (0.74)	0.00
Important statistics		
R-squared	0.99	
Adjusted R-squared	0.99	
Log likelihood	−94.79	
D-W statistics	1.61	

Source: Computed by the author.
Note: Figures within brackets are the elasticities of variables at their mean values.

3.5 PROCUREMENT TRENDS AND DETERMINANTS

The initial objective of procurement of food grains by the government agencies was to ensure remunerative prices to producers and reasonable prices to consumers and to maintain price stability. The food grain stocks procured by the government agencies, i.e., FCI, consist of operational stocks and buffer stocks. The operational stocks are used for distribution through the Public Distribution System (PDS) and for various welfare schemes. In years of shortages, the government has been fixing targets of procurement so as to build a required size of buffer stock and to keep the PDS functioning. Shortfall in procurement was met through imports.

In the last two and half decades, there has been some improvement in the level of price support operations for rice and wheat. Between 1981–82 and 2006–07, while output of rice grew at a rate of 2.27 per cent, its procurement grew at an annual rate of 6.12 per cent. Corresponding figures for wheat are 2.60 and 3.42, respectively. In case of wheat price support purchases increased from 7 million tonnes to 15 million tonnes between 1981–82 and 2005–06. In comparison to wheat, rice procurement by public agencies increased by four times during the period. Since the beginning of economic reform in 1991, some reduction in public procurement took place after 1992–93. Between 1993–94 and 1996–97, the proportion of wheat output procured by the government declined from 21 per cent to 12 per cent. Similarly, public procurement of rice declined from 18 per cent in 1992–93 to about 13 per cent in 1995–96. However, this decline turned out to be reflective of cyclical variations resulting from production fluctuations, and government procurement witnessed a steep increase afterwards and during the year 2000–01 the government procured all-time high shares of wheat and rice produced in the country for the period since the 1980s (Table 3.7).

There has been a sharp change in the relative shares of rice and wheat in procurement. For the triennium ending 1987–88, the share of wheat was 53 per cent. With a steep rise in rice procurement during recent years, the share of wheat declined to 33 per cent for the TE 2006–07. Rice procurement has, by and large, remained above wheat procurement since the early 1990s. Also, in terms of percentage of total output, rice procurement constitutes a higher percentage of total output in comparison to wheat. The government procurement crossed the level of 30 million tonnes in 2006–07, constituting around 35 per cent of total rice production (Table 3.7).

Table 3.7: Production and procurement of rice and wheat by public agencies: 1981–82 to 2006–07

Years	Production million tonnes		Procurement in million tonnes		Procurement as % of production	
	Rice	Wheat	Rice	Wheat	Rice	Wheat
1981–82	53.25	37.45	7.33	6.60	13.77	17.61
1982–83	47.12	42.79	7.05	7.72	14.96	18.04
1983–84	60.10	45.48	7.73	8.29	12.86	18.23
1984–85	58.34	44.07	9.86	9.30	16.91	21.10
1985–86	63.83	47.05	9.88	10.35	15.47	21.99
1986–87	60.56	44.32	9.16	10.54	15.12	23.77
1987–88	56.86	46.17	6.90	7.88	12.14	17.07
1988–89	70.49	54.11	7.73	6.58	10.97	12.16
1989–90	73.57	49.85	11.86	8.94	16.12	17.94
1990–91	74.29	55.14	12.67	11.07	17.06	20.07
1991–92	74.68	55.69	10.25	7.75	13.73	13.92
1992–93	72.86	57.21	13.05	6.38	17.92	11.15
1993–94	80.30	59.84	14.26	12.84	17.76	21.45
1994–95	81.81	65.77	13.71	11.87	16.75	18.05
1995–96	76.98	62.10	10.07	12.33	13.08	19.85

Table 3.7: (*Continued*)

Table 3.7: (*Continued*)

Years	Production million tonnes		Procurement in million tonnes		Procurement as % of production	
	Rice	Wheat	Rice	Wheat	Rice	Wheat
1996–97	81.74	69.35	12.97	8.16	15.86	11.76
1997–98	82.53	66.35	15.59	9.30	18.89	14.01
1998–99	86.08	71.29	12.60	12.65	14.64	17.75
1999–00	89.68	76.37	18.23	14.14	20.33	18.52
2000–01	84.98	69.68	21.28	16.36	25.04	23.47
2001–02	93.34	72.77	22.13	20.63	23.71	28.35
2002–03	71.82	65.76	16.42	19.03	22.87	28.93
2003–04	88.53	72.16	22.83	15.80	25.79	21.90
2004–05	83.13	68.64	24.68	16.80	29.69	24.47
2005–06	91.79	69.35	27.66	14.79	30.13	21.32
2006–07	93.35	75.80	32.40	9.23	34.71	12.17

Source: Bulletin of Food Statistics, Ministry of Agriculture, Government of India, various issues.

A more accurate indicator of government participation in the grain trade is the relative share of marketed surplus purchased by official agencies and the private sector. Figure 3.10 gives the share of public agencies procurement in total marketed surplus of rice and wheat. The share of public procurement in total marketed surplus of rice started declining since 1991–92 and reached the lowest level of 33 per cent in 1995–96. In case of wheat, the share of public procurement started declining since 1993–94 and during the marketing year 1996–97, government agencies purchased less than half of wheat. Since then, the share of public agencies has increased while that of the private sector has declined. This shows that in the late 1990s the private trade played a much-reduced role in the grain trade.

Scholars have given different reasons for the reduction in purchases made by the private sector. Some recent works like Chand (2005) tend to suggest that, first, a lower rate of increase in retail prices compared with procurement prices and wholesale prices gave a signal that demand-side factors did not support increase in procurement and wholesale prices; second, build-up of huge buffer stocks with the government meant that it would be forced to reduce the level of excess stock, which would dampen domestic prices and bring losses to those who bought grains before this happened; and third,

Figure 3.10: Percentage share of government agencies in marketed surplus of wheat and rice: 1981–82 to 1999–2000

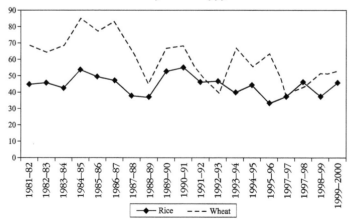

Source: Bulletin of Food Statistics, Ministry of Agriculture, Government of India, various issues.

the private trade found it cheaper to buy rice and wheat from the government when it offered produce for open market sale at heavy discounts during lean period, rather than buying from the market and paying statutory and other charges.

One of the most striking features of procurement is its high regional concentration. Punjab, Haryana and Uttar Pradesh accounted for 96.59 per cent of total procurement of wheat for the TE 2006–07. The share of these states has remained high since the beginning of procurement operations with very little evidence of any other state emerging as a significant contributor to procurement (Table 3.8). States like Bihar, Gujarat, Madhya Pradesh, Karnataka, and Maharashtra, which have experienced sharp increase in marketed surplus of wheat during the 1990s, have hardly benefitted from government procurement (Table 3.9).

Similarly, in case of rice procurement, Punjab, Haryana and Uttar Pradesh have the lion's share of about 50 per cent for the triennium ending 2006–07. This share goes up to 71 if we add Andhra Pradesh. Though the main beneficiaries from public procurement were Punjab,

Table 3.8: Percentage share of different states in total rice and wheat procurement

	TE 1985–86	TE 1990–91	TE 1995–96	TE 2000–01	TE 2006–07*
Rice					
Andhra Pradesh	17.64	22.65	30.74	34.14	17.44
Haryana	9.63	8.35	8.84	5.31	6.72
Madhya Pradesh	4.52	3.90	5.92	3.28	0.39
Orissa	1.34	1.81	3.08	4.39	6.32
Punjab	42.89	39.29	38.84	34.89	35.42
Uttar Pradesh	10.91	12.65	7.21	6.65	11.54
West Bengal	0.89	0.94	1.17	1.78	4.18
Tamil Nadu	9.06	8.07	2.57	6.42	2.37
Wheat					
Punjab	58.48	64.32	56.92	54.23	61.74
Uttar Pradesh	20.66	12.81	13.06	11.46	5.76
Haryana	18.37	21.91	25.93	26.71	29.09
Rajasthan	1.55	1.36	2.74	4.27	1.08

Source: Bulletin of Food Statistics, Ministry of Agriculture, Government of India, various issues.

Note: * TE 2006–07 in case of rice corresponds to TE 2005–06.

Table 3.9: Market arrivals of rice and wheat as percentage of production in select states

	TE 1983–84	TE 1986–87	TE 1990–91	TE 1993–94	TE 1996–97	TE 1999–2000
Rice						
Andhra Pradesh	42.67	43.00	42.33	52.53	62.10	70.97
Bihar	16.13	16.57	14.87	18.10	21.90	24.50
Gujarat	43.57	46.93	50.23	52.33	49.60	60.20
Haryana	91.23	86.47	70.70	83.40	85.97	77.33
Karnataka	18.23	19.77	23.77	24.87	27.63	44.13
Kerala	11.33	9.90	8.53	22.93	24.73	26.30
Madhya Pradesh	13.57	15.30	14.00	27.90	40.57	45.50
Maharashtra	15.87	18.00	22.10	30.13	38.40	45.83
Orissa	4.87	5.37	5.97	5.83	18.80	25.00
Punjab	88.00	86.00	84.80	85.50	81.50	82.83
Rajasthan	34.00	28.23	27.97	43.03	49.73	62.50
Tamil Nadu	34.63	36.40	34.47	36.27	39.47	43.57
Uttar Pradesh	26.20	29.10	28.50	35.00	36.13	40.13
West Bengal	16.37	18.53	15.97	14.83	14.77	15.53
All	31.27	31.67	30.23	37.63	38.47	41.53
Wheat						
Bihar	10.87	10.93	15.20	17.13	16.20	17.13
Gujarat	38.10	38.00	45.70	50.47	52.30	63.20
Haryana	37.80	40.93	41.93	46.17	43.80	44.57
Madhya Pradesh	10.43	10.37	10.77	17.27	24.17	40.50
Punjab	52.97	47.77	47.27	50.77	54.20	51.33
Rajasthan	19.00	20.67	18.87	19.20	18.63	20.33
Uttar Pradesh	15.63	17.07	18.60	17.80	17.67	23.40
All India	26.80	27.27	27.87	29.77	30.27	34.17

Source: Bulletin of Food Statistics, Ministry of Agriculture, Government of India, various issues.

Andhra Pradesh, Haryana, and Uttar Pradesh, states like West Bengal, Orissa and Tamil Nadu have also benefitted to some extent. The remaining states have hardly benefitted from government procurement of grains. For instance, though the states like Bihar, Karnataka and Madhya Pradesh have witnessed substantial increase in marketed surplus over the period, these states have hardly benefitted from government procurement operation (Table 3.9).

3.5.1 Determinants of Procurement

Procurement depends primarily on farmers' capacity to sell and willingness to sell. The capacity to sell is a function of marketable surplus proxied by output and the willingness to sell is determined by difference between procurement price and open market price. Another factor which may have a bearing on procurement volumes is administrative measures such as imposition of levy. Under levy system, producers/traders are required to sell to the government at a fixed price a part of their produce on compulsory basis. The non-levy portion is allowed to be sold in the market. Effectiveness of levy as an instrument of procurement would depend on whether prices fixed by the government are attractive or not and what measures the government adopts to check its evasion. Usually, the difference between procurement price and open market price is not large enough during the post-harvest period (i.e., peak marketing period) to induce a farmer to sell in the open market instead of selling to the government. However, the decision to withhold the surplus in hope of selling it at a higher price in lean season is strongly influenced by the costs entailed in retaining the stocks. Such costs include storage expenses, including storage losses, loss of interest and risk of theft, fire and adverse weather. Most farmers, therefore, find it profitable to sell soon after harvest as indicated by market arrival pattern. It is within this broad framework that we have estimated procurement functions for wheat and rice.

The regression results investigating the above-mentioned hypotheses for wheat are given in Table 3.10 for all of India as well as for Punjab and Haryana, which account for a significant proportion of the entire procurement. All the equations throw light on the importance of output and relative prices (i.e., ratio of procurement price to wholesale price received by farmers). Both the explanatory variables turn out to be statistically highly significant at the all-India as

Table 3.10: Wheat procurement equations

Period	States	Explanatory variable	Coefficient	Probability	Important statistics	
1981–82 to 2005–06	Punjab	Constant	–15.43	0.00	R-squared	0.79
		Output	0.68 (1.22)	0.00	Adjusted R-squared	0.77
		Relative price	14.48 (1.92)	0.00	Log likelihood	–31.77
					D-W statistics	1.28
1981–82 to 2005–06	Haryana	Constant	–10.52	0.00	R-squared	0.82
		Output	0.65 (1.45)	0.00	Adjusted R-squared	0.81
		Relative price	9.62 (2.83)	0.00	Log likelihood	–24.12
					D-W statistics	1.78
1981–82 to 2005–06	All India	Constant	–24.11	0.00	R-squared	0.80
		Output	0.19 (0.94)	0.00	Adjusted R-squared	0.78
		Relative price	27.63 (1.99)	0.00	Log likelihood	–49.77
					D-W statistics	1.60

Source: Computed by the author.

Note: Figures within brackets are the elasticities of variables at their mean values.

well as at state level. At the all-India level, the procurement elasticity with respect to price works out to 1.99, which is substantially higher than the output elasticity of 0.99. However, there are inter-state differences in terms of the elasticity magnitudes, but price elasticity is greater than the output elasticity in both the major states. Therefore, relative prices seem to determine a farmer's willingness to sell to the government. As a matter of fact, a farmer's capacity to withhold stocks is limited due to the cost it entails, so he finds it profitable to sell to the government.

In case of rice, procurement is assumed to be a function of output, relative prices (i.e., ratio of procurement price to wholesale price received by farmers) and levy. The results of different formulations of econometric models are presented in Table 3.11 along with their level of significance and other statistics. As expected, the output turns out to be the most significant factor in explaining the volume of rice procurement in case of major producing states. The coefficients of this variable are particularly large for states like Punjab and Uttar Pradesh which contribute larger shares of their output towards total rice procurement. In all situations, output elasticities are either close to or greater than 1. Levy is significant in all states except Andhra Pradesh, with elasticities greater than 1. In all cases, elasticities with respect to output are less than elasticities with respect to levy. Relative price is not significant in any state except Andhra Pradesh. As a matter of fact, in states with very high levy, such as Punjab where levy had been as high as 90 per cent in certain years and 75 per cent at present, very little surplus is left for open market sale. Therefore, we have no other price to compare the levy price with. For these states, market price becomes redundant and the argument that the weighted average price of levy and non-levy rice is profitable to farmers makes little sense. For such states, levy also captures the price effect. For other states such as Andhra Pradesh where non-levy portion is large, market price (i.e., wholesale price received by farmers) in relation to procurement price becomes a significant factor in explaining procurement volume.

Results on procurement functions for wheat and rice enable us to draw broad conclusions about procurement operations in the country. Elasticities of procurement with respect to relative price or levy rate far exceeded elasticities with respect to output. This is true both in case of wheat and rice. Procurement of wheat can be increased by raising

Table 3.11: Paddy procurement equations

Period	States	Explanatory variable	Coefficient	Probability	Important statistics	
1981–82 to 2003–04	Punjab	Constant	−15.37	0.03	R-squared	0.84
		Output	1.16 (1.30)	0.00	Adjusted R-squared	0.82
		Levy rate	0.16 (1.63)	0.04	Log likelihood	−22.65
					D-W statistics	1.11
1981–82 to 2003–04	Uttar Pradesh	Constant	−2.28	0.08	R-squared	0.47
		Output	0.17 (1.30)	0.00	Adjusted R-squared	0.41
		Levy rate	0.03 (1.43)	0.08	Log likelihood	−6.59
					D-W statistics	0.74
1981–82 to 2003–04	Andhra Pradesh	Constant	−15.23	0.00	R-squared	0.75
		Output	0.78 (2.17)	0.00	Adjusted R-squared	0.72
		Relative price	12.51 (3.20)	0.00	Log likelihood	−28.76
					D-W statistics	1.24
1981–82 to 2003–04	All India	Constant	−31.15	0.00	R-squared	0.82
		Output	0.13 (0.92)	0.01	Adjusted R-squared	0.80
		Relative price	37.57 (2.27)	0.00	Log likelihood	−48.75
					D-W statistics	2.06

Source: Computed by the author.

Note: Figures within brackets are the elasticities of variables at their mean values.

procurement prices in relation to open market prices. Procurement of rice is also most influenced by levy or relative prices rather than output. Therefore, procurement prices played a key role in procurement of wheat and rice during 1981–82 and 2005–06 in the case of wheat and during 1981–82 and 2003–04 in the case of rice.

3.6 Farm Income

Farmers are interested more in the net income from the cultivation of a crop than in the price of the product received by them. The data on gross income and CoC per hectare are available from CACP. Though the CACP uses eight different concepts of costs, we prefer to use cost concept C2 in order to calculate net farm income. The difference between gross income and cost C2 provides a measure for net farm income. Similarly, in order to calculate farm business income we have used cost concept A2. We also looked at trends in the ratio of gross value of output (GVO) to C2 cost, the ratio of GVO to A2 cost, which gives the level of margin over total costs and variable costs, respectively.

The profitability from wheat cultivation in nominal terms has improved during the period 1981–82 and 2006–07 (Table 3.12). However, the net income of farmers fluctuated heavily during the 1990s in comparison to the 1980s. The net income from the cultivation of wheat witnessed a sharp decline from the level of ₹6,269 per hectare to ₹3,270 per hectare during the period 1999–2000 and 2004–05.

If we take the ratios of GVO to C2 costs, the GVO has been more than the cost throughout the period. Nevertheless, the level of margin over total costs declined from 1.38 to 1.16 between 1998–99 and 2004–05. The ratio of GVO to variable costs (i.e., A2 cost) has been more than two in most of the years.

In sharp contrast to wheat cultivation, the profitability from rice cultivation seems to have been going down during the period 1981–82 to 2006–07. The ratios of GVO to costs show that the value of output has been more than all the costs throughout the period (Table 3.13). The ratio of GVO to C2 cost for rice has been maintained around 1.19 till 1995–96 but declined to 1.09 between 1996–97 and 2000–01 and to 1.02 during 2001–02 and 2006–07. Rice farmers got only two per cent returns over their total cost of production during 2000–01 and 2005–06, whereas their counterparts in wheat cultivation got 21 per cent net returns over costs during the same period.

Table 3.12: Cost and returns in wheat per hectare: All India 1981–82 to 2006–07 (in nominal terms, ₹)

Year	CoC–C2	Gross value of output/ha	Net Income/ha	CoC–A2	Farm business income/ha	GVOP/CoC C2	GVOP/CoC A2
1	2	3	4 = 3 − 2	5	6 = 3 − 5	7 = 3/2	8 = 3/5
1981–82	3,273	3,931	657	1,905	2,025	1.20	2.06
1982–83	3,473	4,449	976	2,020	2,429	1.28	2.20
1983–84	3,439	4,009	570	1,990	2,019	1.17	2.01
1984–85	3,739	4,520	781	2,045	2,475	1.21	2.21
1985–86	3,948	5,086	1,139	2,331	2,756	1.29	2.18
1986–87	4,082	5,134	1,052	2,413	2,721	1.26	2.13
1987–88	4,874	6,073	1,200	2,809	3,264	1.25	2.16
1988–89	5,639	6,558	929	3,292	3,275	1.16	1.99
1989–90	5,770	6,880	1,110	3,362	3,518	1.19	2.05
1990–91	6,871	8,259	1,388	3,799	4,460	1.20	2.17
1991–92	7,676	10,712	3,036	4,291	6,421	1.40	2.50
1992–93	8,744	11,553	2,808	4,790	6,763	1.32	2.41
1993–94	NA	NA	NA	NA	NA	NA	NA
1994–95	11,112	13,917	2,805	5,539	8,378	1.25	2.51
1995–96	11,753	14,409	2,656	6,150	8,259	1.23	2.34
1996–97	13,898	18,928	5,030	6,994	11,934	1.36	2.71
1997–98	13,328	17,256	3,928	6,895	10,361	1.29	2.50
1998–99	14,333	19,783	5,450	7,241	12,541	1.38	2.73

Table 3.12: (*Continued*)

Table 3.12: (Continued)

Year 1	CoC-C2 2	Gross value of output/ha 3	Net Income/ha 4 = 3 − 2	CoC-A2 5	Farm business income/ha 6 = 3 − 5	GVOP/CoC C2 7 = 3/2	GVOP/CoC A2 8 = 3/5
1999–00	16,553	22,822	6,269	8,106	14,716	1.38	2.82
2000–01	17,260	21,671	4,411	8,813	12,858	1.26	2.46
2001–02	17,402	21,339	3,937	9,117	12,222	1.23	2.34
2002–03	19,027	22,763	3,736	10,115	12,648	1.20	2.25
2003–04	19,091	23,159	4,068	10,271	12,888	1.21	2.25
2004–05	19,989	23,258	3,270	11,068	12,191	1.16	2.10
2005–06	22,194	26,362	4,168	11,733	14,629	1.19	2.25
2006–07	24,155	34,113	9,958	12,800	21,312	1.41	2.66
Averages							
1981–82 to 1985–86						1.23	2.13
1986–87 to 1990–91						1.21	2.10
1991–92 to 1995–96						1.30	2.44
1996–97 to 2000–01						1.33	2.64
2001–02 to 2006–07						1.23	2.31

Source: Computed from Commission for Agricultural Costs and Prices (CACP) data.

If we take the ratio of GVO to A2 cost, the gross value of output has been twice the variable costs in most of the years except during the period 2000–01 to 2005–06 (Table 3.13). In this context, it may be noted that this ratio was much higher for wheat during the same period. A comparison of the ratios of returns over total costs and variable costs of wheat and rice shows that the ratio of returns over total costs and variable costs were higher for wheat as compared to rice since the mid-1990s.

3.7 CONCLUDING OBSERVATIONS

The analysis in this chapter examined the role of state intervention in procurement of food grains through fixing of support prices and its impact on farm income. The greater emphasis and reliance on price policy in the 1990s and relative exclusion of non-price interventions in the form of public investment shifted the earlier policy regime of 'low-input and low-output' to a 'high-input and high-output' price policy regime. As a result of this policy shift, growth rates in yields have gone down and eventually costs of production started rising. The analysis shows that as a part of the reform strategy, the government not only slashed the subsidies on major inputs in order to discourage environmentally unsustainable practices but also absolved itself of the responsibility to produce or procure and distribute these inputs at farm gates. Consequently, the role played by market forces after the freeing of controls resulted in an unprecedented increase in input costs. The unprecedented rise in input cost along with decline in yield growth rates resulted in high growth in cost of production during the 1990s and beyond. The cost of production in nominal terms, both in case of rice and wheat, during one and a half decades of the reform period, increased three times faster than in the 1980s. The increase in cost of production along with a desire to link domestic prices with international prices with the aim of integrating the domestic economy with the global economy necessitated higher support prices. The trend analysis of MSPs in this chapter shows this phenomenon clearly. As the farmers are interested more in the prices received than MSPs per se, the analysis shows that the ratio of price received to MSPs started declining since the mid-1990s indicating a slower pace of increase in prices received than MSPs.

Our analysis on co-movement of procurement prices along with production cost and wholesale prices received by the farmers shows that past movements of wholesale prices have an influence on

Table 3.13: Cost and returns in paddy per hectare: All India 1981–82 to 2006–07 (in nominal terms, ₹)

Years	CoC–C2	Gross value of output/ha	Net Income/ha	CoC–A2	Farm business income/ha	GVOP/CoC C2	GVOP/CoC A2
1	2	3	4 = 3 – 2	5	6 = 3 – 5	7 = 3/2	8 = 3/5
1981–82	2,856	3,243	387	1,618	1,625	1.14	2.00
1982–83	2,953	3,253	301	1,714	1,540	1.10	1.90
1983–84	3,546	4,275	729	1,996	2,279	1.21	2.14
1984–85	3,670	4,201	531	2,029	2,172	1.14	2.07
1985–86	3,561	4,838	1,277	1,932	2,906	1.36	2.50
1986–87	4,076	4,816	739	2,329	2,486	1.18	2.07
1987–88	4,938	5,588	650	2,792	2,796	1.13	2.00
1988–89	5,934	6,558	624	3,271	3,287	1.11	2.00
1989–90	5,880	6,770	891	3,246	3,524	1.15	2.09
1990–91	6,987	7,559	573	3,717	3,842	1.08	2.03
1991–92	7,680	9,441	1,761	4,115	5,326	1.23	2.29
1992–93	7,637	9,170	1,532	4,019	5,151	1.20	2.28
1993–94	NA	NA	NA	NA	NA	NA	NA
1994–95	12,092	14,195	2,103	6,344	7,851	1.17	2.24
1995–96	12,059	13,785	1,726	6,318	7,466	1.14	2.18
1996–97	14,169	16,117	1,948	7,101	9,017	1.14	2.27
1997–98	14,832	16,006	1,174	7,646	8,360	1.08	2.09

1998–99	16,791	18,627	1,836	8,725	9,902	1.11	2.13
1999–00	17,469	18,970	1,501	8,745	10,225	1.09	2.17
2000–01	18,493	18,978	486	9,598	9,380	1.03	1.98
2001–02	19,892	20,131	238	10,591	9,540	1.01	1.90
2002–03	21,594	20,186	–1,408	11,858	8,328	0.93	1.70
2003–04	21,858	23,087	1,229	11,759	11,328	1.06	1.96
2004–05	23,056	24,144	1,087	12,432	11,712	1.05	1.94
2005–06	23,566	24,274	708	12,357	11,917	1.03	1.96
2006–07	24,183	25,839	1,655	12,681	13,158	1.07	2.04
Averages							
1981–82 to 1985–86						1.19	2.12
1986–87 to 1990–91						1.13	2.04
1991–92 to 1995–96						1.19	2.25
1996–97 to 2000–01						1.09	2.13
2001–02 to 2006–07						1.02	1.92

Source: Computed from Commission for Agricultural Costs and Prices (CACP) data.

procurement price fixation. There has been a systematic attempt to cover cost of production, and in the case of wheat and paddy procurement prices have remained well above the cost of production. Regression analysis results bring out the importance of the past trend in wholesale prices received by the farmers in the determination of procurement prices. The past trend in wholesale prices turns out to be significant with elasticities of 0.72 for wheat and 0.74 for rice, which is substantially higher than the cost of production elasticity of 0.33 and 0.32 in the case of wheat and rice, respectively.

Trends in procurement reveal the fact that there has been positive development in the level of price support operations for rice and wheat. Between 1981–82 and 2006–07, while output of rice grew at a rate of 2.27 per cent, rice procurement grew at an annual rate of 6.12 per cent. Corresponding figures for wheat are 2.60 and 3.42, respectively. However, there has been a sharp change in the relative shares of rice and wheat in procurement. For the triennium ending 1987–88, the share of wheat was 53 per cent. With a steep rise in rice procurement during the recent years, the share of wheat declined to 33 per cent for the triennium ending 2006–07. One of the most striking aspects of the procurement operation was its high regional concentration. Punjab, Haryana and Uttar Pradesh accounted for 96.59 per cent of total procurement of wheat for the triennium ending 2006–07. Similarly, in case of rice procurement, Punjab, Haryana, Uttar Pradesh, and Andhra Pradesh have the lion's share of about 71 per cent for the triennium ending 2006–07.

In order to find out what determines the procurement volume, our regression analysis shows that the difference between procurement price and open market price determines a farmer's willingness to sell to the government. Elasticities of procurement with respect to relative prices or levy rates far exceeded elasticities with respect to output in the case of both wheat and rice. Procurement of wheat can be increased by raising procurement prices in relation to open market prices, whereas in the case of rice, procurement was most influenced by levy or relative prices rather than by output.

However, agricultural price policy on an average has been largely successful in playing a major role in regard to providing reasonable level of margins over total costs to the farmers of both rice and wheat. Nonetheless, the margin over total cost and variable cost has declined since the late 1990s in the case of both wheat and rice. Not only the level of margin, but the net income in absolute terms has also declined since the late 1990s in the case of both wheat and rice. The net income from the cultivation of wheat witnessed a sharp decline from the level of ₹6,269 per hectare to ₹3,270 per hectare during the period 1999–2000 and 2004–05, whereas in case of rice it declined from the level of ₹2,103 per hectare in 1994–95 to reach an insignificant level in 2002–03 leading to distress among farmers. The decline in profitability has discouraged the farmers to increase spending on yield augmenting technology, which resulted in poor yield growth rates and, in turn, to a decline in production growth rates.

4

International Price Trends
and Volatility

The move towards a liberal and open trade regime, particularly after India became a signatory to the new world trade arrangement, resulted in increased integration of the domestic agricultural economy with the world economy in which the behaviour of international prices has a greater influence on domestic food prices and production than before. For example, changes in international prices exert a significant direct and indirect influence on domestic food prices through trade as well as through adjustments in domestic policies in order to keep some balance with global prices. To elaborate, a decline in international prices implies relatively cheaper imports and if the domestic prices are higher than the imported commodity's prices, it would result in more imports into the domestic market. An increase in imports enhances supplies, and for agricultural commodities — the prices of which are determined by supply and demand — may be expected to lower the price relative to the counterfactual equilibrium. The decline in domestic food prices also puts pressure on agriculture price policy to increase support prices in order to protect the domestic producers from low market prices. Therefore, in the changed economic scenario, the behaviour of international prices becomes all the more important as it exerts a strong influence on domestic food prices and production.

However, integration with the world economy also has a potential consequence that can damage agricultural growth independent of its influence on the level of domestic prices, as it can increase the volatility of domestic prices. Many economists have argued that commodity prices are notoriously volatile creating instability in global commodity markets (Blandford 1983; Heifner and Kinoshita 1994). In the Indian context, one of the major arguments advanced against agricultural trade liberalisation is that it would lead to transmission of international price volatility into domestic markets. Since the international prices of agricultural commodities are more volatile compared to domestic prices (Nayyar and Sen 1994), a more liberal and open trade regime is likely to lead to greater price instability in the domestic market. Increased volatility can adversely affect producers, especially if they are smallholders, by generating instability in farm income. It is in this context that high price volatility has been used to justify commodity stabilisation programs, such as price support, buffer stocking and provision of producer subsidies. Apart from trade, the new economic environment, which seeks to rely heavily on market forces by curtailing the role of the government in markets ranging from input to agricultural produce markets, could also be responsible for generating instability in domestic market prices. To elaborate, a market-based agricultural transformation is based on the assumption of effectively functioning markets in which transaction costs are not prohibitively high, market access is even across the population, and neutral market intermediaries absorb risk. However, if there is market power or market failure of any sort, in inter-seasonal storage, transport, wholesaling, processing, *inter alia*, especially if this is due to minimum efficient scales of investment and operation coupled with fixed capacity limits, then market failure can have especially negative effects on grain prices. This is a more common characteristic of developing and transition economies including India. Government intervention in the food grain market in terms of buffer stock operation and price support programmes have been a major factor for ensuring greater stability in Indian domestic market prices compared to international prices (Chand 1998). Some studies suggest that trade liberalisation is a better measure than buffer stock operations for stabilisation of domestic food prices (Jha and Srinivasan 1999). On the other hand, some scholars have argued that in an international trade context, the welfare of all countries taken together increases by price stabilisation through the use of storage, i.e., what the gainers gain is more than what the losers lose. The distributional effects depend upon the source of the instability (whether generated within or outside the country) and the height of tariffs (Hueth and Schmitz 1972).

It is in this context that the present chapter seeks to analyse, first, the long-term price behaviour of selected agricultural commodities and factors that have influenced the movements of the prices, and second, measures the volatility in world prices of selected agricultural commodities and then compares it with the volatility in domestic market prices under different degrees of government intervention. The chapter is organised into four sections. Section 4.1 of the chapter deals with the methodological issues involved in the measurement of volatility in agricultural commodity market prices. The long-run trend in world market prices of selected agricultural commodities is discussed in section 4.2. Section 4.3 tries to measure the volatility in domestic and international market prices of agricultural commodities. Section 4.4 presents some concluding observations. As mentioned in the Introduction (Chapter 1), the analysis is confined to six principal agricultural commodities. Two of these — rice and wheat — are from the group of cereals crops; the remaining four — of which groundnut, rape/mustard seed and soybean are important oilseeds, and sugarcane a leading crop among the rest — belong to the group of cash crops.

4.1 Methodology for Measuring Price Volatility

A number of different methods have been used to measure volatility, including the standard deviation of prices, the coefficient of variation, and the Black-Scholes-Merton model. Other methods evaluated by Offutt and Blandford (1986) include the percentage range, the average percentage change, the moving average, and the Coppock index. Previous studies have typically measured commodity price volatility using the unconditional standard deviation or the coefficient of variation. Implicit in this measurement is the idea that past levels of price and volatility have no influence on current or future realisations. Therefore, the unconditional standard deviation does not distinguish between the known and unknown components of price series, leading to the overestimation of the degree of uncertainty.[1] The Black-Scholes-Merton model is one that distinguishes between predictable and unpredictable components of price series, but the price volatility is assumed to remain time-invariant. Thus, the Black-Scholes-Merton model is unable to account for periods of changing volatility. The methods used by Offutt and Blandford (ibid.) centralise around the fact that they do not take into account either the

---

[1] Two key connotations of volatility are variability and uncertainty. Variability refers to all movement, while uncertainty refers to unknown movement. Conceptually, volatility at a given time can be decomposed into a predictable component (such as the effects of inflation, trend and seasonality) and an unpredictable component. Policy makers are, however, typically better able to cope with predictable variation. The primary concern thus tends to rest with unpredictable movement. The methods used to separate out the predictable component from the data series is discussed in Appendix I.

predictable and unpredictable components in the price process, or all the information available to quantify the volatility. One method that distinguishes not only between predictable and unpredictable components in the price process but also allows the variance of the unpredictable component to be time varying, is the Generalised Autoregressive Conditional Heteroscedasticity (GARCH) approach developed by Bollerslev (1986). In the present analysis, the variability of the price series was measured by using the GARCH model. The basic framework that was followed to quantify the volatility in the price series by using GARCH model is presented in Appendix I.

Apart from these, the ratio method has also been used to measure the volatility of the price series. In this method, the instability of the series is calculated by measuring the standard deviation of log (P_t/P_{t-1}) over a period, where P_t is price in period 't' and P_{t-1} is the price in period '$t-1$'.

The international monthly price data for agricultural commodities are from various sources, viz., ERS-USDA, IFS and UNCTAD. For domestic prices, data on agricultural commodities were collected from *Agricultural Prices in India* and *Agricultural Situation in India*, published by the Directorate of Economics and Statistics, Ministry of Agriculture, Government of India.

4.2 LONG-RUN PRICE TRENDS

4.2.1 Trends in Wheat Price

Trends in the international price of wheat show a cyclical movement. Figure 4.1 enables a visual grasp of such cyclical movements over the years, i.e., 1981–82 to 2004–05 (for the period April to March). The international price of wheat has a tendency to rise for four to five years and then decline for about the same number of years. Thus, the price cycle is completed in about eight to 10 years. During the last 25 years, wheat prices reached a trough in 1987 and they were again at their lowest during 2000.

There are two major factors responsible for this cyclical movement. First, the inherent difficulty in predicting the world import demand and, second, increases in exportable surpluses are highly correlated with contraction in import markets. Subsequent to periods of high prices and low stocks, major exporters expand their production because they believe that high prices will persist and at the same time high prices also provide an incentive for importing countries to expand production and decrease reliance on imports. This results in

Figure 4.1: Trend in nominal world price for wheat: 1981–82 to 2004–05

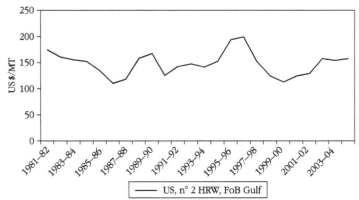

Source: UNCTAD commodity price data set.

a contraction of the export market at the same time as the exportable surplus is increased. For instance, the international price of wheat increased rapidly during the year 1995 and the first half of 1996. The price of wheat peaked in May 1996 at around $260 per tonne, about 65 per cent higher than the price a year earlier and more than double the price in May 1994. This steep rise in prices resulted from a combination of demand and supply side factors.

On the supply side, between 1994–95 and 1995–96, global cereal production declined by 3.0 per cent (accounting to 1,728 million tons), driven by a 9.6 per cent reduction in production in developed countries. Due to poor weather in some major cereal-producing countries such as Australia, Canada and the United States, policy-induced reductions in price subsidies in Western Europe and North America that diminished production and stock-holding incentives, and significant declines in food production in the former Soviet Union, were recorded. At the same time, on the demand side, global consumption of cereals outstripped production for the third year in a row, considerably depleting stocks and contributing to a rapid increase in prices (Pinstrup-Andersen, Pandya-Lorch and Rosegrant 1997). By 1995–96, there was a substantial reduction in global cereal stocks, which reached a 20-year low of 258 million tonnes. This constituted only 14 per cent of global cereal consumption, well below the 17 per cent considered by the Food and Agricultural Organization (FAO) to provide the necessary margin of safety for world food security. Much of the drawdowns occurred in the traditional exporting or stockholding countries like Canada, US and Australia.

This trend was completely reversed in the next two years. Wheat prices, which rose by about 70 per cent between April 1995 and May 1996, dropped to less than half of its 1996 level by July 1999. In this context, it must be noted that policies of major exporting economies also exacerbated the fall in the international price by generating artificial export surpluses. For example, the United States increased its support payments from US $ 15 in 1996 to US $ 55 per MT in 1999. In the European Commission, too, while substantial direct payments were maintained at the rate of 54 Euro per MT during the period, there was an increase in export refunds also. As a result of increased farm support in major exporting countries along with high world prices of 1995–96, worldwide, wheat area cultivated increased by 5 per cent between 1995–96 and 1996–97. The world grain stocks were rebuilt and reached 337 million tonnes by 1999, corresponding to 17.9 per cent of annual world cereal consumption and consequently the grain prices fell (Sekhar 2008).

4.2.2 Trends in Rice Price

Looking at rice price data from the beginning of 1980s, three different periods can be seen. First, between the years 1980–81 and 1986–87, world rice prices showed a downward trend (Figure 4.2). During this period, the decline in prices was more than 50 per cent; from US $ 492 in 1980–81 to US $ 212 in 1986–87. The main reason for this fall in price was the huge growth in per capita rice production in Asian countries. The production in Indonesia had increased by about 16 per cent from 1981 to 1984. Rapid increases in rice production were also witnessed in China, India and Vietnam. Also, the increasing per capita income around this time in several Asian countries had led to a decline in the income elasticity of demand. Second, between the mid-1980s until the beginning of WTO in 1995, rice prices were relatively stable; fluctuating between US $ 295 per metric tonnes to US $ 349 per metric tonnes. The magnitude of year to year fluctuations in per-capita rice production in Asia has been markedly lower in this phase than previously observed (BAPPENAS 1999). Third, during the post-WTO period beginning with the year 1996–97, international rice prices again faced a severe downward pressure and touched, in 2000–01, the lowest level since the 1960s of US $ 176 per metric tonne. International rice prices, pressured by ample exportable supplies that exceeded the prevailing global import demand, declined by 50 per cent during this period. On the supply

Figure 4.2: Trend in nominal world price for rice: 1980–81 to 2005–06

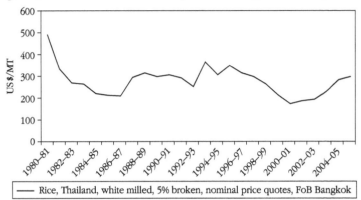

— Rice, Thailand, white milled, 5% broken, nominal price quotes, FoB Bangkok

Source: UNCTAD commodity price data set, for the period October to September.

side, this was the time when major exporting countries had bumper harvests. Rice production in Asia increased continuously, breaking records every year through 1999, and reaching 371 million tonnes. Total world production, reflecting the situation in Asia, reached a new record at slightly over 400 million tonnes in 1999, the first time in history for production to reach the 400 million tonne level. The increased exports from countries like India, China and Pakistan have ensured low world prices. For example, in 1998, the world rice market saw the entry of China as a major exporter with a supply of more than 3.5 million tonnes, Vietnam also re-entered the world rice market with exports of about 20 per cent of its production, in the late 1990s. As a result, between 1996–97 and 1998–99, the ratio of world rice trade to total rice production has exceeded 5 per cent in every single year with an average of 5.9 per cent.

On the demand side, following the East Asian crisis, demand from Asian importers got weakened. The crisis affected Latin America too, and reduced global agricultural commodity prices, consumption and trade. Domestic policies in the developed countries exacerbated the situation arising from the decline in prices. During the period when international rice price was declining, a massive dose of counter-cyclical subsidies were provided to the US rice farmers. The United States increased its support payments from US$ 53.99 in 1997 to US$ 172.70 per MT in 2000. As a result, US rice producers were insulated from the price shock and they managed to maintain their high trading volumes. As USA is a major rice exporting country, this resulted in oversupply of rice in the international market and exacerbated the decline in international rice prices (Hoda and Gulati 2008). Despite a decline of eight million tonnes in global production in 2000 over the previous year, international rice prices continued on the downward path in 2000. The reason underlying such a slide in price was fundamentally the same as in the previous year, as import demand continued to shrink in most of the traditional importing countries such as Bangladesh, Indonesia, the Philippines, and Sri Lanka (FAO 2002).

Global rice production decreased three years in a row to as little as 381 million tonnes in 2002, a 7.3 per cent decrease from the record level in 1999, reflecting adverse weather conditions in several important producing countries. Although rebounding, production still fell short of consumption in 2003 and 2004, resulting in depleted world rice inventories. Reduced stocks along with a brisk demand for imports sustained world prices, which started recovering by mid-2003 after four years of decline.

4.2.3 Trends in Oilseeds and Edible Oil Prices

International prices for oilseeds and oils during the last two and half decades exhibit three distinct patterns (see Figures 4.3 to 4.8). First, beginning with the year 1980–81, world prices for oilseeds followed

Figure 4.3: Trend in nominal world price for groundnut (shelled), CIF Europe: 1980–81 to 2003–04

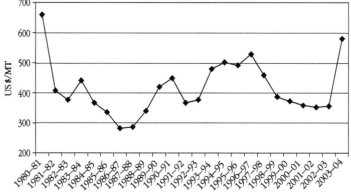

Source: Oil world, Hamburg, Germany, for the period October to September.

Figure 4.4: Trend in nominal world price for rapeseed, CIF Europe: 1980–81 to 2004–05

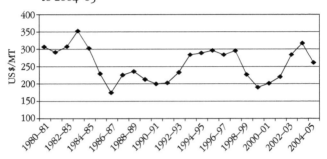

Source: ERS-USDA, Washington, DC, for the period October to September.

Figure 4.5: Trend in nominal world price for soybean, CIF Rotterdam: 1980–81 to 2004–05

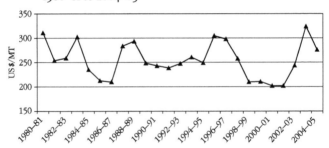

Source: UNCTAD commodity price data set, 2007, for the period October to September.

Figure 4.6: Trend in nominal world price for groundnut oil, CIF Rotterdam: 1980–81 to 2004–05

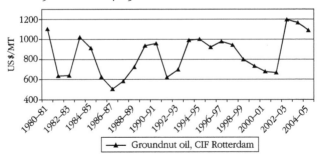

Source: International Financial Statistics, IMF, 2007 data set, for the period November to October.

Figure 4.7: Trend in nominal world price for rapeseed oil, FoB ex-mill, Dutch: 1980–81 to 2004–05

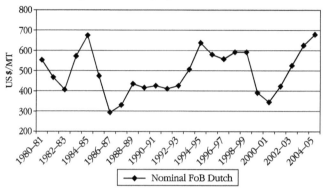

Source: ERS-USDA, Washington, DC, for the period April to March.

Figure 4.8: Trend in nominal world price for soybean oil, FoB ex-mill, Dutch: 1980–81 to 2004–05

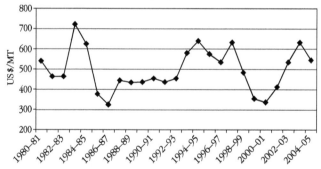

Source: UNCTAD commodity price data set, 2007, for the period October to September.

a downward trend until the year 1986–87, with the exception of the year 1984. During the period, groundnut prices declined by more than 55 per cent, from US $ 662 per tonne in 1980–81 to US $ 283 per tonne in 1986–87, whereas in the case of rapeseed/mustard and soybean, the decline was 43 per cent and 33 per cent, respectively. In the case of oils, prices reached their lowest level in 1986–87, following the pattern of seed prices. Second, the period between 1987–88 and 1996–97, barring few exceptions, witnessed an upward movement in prices, in the case of both oilseeds and oils. During this period, prices increased by more than 80 per cent from US$ 289 per tonne to US$ 530 per tonne, in the case of groundnut, while rapeseed/ mustard and soybean prices witnessed an increase of 30 per cent and 7 per cent, respectively. Oil prices have also followed a similar pattern. Third, international prices for oilseed and edible oils were again subject to strong downward pressure during the years 1997 to 2002. Until the end of 2001, the international market for oilseeds and oils were oversupplied relative to demand, which resulted in above average stocks and downward pressure on prices. The period was characterised by increased direct support to domestic producers and increase export promotion efforts by major exporting countries. During the period, prices for oilseeds declined by 34 per cent, 36 per cent and 34 per cent in the case of groundnut, rape/mustard seed and soybean, respectively, reaching their lowest level since 1992–93.

Whereas, decline in oil prices has been caused by unusually sharp, but temporary, increases in palm oil production, as oil palm plantations in Asia recovered from the 1998 weather anomalies. In the case of three major edible oils, namely, groundnut, rapeseed/ mustard and soybean, prices declined by 32 per cent, 42 per cent and 48 per cent, respectively, during the period and touched their lowest level since 1987–88.

In 2002, by contrast, production growth declined and global stocks were drawn down leading to a partial recovery in international prices and less policy support. As a result, after several years of falling prices, the 2002–03 season marked the beginning of an oilseed price recovery in which prices in the 2003–04 seasons returned to their high level of the mid-1990s. The increase in prices was triggered mainly on account of production shortfalls and exceptionally low stock levels, which coincided with sustained growth in demand. During the marketing season, 2003–04 prices in the oil crop complex were strongly influenced by tight soybean supplies and by a slower growth in palm oil production. However, prices for oilseeds and oils came under considerable downward pressure in the following year due to record global oilseeds production, particularly soybean.

4.2.4 Trends in Sugar Price

Figure 4.9 shows the average annual world free market prices for raw sugar for the sugar years (October–September) 1980–81 to 2005–06. Beginning with the year 1981, world prices for raw sugar showed a downward trend and reached its minimum in 1985. During the

Figure 4.9: Trend in nominal world price for raw sugar: 1980–81 to 2005–06

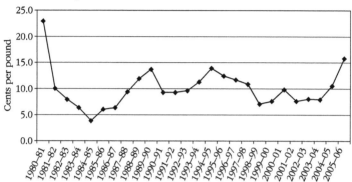

Source: ERS-USDA, Washington, DC, for the period October to September.

period, world prices declined by 83 per cent, i.e., from 23 US cents per pound to 4 US cents per pound.

The period between 1986 and 1996 was characterised as a period of relatively stable world sugar prices. The annual price averaged 10.25 US cents per pound between the years 1986 and 1996. For many of the world's sugar exporting countries, the period was viewed as a 'golden era' for sugar prices with prices at comfortably high levels. The declining import market share of developed countries and increasing share of developing countries, on the other hand, was perceived as the main factor behind the increased price stability during the period. The share of developed economies in world imports declined from two-thirds in the 1970s to 35 per cent by 1995. The sheer volume of imports by developed countries with their policy of obtaining neces- sary supplies, irrespective of prices, helped to drive prices up to the peaks in the past. However, from 1980, developed country imports declined sharply as large high fructose corn syrups (HFCS) industries developed, encouraged by price booms of 1974 and 1980, in the USA, in particular, and Japan. At the same time, imports of develop- ing countries rose, partly because of the rise in oil prices from 1973, and partly reflecting the very low sugar prices in the mid-1980s. The result was that by the late 1980s, two-thirds of world sugar imports were accounted for by developing countries with demand that was highly price elastic. Their reaction to high prices was to purchase less, bringing more stability to world sugar prices.

World sugar prices crashed in 1999 to levels not seen for more than a decade. World sugar production grew between 1994–95 and 2000–01 by 16 per cent, whereas consumption increased by only 11 per cent, leading to a substantial build-up in stocks and continued downward price pressure. By August 2000, surplus stocks had risen to 18 million tonnes, an all time high. High average world sugar prices during the 1990s drew the biggest response from Latin America and Brazil in particular. In fact, Latin America's export increased by 51 per cent during the 1994–95 to 2000–01 period to reach 17.6 million tonnes, whereas Brazil's export alone grew by 6.8 million tonnes during the period. In hindsight, the price crash of 1999 occurred because the Asian financial crisis curtailed demand in several large sugar importers while Brazil continued to export record amounts, aided by the devaluation of the country's currency. Prior to the 1999 crash, the impact of Brazil's export of raw sugar was not felt immediately in the global market because higher Brazilian exports were counterbalanced by a dramatic decline in Cuba's exports. In addition, the decrease in Russia's domestic production in the mid-1990s was filled almost exclusively by imports from Brazil. This Brazil–Russia nexus helped to keep the sugar market near balance and prices from collapsing, despite a steady build-up of stocks.

In 2000, world sugar prices were strengthened by a supply deficit and continued recovery in the economies of some major sugar importers. World sugar prices, which reached 14-year lows in February 2000, recovered nearly 90 per cent to an average of 11 US cents per pound in October 2000. The rise in sugar prices seen in 2000 continued into 2001. World prices averaged 9.8 US cents per pound for the sugar year 2001. However, prices began to fall thereafter and reached a low of 7.60 US cents per pound in the year 2002. This trend was largely due to the weakening import demand, particularly in the Russian Federation because of high stock levels and higher tariff rates, and uncertainty in the market place after the terrorist attacks on 11 September 2001. Surplus stocks of sugar continued to expand throughout the 2002–03 marketing year, exacerbated by record output in several key producing nations, notably Brazil. In the second half of 2002, prices improved slightly, but throughout 2003 they stayed well below the level of the early to mid-1990s. The strengthening in world sugar prices started in 2004 and continued in 2005 as well. This increase in sugar prices was underpinned by the strong growth in consumption against slower growth in production, resulting in declining global inventories. World sugar prices increased significantly during the period October 2005 to September 2006 and reached a 23-year high with price averaging 15.8 US cents per pound, largely due to a substantial rise in crude oil prices, as well as a world supply deficit for the third consecutive year.

In summary, the long-run price trends of major agricultural commodities during the last two and half decades show that output and stockholding policies of major exporters have a crucial bearing on world prices. Any movement, whether that of the aggregate world supply curve to the left (due to poor weather or policy induced reduction) or the world demand curve to the right, leads to the depletion of global stocks and an increase in world prices. The higher world price provides incentive to exporting countries to increase exports by drawing down their stocks and even by increasing the cropped area in subsequent years. At the same time, high prices also provide an incentive for importing countries to expand production and decrease reliance on imports. This results in a contraction of the export market at the same time as the exportable surplus is increased. It puts downward pressure on world prices leading to decline in prices. The situation arising from the decline in prices gets further exacerbated by the policies of major exporting countries when they try to maintain their market share in export markets even at low prices. This has been the case during the post-WTO period when a massive dose of counter-cyclical subsidies were provided to the farmers by major exporting countries like the United States and the European Community (EC), in order to insulate them from the price shocks and help them maintain their high trading volumes. Therefore, the output and stockholding policies of major exporting countries still hold the key to stability of commodity market prices in world markets.

4.3 PRICE VOLATILITY

In the literature on volatility, the measure most commonly used for price instability is inter-year variability. However, as the prices used in calculating this measure are the annual averages, they tend to conceal short-run price fluctuations which arise mainly due to seasonality in production. Government intervention in the food grain market by way of procurement and release of stocks to mitigate acute declines and increases in prices also impacts on short-run fluctuations in prices.

In this context, the subsequent section first gives the comparative picture of price variability (both intra-year and inter-year variability) in major international and domestic markets, by using the ratio method. This is followed by a detailed analysis of the variability patterns by using the GARCH model to look at the pattern of both short-run and long-run fluctuations in market prices.

To calculate intra-year variability, first, monthly growth rates in nominal prices are calculated. Then annual intra-year variability is calculated as the standard deviation of the 12-monthly growth rates in the year. The decadal average is calculated as the average of annual intra-year variability of all the years in the decade. For calculating the inter-year variability, however, the methodology is slightly different. First, the annual average prices are calculated as a simple average of the 12-monthly prices. Then the growth rates of annual prices are calculated as $\log (P_t/P_{t-1}) \times 100$. The average inter-year variability of annual prices for the decade is then calculated as the standard deviation of all the annual growth rates in the decade.

4.3.1 Patterns in Agricultural Price Volatility

This section gives a comparative picture of price variability in the major international and domestic markets (Tables 4.1 and 4.2).

Wheat

Although the inter-year variability of annual prices is considerably higher for international markets compared with domestic markets in both the decades (Table 4.1), the gap has considerably narrowed in recent years. The intra-year variability is higher in the domestic markets than in the international market, indicating higher degree of within-the-year fluctuations of wheat prices in Indian markets (Table 4.2). In the case of international market, intra-year variability was highest in the 1990s followed by the most recent sub-period indicating that the 1980s were a relatively stable period. The monthly movement in US Gulf port prices shows that prices are generally stable between January to March after which there is a slight decline between April to August. The prices again reverse the trend and start rising from September to December. The higher volatility observed in the 1990s and beyond, compared to a relatively tranquil 1980s, can be analysed better in the backdrop of the developments in world wheat market during these decades as discussed in section 4.2.1. Unlike the pattern observed in international markets, a majority of the domestic markets showed lowest intra-year variability in the most recent sub-period followed by the 1990s, leaving

Table 4.1: Inter-year variability in annual prices (in percentage)

		1980–81 to 1989–90	1990–91 to 1999–00	2000–01 to 2004–05	Overall
Wheat[i]	Moga	8.26	8.48	5.52	8.27
	Ludhiana	8.85	8.33	6.84	8.53
	Karnal	9.46	8.45	6.73	8.96
	Hapur	9.14	13.50	8.96	11.52
	US, n° 2 HRW, FoB Gulf	14.98	17.44	8.55	15.04
Rice[ii]	Kakinada	8.72	9.89	12.13	9.66
	Patna	13.07	6.88	13.30	10.17
	Amritsar	13.85	7.85	5.79	10.68
	Kanpur	9.96	12.67	3.96	10.42
	Sainthia	12.79	12.37	14.01	12.25
	Thailand, FoB Bangkok, white milled, 5% broken	19.89	17.18	14.54	17.28
Groundnut seed[ii]	Nandyal	13.62	9.12	14.70	11.37
	Rajkot	17.09	10.36	19.52	14.02
	Madras (kernels)	12.18	10.75	21.74	12.59
	CIF, Rotterdam	24.83	29.95	17.92	25.78
Groundnut oil[ii]	Madras	11.34	15.40	17.30	13.75
	Rajkot	12.42	14.59	16.34	13.35
	Hyderabad	12.74	14.14	15.49	13.38
	CIF, Rotterdam	32.77	20.23	36.80	27.49
Rape/mustard seed	Hapur	23.49	18.15	15.35	19.03
	Kanpur	22.21	17.34	12.16	17.76
	Calcutta	21.61	14.86	10.52	16.38
	Delhi	24.13	15.52	15.60	18.42
	CIF, Hamburg	18.01	13.62	16.17	15.70
Rapeseed oil	Kanpur	21.54	22.83	19.32	20.80
	Calcutta	21.83	22.28	19.48	20.71
	Delhi	21.44	21.91	20.10	20.48
	Rapeseed oil, Dutch, FoB ex-mill	28.12	17.28	14.51	21.40
Soybean seed[iii]	Madhya Pradesh (yellow)	NA	11.63	19.01	14.98
	US, n° 2 yellow, CIF Rotterdam	17.88	11.01	18.14	15.02

Table 4.1: (*Continued*)

Table 4.1: (*Continued*)

		1980–81 to 1989–90	1990–91 to 1999–00	2000–01 to 2004–05	Overall
Soybean oil[iii]	Madhya Pradesh	NA	14.59	16.41	16.76
	The Netherlands, FoB ex-mill	27.63	17.78	17.88	21.56
Sugar[iv]	Kanpur	12.94	9.16	12.19	10.83
	Bombay	9.11	9.37	11.78	9.50
	Madras	15.63	10.35	10.27	11.87
	Raw Sugar, FoB Caribbean port	33.95	20.98	24.48	26.65

Source: Author's own computation.
Note: [i] In case of wheat, 1980s corresponds to 1981–82 to 1989–1990.
[ii] In case of rice, groundnut seed and groundnut oil, period 2000 onwards refers to 2000–01 to 2002–03.
[iii] In case of domestic price of soybean seed and oil, analysis is confined to 1991–92 to 2004–05.
[iv] In case of sugar, 1980s corresponds to 1981–82 to 1989–90, and period 2000 onwards refers to 2000–01 to 2005–06.

Table 4.2: Intra-year variability in annual prices (in percentage)

		1980–81 to 1989–90	1990–91 to 1999–00	2000–01 to 2004–05	Overall
Wheat[i]	Moga	6.37	6.51	4.13	5.96
	Ludhiana	7.52	7.34	3.89	6.69
	Karnal	7.20	6.75	4.80	6.51
	Hapur	7.80	7.38	5.22	7.09
	US, n° 2 HRW, FoB Gulf	3.29	4.97	4.83	4.31
Rice[ii]	Kakinada	5.90	6.05	5.72	5.94
	Patna	5.81	5.21	7.19	5.73
	Amritsar	6.01	3.42	1.29	4.27
	Kanpur	5.79	5.29	6.66	5.69
	Sainthia	7.72	5.67	5.62	6.55
	Thailand, FoB Bangkok white milled, 5% broken	3.75	5.49	3.26	4.44

Table 4.2: (*Continued*)

Table 4.2: (*Continued*)

		1980–81 to 1989–90	*1990–91 to 1999–00*	*2000–01 to 2004–05*	*Overall*
Groundnut seed[ii]	Nandyal	7.85	10.14	7.30	8.77
	Rajkot	9.70	7.30	8.14	8.45
	Madras (kernels)	8.60	7.89	10.82	8.58
	CIF, Rotterdam	8.69	6.14	3.26	6.87
Groundnut oil[ii]	Madras	7.12	6.59	8.22	7.03
	Rajkot	7.05	5.89	7.35	6.58
	Hyderabad	7.13	6.67	8.79	7.15
	CIF Rotterdam	6.99	3.09	6.16	5.18
Rape/mustard seed	Hapur	9.81	8.66	6.65	8.72
	Kanpur	7.34	7.76	6.45	7.33
	Calcutta	6.99	6.40	6.03	6.56
	Delhi	7.58	7.56	4.95	7.05
	CIF, Hamburg	6.00	4.62	5.63	5.38
Rapeseed oil	Kanpur	5.96	7.41	4.43	6.23
	Calcutta	6.39	6.70	5.60	6.36
	Delhi	6.69	6.68	6.05	6.56
	Rapeseed oil, Dutch, FoB ex-mill	7.27	4.17	4.78	5.53
Soybean seed[iii]	Madhya Pradesh (yellow)	NA	6.66	7.67	7.02
	US, n° 2 yellow, CIF Rotterdam	4.38	4.19	5.49	4.52
Soybean oil[iii]	Madhya Pradesh	NA	5.17	4.46	4.92
	The Netherlands, FoB ex-mill	6.55	4.11	5.96	5.46
Sugar[iv]	Kanpur	3.86	3.88	3.78	3.85
	Bombay	5.80	4.53	3.20	4.67
	Madras	6.44	4.57	3.90	5.08
	Raw Sugar, FoB Caribbean port	10.62	6.47	6.64	8.01

Source: Author's own computation.

Note: [i] In case of wheat, 1980s corresponds to 1981–82 to 1989–1990.

[ii] In case of rice, groundnut seed and groundnut oil, period 2000 onwards refers to 2000–01 to 2002–03.

[iii] In case of domestic price of soybean seed and oil, analysis is confined to 1991–92 to 2004–05.

[iv] In case of sugar, 1980s corresponds to 1981–82 to 1989–90, and period 2000 onwards refers to 2000–01 to 2005–06.

the 1980s as a decade of higher intra-year variability.[2] The monthly price movements show a distinct pattern in all the markets. There is general dip between February and April/May and then a steady rise till January. The observed pattern in monthly prices may be due to arrival of harvests in the wheat markets between February and April/March.

Rice

In the case of rice, the inter-year variability of annual prices is substantially lower in all the rice producing domestic markets such as Kakinada, Patna, Amritsar, and Kanpur than in the international market (Table 4.1).

However, the intra-year variability is higher in the domestic markets than in the international market with the exception of the decade of the 1990s (Table 4.2). This shows that Indian rice prices were more prone to within-the-year fluctuations during the 1980s and the recent sub-periods compared to international prices. The intra-year variability analysis of international prices shows the 1990s as being the most variable decade followed by the 1980s. However, in one year in the 1990s (1993–94) out of 10, the intra-year variability was greater than 200 per cent of the decadal average, while in the 1980s there was none. The most recent sub-period shows lowest variability. The monthly movement in international market prices shows that prices were generally higher during October to December compared to the rest of the months. In case of domestic markets, with the exception of Kakinada, the intra-year variability was less during the 1990s than in the 1980s. A similar trend was observed in the case of inter-year variability as well between the 1980s and 1990s with the exception of Kakinada and Kanpur market prices.

Groundnut seed

The overall inter-year variability is substantially lower in domestic markets than in the international market. However, the intra-year variability is higher in the domestic markets. This shows that the average annual prices perhaps conceal the true fluctuations in monthly prices due to offsetting movements in opposite directions. The intra-year

---

[2] The only exception was the Moga market which showed higher intra-year volatility in monthly prices during the 1990s compared to the 1980s.

variability in international price was the highest in the 1980s followed by the 1990s and beyond. A similar trend was observed in case of domestic markets as well between the 1980s and 1990s with one exception of Nandyal market.

Groundnut oil

As in the case of groundnut seed, inter-year variability was substantially lower in domestic markets than in the international market, whereas the intra-year variability was higher in the domestic markets. In the case of intra-year variability, both international and domestic markets followed similar patterns showing higher volatility in the 1980s compared to the 1990s.

Rape/mustard seed

In the case of rape/mustard seeds, domestic markets show higher levels of variability than in the international markets. This is true for inter-year variability as well as intra-year variability. The intra-year variability in domestic markets was highest in the 1980s followed by the 1990s and beyond, whereas in the case of international prices, variability has declined in the 1990s compared to the 1980s but increased again in the most recent sub-period.

Rapeseed/mustard oil

During the 1980s, domestic markets show lower level of variability than in international markets, but in subsequent periods, prices were more volatile in domestic markets compared to international markets, both in terms of inter-year and intra-year. The intra-year variability in international oil price has followed the trend of seed prices. In case of domestic markets, intra-year volatility was lowest in most recent sub-period following the 1980s and 1990s.

Soybean seed

In case of inter-year variability, both domestic as well as international markets turn out to be equally volatile. However, the intra-year variability is higher in the domestic market. The decade of the 1990s has been relatively milder with lower average intra-year and inter-year variability compared to the most recent sub-period and the decade of the 1980s in the case of both international and domestic prices.

Soybean oil

Both inter-year and intra-year variability is lower in domestic markets than in international markets. As was the case with soybean seed, both inter-year and intra-year variability were lowest in the 1990s in the case of international markets. In the case of domestic markets, intra-year variability was high during the 1990s compared to the most recent period.

Sugar

In the case of sugar, the domestic markets show a much lower level of variability than international markets. This is true for inter-year variability as well as intra-year variability. In the case of the international market, the decade of the 1980s exhibited highest variability followed by the most recent sub-period. The decade of the 1990s has been relatively tranquil. The intra-year variability in case of domestic markets is highest in the 1980s followed by the 1990s and the most recent sub-period.

In summary, what emerges from this analysis is: first, comparing domestic and international market prices, it has been found that in a majority of the cases, inter-year variability is generally lower in domestic markets (except rapeseed) than in the international markets. On the other hand, intra-year variability is higher in domestic markets (except sugar) than in the international markets. This shows that Indian domestic market prices are more prone to within-the-year fluctuations. Second, the decade of the 1990s turned out to be relatively stable compared to the 1980s in the case of both domestic as well as international market prices. The exceptions to this were international market prices of wheat and rice where intra-year variability has gone up in the 1990s compared to the 1980s. Third, the most recent sub-period (i.e., 2000–01 to 2004–05) showed further decline in within-the-year fluctuations in a majority of domestic market prices (except groundnut seed and oil). In sharp contrast to domestic markets, international market prices again witnessed an increase in intra-year volatility after remaining relatively stable during the decade of the 1990s. The only exceptions to this were wheat and rice where intra-year variability has gone down.

One drawback of using the ratio method to measure variability is that it assumes that past realisations of price and volatility have no influence on current or future realisations and does not distinguish between the known and unknown components of the price series. Therefore, it leads to overestimation of the degree of uncertainty. In order to get a more reliable estimate, the predictable components (such as the effect of inflation, seasonality and trend) of the data series should be removed, leaving only unpredictable or stochastic components for further analysis. In this context, the next section of the chapter deals with the price variability in major domestic and international markets using the GARCH model.

4.3.2 Agricultural Price Variability: GARCH Approach

Following the basic framework discussed in Appendix I, this section quantifies the variability in the prices of international and domestic markets, where price volatility is considered to be only the stochastic or unpredictable component in the price of the crop under consideration.

Wheat

In case of wheat, the analysis of variability in market prices shows that the variability in prices (in both domestic as well as international markets) has declined substantially after removing the predictable components of the data series. In the case of international market prices, with the removal of the trend component[3] of the data series, variability has declined substantially. On the other hand, in the case of domestic markets, variability declined by 50 per cent after removing the seasonal component of the data process (Table 4.3). Out of four domestic markets and one international market, only two markets, namely, Karnal and Ludhiana, reported presence of conditional volatility.

The long-run volatility[4] (i.e., inter-year volatility), as measured by taking the medians of the conditional standard deviations for the markets with varying volatility or standard error of ARIMA process,[5] shows higher volatility in domestic market prices (varying from 0.05 to 0.06) in comparison to the international market (i.e., 0.04).

The short-run volatility (intra-year volatility), as computed by taking the medians of the conditional standard deviations of monthly

---

[3] This is obtained from first-order differencing of the series.

[4] Volatility of whole time period.

[5] In markets where variability was not time varying.

Table 4.3: Estimates of price volatility for wheat markets

Series Name (log real prices) (1)	Unit (2)	Periods (3)	Presence of Seasonality (4)	Data Process of the Series (5)	STDEV of column (1) (6)	STDEV of De-seasonalised Series (7)	Unconditional STDEV (8)	Conditional STDEV (9)	Models used for columns (8) & (9) (10)
Domestic market									
Hapur	₹/qtl	1981M04–2005M03	Yes	Stationary	0.12	0.10	0.06	Not present	ARIMA (1,0,0)
Karnal	₹/qtl	1981M04–2005M03	Yes	Stationary	0.11	0.10	0.06	0.05	ARIMA (1,0–11,0,0) GARCH (0,1)
Ludhiana	₹/qtl	1981M04–2005M03	Yes	Stationary	0.10	0.09	0.06	0.05	ARIMA (1,0,0) GARCH (0,1)
Moga	₹/qtl	1981M04–2005M03	Yes	Stationary	0.10	0.09	0.06	Not present	ARIMA (1,0,1)
International market									
US, n° 2 HRW	US$/MT	1981M04–2005M03	No	Difference stationary	0.28	0.05[+]	0.04	Not present	ARIMA (1,1,0)

Source: Author's own computation.

Note: + Standard deviation of differenced price series.

prices of the markets with varying volatility[6] can be observed from Figure 4.10. The short-run volatility in market prices shows higher variability in Karnal compared to Ludhiana. The monthly conditional standard deviation also shows that both the markets had spikes (i.e., sharp rise) in 1988, 1989, 1991, 1992, and again in 1996 exceeding the one standard deviation boundaries (Appendix, Figures A-4.1a and b). This is an indication of high volatility during these periods. The only difference was that the Karnal market showed spikes in monthly prices even after 1996 whereas there was no spike in Ludhiana after 1996, indicating a low level of volatility after 1996. In short, the general trend indicates higher level of volatility in domestic market prices than in the international market price both in the short-run as well as the long-run.

Figure 4.10: Medians of the conditional standard deviation in wheat market prices: 1982–83 to 2004–05

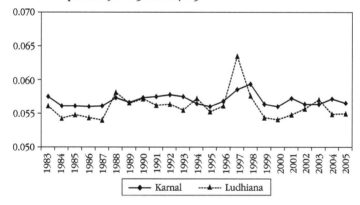

Source: Author's own computation.

Rice

The measure of price variability in case of rice markets shows that none of the markets reported presence of conditional variability (Table 4.4). As observed in the case of wheat, variability in case of rice prices has also declined substantially after removing the predictable

---

[6] In this context, it must be noted that, in case of markets where variability was not time varying, the short-run volatility remains constant over the years at a level of SE of ARIMA process of the series.

components (i.e., trend) of the data series. In case of international market prices with the removal of trend component, variability has declined substantially. On the other hand, in the case of domestic markets, variability declined by 50 per cent after removing the trend component of the data process. As a matter of fact, with the removal of the trend component, domestic market prices showed higher level of variability than the international market prices.

The long-run volatility,[7] as measured by standard error of ARIMA process, shows higher instability in Indian market prices (varying from 0.05 to 0.06) than the international prices (i.e., 0.05). Among the Indian markets, prices at Amritsar in Punjab and Kanpur in Uttar Pradesh showed lower variability than the prices at other domestic markets.

Data for international market prices is I(1). An ARIMA (1, 2) model fits the data well. On the other hand, prices in domestic markets were trend stationary, except the price at Kakinada market, which was stationary. An ARIMA (3, 2) model has been fitted to the data of Kakinada market price.

Groundnut seed and oil

In case of groundnut seed and oil prices, out of three domestic markets studied, only two, namely, Nandyal and Madras in case of seed, and Madras and Hyderabad in case of oil, show presence of conditional variability. On the other hand, variability was time varying in both the international markets (i.e., seed as well as oil market prices).

With the exception of the international market price for groundnut oil, price data in other markets are trend stationary. The international price for groundnut oil is I(1). Models fitted to the data for different markets are mentioned in Table 4.5. Analysis further shows that with the removal of predictable components from the data process variability has come down. Decline was substantial in case of international prices with the removal of the trend component and this has also lowered the difference between domestic and international market price variability.

The long-run volatility as measured by taking the medians of the conditional standard deviations for the markets with varying volatility

---

[7] In this context, it must be noted that since none of the market reported presence of conditional volatility, therefore, the short-run volatility remains constant over the years at a level of SE of ARIMA process of the series.

Table 4.4: Estimates of price volatility for rice markets

Series Name (log real prices) (1)	Unit (2)	Periods (3)	Presence of Seasonality (4)	Data Process of Series (5)	STDEV of column (1) (6)	STDEV of Detrended+ or Differenced Series (7)	Unconditional STDEV (8)	Conditional STDEV (9)	Models used for columns (8) & (9) (10)
Domestic market									
Amritsar	₹/qtl	1980M10–2003M09	No	Trend stationary	0.16	0.08	0.05	Not present	ARIMA (1,0,2)
Kakinada	₹/qtl	1980M10–2003M09	No	Stationary	0.10	NA	0.06	Not present	ARIMA (3,0,2)
Kanpur	₹/qtl	1980M10–2003M09	No	Trend stationary	0.14	0.08	0.05	Not present	ARIMA (2,01)
Patna	₹/qtl	1980M10–2003M09	No	Trend stationary	0.16	0.08	0.06	Not present	ARIMA (1,0,0)
Sainthia	₹/qtl	1980M10–2003M09	No	Trend stationary	0.18	0.08	0.06	Not present	ARIMA (1,0–12,0,0)
International market									
Thai Rice 5% broken	US$/MT	1980M10–2003M09	No	Differenced-stationary	0.39	0.05	0.05	Not present	ARIMA (1,1,2)

Source: Author's own computation.

Note: + Detrending was done by taking the difference between a series and its trend estimated with the Hodrick–Prescott Filter.
'NA' means series was stationary without trend.

Table 4.5: Estimates of price volatility for groundnut seed/oil markets

Series Name (log real prices) (1)	Unit (2)	Periods (3)	Presence of Seasonality (4)	Data Process of Series (5)	STDEV of column (1) (6)	STDEV of Detrended[+] or Differenced Series (7)	Unconditional STDEV (8)	Conditional STDEV (9)	Models Used for columns (8) & (9) (10)
Groundnut Seed									
Domestic market									
Nandyal	₹/qtl	1980M10–2003M09	No	Trend stationary	0.17	0.11	0.08	0.07	ARIMA (1,0,0) GARCH (1,1)
Madras	₹/qtl	1980M10–2003M09	Yes	Trend stationary with seasonality	0.18	0.10	0.07	0.06	ARIMA (2,0,0) GARCH (0,1)
Rajkot	₹/qtl	1980M10–2003M09	No	Trend stationary	0.17	0.11	0.08	Not present	ARIMA (1,0,0)
International market									
CIF, Rotterdam	US$/MT	1980M10–2003M09	No	Trend stationary	0.40	0.17	0.07	0.05	ARIMA (2,0,0) GARCH (1,1)

Groundnut Oil

Domestic market

Madras	₹/qtl	1980M11–2003M10	No	Trend stationary	0.22	0.10	0.07	0.06	ARIMA (1,0,0) GARCH (1,1)
Hyderabad	₹/qtl	1980M11–2003M10	No	Trend stationary	0.19	0.10	0.07	0.06	ARIMA (1,0,0) GARCH (1,1)
Rajkot	₹/qtl	1980M11–2003M10	No	Trend stationary	0.21	0.10	0.06	Not present	ARIMA (1,0,1)

International market

CIF, Rotterdam	US$/MT	1980M11–2003M10	No	Non-stationary with drift	0.31	0.06	0.06	0.05	ARIMA (1,1,0) GARCH (0,1)

Source: Author's own computation.

Note: + Detrending was done by taking the difference between a series and its trend estimated with the Hodrick–Prescott Filter.

or standard error of ARIMA process shows that prices in international markets were less volatile compared to domestic markets. Among the domestic seed markets, Rajkot was the most volatile, followed by Nandyal and Madras. On the other hand, in case of oil, domestic markets were equally volatile.

The short-run volatility (intra-year volatility), as computed by taking the medians of the conditional standard deviations of monthly prices of the markets with varying volatility, shows higher risk in international seed markets during the 1980s, whereas domestic markets turned more volatile during the 1990s and beyond compared to the international market (Figure 4.11). Our standard deviation estimates also confirm these results. The presence of spikes in monthly conditional standard deviation in international market price during 1983, 1986, 1988, and 1991 also indicates clustering of volatility during the 1980s (Appendix, Figures A-4.2a, b and c). In case of domestic markets, the short-run volatility shows higher risk in Nandyal compared to Madras.

In the case of oil, domestic markets were more volatile in the short-run compared to international markets during the 1990s and onwards (Figure 4.12). The frequency of the spikes exceeding the one standard deviation boundaries was also high during the period in domestic market prices. Our estimates of intra-year volatility using ratio method

Figure 4.11: Medians of the conditional standard deviation in groundnut seed market prices: 1980–81 to 2002–03

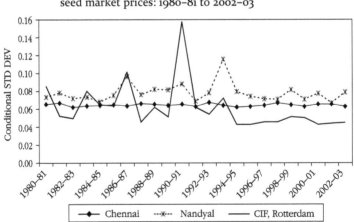

Source: Author's own computation.

Figure 4.12: Medians of the conditional standard deviation in groundnut oil market prices: 1980–81 to 2002–03

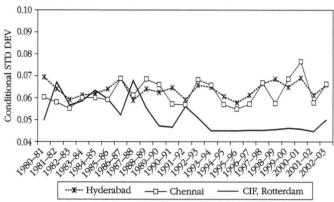

Source: Author's own computation.

also confirm these results. The presence of spikes in 1983, 1988, 1989, 2001, and 2003 in international market prices shows higher volatility during the period (Appendix, Figures A-4.3a, b and c). The short-run volatility also shows that both the domestic markets were equally volatile. Standard deviation results also confirm this finding.

Rape/mustard seed and oil

In the case of rape/mustard seed and oil prices, except for the Delhi market in the case of seed and Kanpur market in the case of oil, all other studied domestic markets showed presence of conditional variability. On the other hand, in the case of international markets, only oil market prices showed time-varying variability. Data on domestic market prices are trend stationary, whereas international price data both for rape/mustard seed and oil are integrated of order one, i.e., I (1). Models fitted to the market price data for both seed and oil are mentioned in Table 4.6.

With the removal of trend component from the price data, variability has declined significantly in all the studied markets. However, compared to domestic markets, decline was higher in case of international market prices. And with the removal of trend components, prices in the domestic markets became more volatile in comparison to international market prices.

Table 4.6: Estimates of price volatility for rapeseed/oil markets

Series Name (log real prices) (1)	Unit (2)	Periods (3)	Presence of Seasonality (4)	Data Process of Series (5)	STDEV of column (1) (6)	STDEV of Detrended+ or Differenced Series (7)	Unconditional STDEV (8)	Conditional STDEV (9)	Models Used for columns (8) & (9) (10)
Rapeseed									
Domestic market									
Hapur	₹/qtl	1980M10–2005M09	No	Trend stationary	0.22	0.14	0.08	0.08	ARIMA (1,0,0) GARCH (1,1)
Kanpur	₹/qtl	1980M10–2005M09	No	Trend stationary	0.23	0.13	0.07	0.06	ARIMA (2,0,1–10) GARCH (1,1)
Calcutta	₹/qtl	1980M10–2005M09	No	Trend stationary	0.19	0.12	0.06	0.05	ARIMA (2,0,1–10) GARCH (1,1)
Delhi	₹/qtl	1980M10–2005M09	Yes	Trend stationary with seasonality	0.20	NA	0.06	Not present	ARIMA (3,0,2)
International market									
Europe, '00', CIF Hamburg	US$/MT	1980M10–2005M09	No	Non-stationary with drift & trend	0.33	0.06	0.05	Not present	ARIMA (1,1,0)

Rapeseed Oil
Domestic market

Kanpur	₹/qtl	1980M04–2005M03	No	Trend stationary	0.24	0.13	0.06	Not present	ARIMA (1–3,0,2)
Calcutta	₹/qtl	1980M04–2005M03	No	Trend stationary	0.23	0.12	0.06	0.06	ARIMA (1,0,0) GARCH (1,1)
Delhi	₹/qtl	1980M04–2005M03	No	Trend stationary	0.23	0.12	0.06	0.06	ARIMA (1,0,0) GARCH (1,1)

International market

Dutch FoB, ex-mill	US$/MT	1980M04–2005M03	No	Non-stationary, with drift	0.31	0.06	0.06	0.05	ARIMA (2,1,0) GARCH (1,1)

Source: Author's own computation.

Note. + Detrending was done by taking the difference between a series and its trend estimated with the Hodrick–Prescott Filter.
'NA' means series became stationary without drift and trend after deseanilizing.

The long-run volatility shows that oil prices in international markets were less volatile as compared to domestic markets, whereas in the case of seed, variability in domestic market prices was high, if not higher, than the international market prices. Among the domestic rape/mustard seed markets, Hapur was the most volatile market followed by Kanpur and Calcutta. Unlike the seed market prices, domestic oil markets were equally volatile. Our estimates of standard deviation of domestic market prices also confirm this result (Table 4.1, last column).

The short-run volatility shows that among the domestic seed markets, Hapur was more risky even in the short-run also followed by Kanpur and Calcutta (Figure 4.13) and can also be confirmed with the estimates of standard deviation (Table 4.2). The presence of spikes in monthly conditional standard deviation during 1983–84, 1986–87, 1990–91, and 1998–99 indicates clustering of volatility in the prices during the period (Appendix, Figures A-4.4a, b and c). In case of oil (Figure 4.14), the prices in international markets were more volatile during the 1980s compared to the 1990s. In comparison to domestic markets, volatility in international market prices was less during the 1990s and can also be verified with the presence of spikes in monthly conditional standard deviation of prices (Appendix, Figures 4.5a, b and c). The standard deviation results also substantiate the GARCH estimate.

Figure 4.13: Medians of the conditional standard deviation in rape/mustard seed market prices: 1980–81 to 2004–05

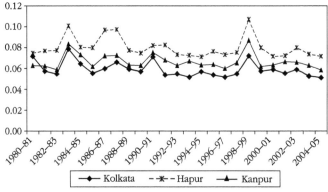

Source: Author's own computation.

Figure 4.14: Medians of the conditional standard deviation in rapeseed/
mustard oil market prices: 1980–81 to 2004–05

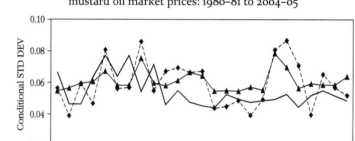

Source: Author's own computation.

Soybean seed and oil

In case of soybean seed and oils, only international market prices
showed presence of conditional variability. However, data on domestic and international market prices both in case of seed and oil are
I(1). With the removal of predictable components of the price process,
variability has declined substantially both in international and domestic market prices. And with the removal of trend component, seed
prices in domestic markets turned out more volatile in comparison
to international market prices (Table 4.7).

The long-run volatility, as measured by taking the medians of
the conditional standard deviations for the markets with varying
volatility or standard error of ARIMA process shows less variability
in international market prices compared to domestic markets in the
case of both seed and oil.

The short-run volatility shows that in comparison to oil prices,
seed prices in international markets are more volatile (Figure 4.15).
The presence of spikes in monthly conditional standard deviation of
seed market prices, during 1993–94, 1996–97, 2000–01, 2003–04 and
2004–05 indicates higher volatility in the prices during the periods
(Appendix, Figure A-4.6a and b). Standard deviation results confirm
this finding. The volatility in domestic prices of soybean seed and
oil remained constant at the level of 0.07 and 0.05, respectively,
throughout the period.

Table 4.7: Estimates of price volatility for soybean seed/oil markets

Series Name (log real prices) (1)	Unit (2)	Periods (3)	Presence of Seasonality (4)	Data Process of Series (5)	STDEV of column (1) (6)	STDEV of Detrended[+] or Differenced Series (7)	Unconditional STDEV (8)	Conditional STDEV (9)	Models Used for columns (8) & (9) (10)
Soybean seed									
Domestic market									
Madhya Pradesh, yellow	₹/qtl	1991M10–2005M09	No	Non-stationary, with drift	0.20	0.07	0.07	Not present	ARIMA (1,1,2)
International market									
US, n° 2 yellow, Rotterdam Soybean oil	CIF US$/MT	1991M10–2005M09	No	Non-stationary, with drift	0.19	0.05	0.05	0.04	ARIMA (0,1,1) GARCH (0,1)
Domestic market									
Madhya Pradesh, yellow, refined oil	₹/qtl	1991M10–2005M09	No	Non-stationary, with drift	0.24	0.05	0.05	Not present	ARIMA (0,12)
International market									
The Netherlands FoB ex-mill	US$/MT	1991M10–2005M09	No	Non-stationary, with no drift and trend	0.25	0.05	0.05	0.04	ARIMA (2,1,2) GARCH (0,1)

Source: Author's own computation.

Note: + Detrending was done by taking the difference between a series and its trend estimated with the Hodrick–Prescott Filter.

Figure 4.15: Medians of the conditional standard deviation in international market prices of soybean seed and oil: 1991–92 to 2004–05

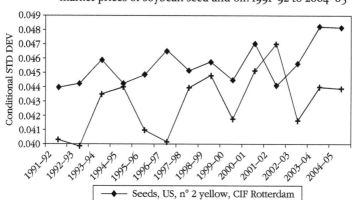

Source: Author's own computation.

Sugar

The prices included in the analysis are for Bombay, Kanpur and Madras in the case of domestic markets and raw sugar price at the Caribbean port for the international market. Out of the four markets studied, with the exception of Madras, prices in all other markets showed presence of conditional variability in monthly data.

In the case of domestic markets, data is trend stationary in all the markets. On the other hand, international price data was integrated of order one, i.e., I(1). The model that fits the data well is specified in Table 4.8. With the removal of trend component from the price data, variability has declined significantly in all the studied markets. However, compared to domestic markets, decline was higher in case of international market prices. The elimination of trend component has also narrowed the difference between domestic and international market variability.

The long-run volatility as measured by taking the medians of the conditional standard deviations or standard error of ARIMA process indicates that price risk associated with the international market is higher in comparison to domestic markets. Among the domestic markets, price in the Madras market was most volatile followed by the Bombay and Kanpur markets.

The short-run volatility (intra-year volatility), as computed by taking the medians of the conditional standard deviations of monthly

Table 4.8: Estimates of price volatility for sugar markets

Series Name (log real prices) (1)	Unit (2)	Periods (3)	Presence of Seasonality (4)	Data Process of the Series (5)	STDEV of column (1) (6)	STDEV of De-trended Series (7)	Unconditional STDEV (8)	Conditional STDEV (9)	Models Used for columns (8) & (9) (10)
Domestic market									
Bombay	₹/qtl	1981M10–2006M09	No	Trend stationary	0.20	0.07	0.05	0.04	ARIMA (1,0,0) GARCH (0,1)
Kanpur	₹/qtl	1981M10–2006M09	No	Trend stationary	0.19	0.07	0.04	0.03	ARIMA (1,0,0) GARCH (0,2)
Madras	₹/qtl	1981M10–2006M09	No	Trend stationary	0.19	0.09	0.05	Not present	ARIMA (1,0,0)
International market									
Raw sugar, FoB Caribbean port	US cents per pound	1981M10–2006M09	No	Difference stationary	0.34	0.09[+]	0.08	0.07	ARIMA (0,1,1) GARCH (0,1)

Source: Author's own computation.

Note: + Standard deviation of differenced price series.

prices, shows higher variability in international prices in comparison to domestic prices. Regarding domestic markets, Kanpur market was less risky compared to Bombay market even in the short-run (Figure 4.16). The standard deviation result also confirms this finding (Table 4.2).

Figure 4.16: Medians of the conditional standard deviation in international and domestic market prices of sugar: 1981–82 to 2005–06

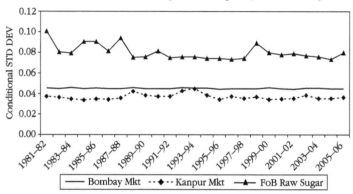

Source: Author's own computation.

In the case of the international market, the intra-year volatility was substantially higher in the 1980s than in the 1990s. The Kanpur and Bombay markets also display a trend similar to that in the international market, i.e., presence of higher volatility during the 1980s than in the 1990s. Clustering of spikes in monthly conditional standard deviation during the 1980s indicates clustering volatility in the price during the period (Appendix, Figure A-4.7a, b and c). The standard deviation result also verifies this finding (Table 4.2).

The pattern was slightly different during the 1990s. The international market witnessed a substantial decline in intra-year volatility since early-1990, whereas domestic market prices shows clustering of volatility during the first half of the 1990s. Nevertheless, compared to the 1980s, the decade of 1990s was relative stable in the case of both domestic as well as international market prices (Appendix, Figure A-4.7a, b and c). Standard deviation results also validate the finding.

After having analysed the volatility in detail by using the standard deviation and GARCH estimate, we now put the results from both the estimates together and see what comes up. The first striking observation is decline in volatility significantly across the commodities with the removal of predictable component from the price data. In case of international market prices, a significant proportion of volatility as observed in the standard deviation estimate was largely because of the presence of trend component in the monthly price series. After removing the trend component, the overall volatility in international prices turned lower than in the domestic market, the only exception to this was volatility in the international market price of sugar, which remained higher than the domestic market even after removing the trend component. Another important observation is that in the case of within-the-year variability, the results from GARCH model confirm the results obtained by using standard deviation method and shows similar pattern of intra-year variability across commodities as observed by standard deviation method.

4.4 Summary

We summarise the analysis of this chapter with the following observations:

First, the behaviour of international market prices of agricultural commodities clearly shows that a country like India cannot afford to excessively rely on the international market. Doing so will make domestic agriculture vulnerable to the developments/policies of the major exporting countries. Although the world demand and supply situation determines the movements in world prices, the output and stockholding policies of major exporting countries still holds large implications for world price movement and stability. To elaborate, in the case of rice, just after the Asian crisis, international price of rice started declining. Low demand from some big importers of rice from Asia and Latin America was one of the reasons behind this decline. On the supply side, India and China's entry as exporters in the international rice market and domestic policies undertaken by developed countries increased the supply–demand gap. This decline in international prices of rice was accentuated by heavy subsidisation of rice farmers in the USA. The increased direct support to US rice producers by way of counter-cyclical payments to absorb the shock of low prices and maintain their high trading volumes resulted in oversupply of rice in the international market and exacerbated the decline in international rice prices.

Second, the broader conclusion that one can draw from the volatility analysis is lower inter-year variability in domestic market prices compared to international market prices. On the other hand, the higher intra-year variability in domestic markets (except sugar) than the international markets highlights the fact that Indian market prices are more prone to within-the-year fluctuations. The decadal analysis of intra-year variability shows that domestic market prices have witnessed a continuous decline in volatility. In domestic markets, highest volatility was observed in the 1980s followed by the 1990s and the most recent sub-period. The only exception to this was groundnut seed and oil where volatility has increased slightly during the most recent sub-period. In contrast to domestic markets, international market prices showed cyclical movement in intra-year volatility. The decade of the 1990s turned out to be a relatively stable period compared to the 1980s in the case of international market prices for most of the commodities except for rice and wheat. After the 1990s, international market prices again witnessed an increase in volatility with the exception of rice and wheat where volatility has declined relative to the decade of the 1990s. The results from the GARCH model confirm the results obtained by using standard deviation method and show similar pattern of intra-year variability across commodities as observed by the standard deviation method. In sum, comparing data across periods for India and the world separately, we find volatility reduced for most crops in the Indian market, but not so in the global, implying that the world market has become more volatile whereas the Indian market has become less so in recent periods.

Therefore, from the analysis of price volatility, we do not see much ground for granting price volatility a significant role in determining the trajectory of agricultural growth since 1991 because of continuous decline in within-the-year fluctuations in domestic market prices. However, the long-run trend of international prices has a possible effect that can damage domestic agriculture independent of volatility by affecting the level of domestic prices (this issue is discussed in Chapter 6).

5

Agricultural Trade

Policies and Patterns

In India, like any other developing country, the central problem of food policy is how to reconcile the conflicting objectives of providing low food prices to consumers and remunerative prices to farmers. Maintaining stability in these prices is an equally important objective of food policy. Trade policies that are designed to regulate the volume of trade flows are found to be an effective instrument in imparting stability to domestic prices along with affecting the performance of the marketing system by influencing the average level of prices, intercrop price ratios and the price spread in the domestic market. As the policy reconciles the objectives of growth and equity, it has always occupied an important place in economic and political debates.

The volatility analysis of the previous chapter highlights the fact that during the post-reform period, volatility in domestic market prices of agricultural commodities has come down compared to the decade of the 1980s. However, the long-run trend of international prices, particularly after the mid-1990s, has a possible effect that can damage domestic agriculture independent of volatility by affecting the average level of domestic prices. This raises an obvious question regarding the role played by trade policy during the post-reform period in terms of imparting stability to domestic prices and influencing the average level of prices. It is in this perspective that the present chapter considers the trade policy regime for agriculture in the national context outlining its rationale and structure over the past quarter of a century. To this end, evolution of agriculture trade policy is discussed in section 5.1. This is followed by commodity specific developments in the external trade policies in section 5.2. An attempt is made to analyse the performance of agricultural export and import along with changes in composition of the agriculture trade basket in section 5.3. Since the actual trade outcome is dependent on many factors and trade policy at best gives an idea about government intentions, therefore, an attempt is made to analyse the export and import pattern of selected agricultural commodities in section 5.4, in the light of the domestic demand and supply situation along with changes in international prices and India's agriculture trade policy. Section 5.5 draws together some conclusions that emerge from the analysis.

5.1 EVOLUTION OF AGRICULTURE TRADE POLICY

India's foreign trade policy in the sphere of agriculture which regulated the volume of both exports and imports till the reform initiated in 1991 was primarily dictated by two important considerations, a quest for import substitution and a concern for food self-sufficiency. In most of the commodities,[1] foreign trade flows have been perceived as a residual whether we consider exportables or importables. For exportables, the difference between actual domestic production and estimated domestic consumption has determined the surplus available for export. For importables, the difference between estimated domestic production and desired domestic consumption has determined the volume of imports. The major instruments used to implement these policy goals comprise quantitative restrictions (QRs) (either in the form of licences or quotas), canalisation or a combination of both. The role of the State Trading Corporation (STC) and the co-operative federations was emphasised as canalising agencies for agricultural trade.

However, this scenario has witnessed significant changes after 1991 when India started a process of stabilisation and adjustment. Under the structural adjustment programme, the rupee was devalued by 18 per cent against the dollar and the exchange rate was left to be determined by market forces. Following this, new initiatives were taken in the trade policy area to create an environment that provides a stimulus to export while at the same time reducing the degree of regulation and licensing control on foreign trade. The scope of canalisation for both exports and imports was narrowed. The aim of these policy changes was to (*i*) strengthen export incentives, (*ii*) eliminate substantial import licensing and (*iii*) ensure optimal import compression as necessitated by the balance of payments situation.

---

[1] Traditional exports that originate in the agricultural sector, both plantation crops such as tea or coffee and cash crops such as tobacco or spices, which have always been an important source of foreign exchange earnings for the economy since the colonial era, constitute the exception to the rule.

The new export–import policy announced on 31 March 1992 for the period 1992–97 introduced by far the most liberal trade policy regime the country has seen since Independence. The main feature of the policy was that trade was free except for a small negative list of imports and exports. Imports of three items were banned, 80 items restricted, and eight items canalised. Till 1992, agricultural exports and imports in the country were strictly regulated through QRs, such as quotas and licenses, or channelled through some trading organisation or some combination of both. With the new trade policy initiated in 1992, three major changes were effected in agricultural trade. First, channelling of trade was abandoned and the government stopped determining the value or nature of the imports or exports, except for exports of onion and import of cereals, pulses and edible oils. Second, most of the quantitative restrictions on agricultural trade flows were dismantled. Third, there was some reduction in tariffs.

The move towards trade liberalisation during the period was triggered both by internal policy assessments as well as external developments such as the WTO Uruguay Round Agreements. Beginning in 1996, strong pressure was put on India by several developed countries to remove all kinds of quantitative restrictions on imports as it was found that India was not suffering from a balance-of-payments problem and this required a WTO member country to remove quantitative restrictions. Thus, in order to make its policy consistent with WTO obligations, India removed the QRs on 714 items including 142 commodities belonging to the category of agricultural commodities during 1999–2000. On 1 April 2001, India eliminated the last quantitative restrictions on 715 six-digit tariff lines including 142 tariff lines pertaining to agriculture.

The trade policy announced for the period 2002–07 has taken a number of measures to prevent any negative impact of QR removals on the agricultural sector. Import of agricultural products like rice, wheat, maize, other coarse cereals, copra, and coconut oil were placed in the category of 'State Trading'. The government also monitors imports of a number of agricultural products considered to be sensitive, including milk products, fruit and nuts, coffee, tea, spices, cereals, and edible oils. The authorities maintain that the only measure that can be taken in case of a surge in imports of these products is an increase in the applied rates of customs duties within their respective bound rates.

In recent years, agricultural exports have received special attention from the government. Under the Special Focus Initiative package for agriculture, in its export–import policy 2002–07, India took additional steps to boost exports of agricultural products. Agri-export zones were established to encourage exports of certain products. The Vishesh Krishi Upaj Yojana (special agricultural products scheme), which was introduced in 2004, promotes exports of fruit, vegetables, flowers, minor forest produce, dairy, poultry, and their value-added products.[2] Although over the years India has gradually removed prohibitions, licensing, and other restrictions on exports in order to maintain domestic supplies and stability in domestic prices, notifications were made from time to time to restrict exports or lift export restrictions.

In summary, though the protection in agricultural trade has declined over time, India continues to use trade policy instruments to support its overall goals of food self-sufficiency and price stability. Thus, tariffs, import licences and export restrictions as the main instruments of trade policy continue to be used from time to time to ensure sufficient domestic supply of key products. The following section analyses how these key trade policy instruments were used over time in case of key crops, such as wheat, rice, oilseeds and sugarcane, in order support the overall goals of food self-sufficiency and price stability.

5.2 Commodity-specific External Trade Policy

5.2.1 Wheat

From the 1980s to early 1990s India protected its wheat sector with quantitative restrictions on both imports and exports. Wheat trade has been under government control, and the import and export quantities reflect government decisions made during each year as well as across the years in managing supply, demand, stocks and food prices to strengthen domestic food security. Quantitative controls on exports were administered through the Food Corporation of India. According to the trade policy followed from 1988 to 1991, the export of wheat was restricted through licensing. During 1992–97, wheat was kept

---

[2] The full list of products may be viewed in the Foreign Trade Procedures, Appendix 37A. See http://dgft.delhi.nic.in/ (accessed 21 March 2014).

under the 'negative list'[3] but the export was allowed freely, as long as it did not exceed the ceiling limit stipulated from time to time, at a price above MEP. This policy was followed till 1997, except for the period between 1995 and 1996 when the government attempted to boost wheat exports. In 1995, the government placed wheat export in the open category and released an export ceiling of 2.5 million tonnes for export of non-Durum wheat from the open market without any MEP during the year 1995–96. But as exports picked up, domestic prices of wheat rose and the government, fearing unrest, put a ban on wheat export. Therefore, till 1997, export of wheat from India was restricted and subjected to minimum export price. Since then, export restrictions were removed in a phased manner, first, by abolishing the condition of MEP in 1998 and second, by removing the ceiling limit on export of wheat and its products in April 2002, subject to the condition that stocks in the central pool are not lower than 14.3 million tonnes at any point of time. The government started providing budgetary subsidies since 2000 to support exports of surplus wheat when the combination of declining world prices[4] and higher domestic prices made Indian wheat uncompetitive in world markets. Table 5.1 shows that during 2001–05, substantial amount of export subsidies were paid to make it worthwhile for private traders to help dispose of large excess wheat stocks. In 2005, the government halted export subsidies because of tightening domestic supplies and increased Indian competitiveness in international markets, although private traders remain free to export wheat. Following a sharp fall in the government's annual food grain procurement because of good open market prices and lower production, India banned exports of wheat and wheat products in 2007.

In the case of import, trade policies were changed when quantitative restrictions on imports were lifted and replaced by tariffs in the mid-1990s. There was zero customs duty on import of wheat until 1999 and a check on imports was kept through quantitative restrictions and canalisation. Removal of QRs and freeing of imports in mid-1999 led

---

[3] Importation/exportation under the category is subject to restriction on total quantity or on price, such as Minimum Export Price (MEP) issued as public notice by the competent authority from time to time. It also includes the items kept under canalised list, where goods can be exported/imported only by a government-designated agency.

[4] Please refer to the section under 'Trends in Wheat Price' in Chapter 4.

Table 5.1: Wheat export quantities and amount of subsidy provided by the Food Corporation of India: 2000–01 to 2004–05

	Quantity lakh tonnes	Rate of Subsidy ₹/Qtl	Amount of Subsidy ₹ lakh
2000–01	21.53	468.40	100,850.53
2001–02	37.95	430.15	163,242.56
2002–03	73.91	445.27	329,098.71
2003–04	71.75	379.15	272,003.54
2004–05	8.45	353.19	29,844.62

Source: Annual reports of the Food Corporation of India, various issues.

to sudden importation of wheat. This forced the country to impose varying rate of tariff to regulate wheat importation. As a result, the wheat tariff, which was initially set at zero, was raised to 50 per cent on 1 December 1999 to curb imports into southern India at a time when surpluses were growing in the north,[5] which continued till January 2006. In view of inadequate stocks with public agencies, it was decided in February 2006 that government-run agencies can import wheat at zero duty. Later on during the year, the previous major role of State Trading Enterprises (STEs) in import was eliminated in June 2006 by announcing that wheat imports would no longer be a monopoly of the Food Corporation of India (FCI). Reacting to the surge in wheat prices, initially, the government on 28 June 2006 decided to reduce the customs duty from 50 per cent to 5 per cent for private agencies along with the standards of quality applicable only to the imports made by the public sector, and after that, in September 2006, the government allowed private traders to import wheat at zero duty.[6] Therefore, there appears to be a tendency in food policy to use trade policy instruments more frequently since 2000 compared to earlier decades.

5.2.2 Rice

Before liberalisation, a restrictive trade policy was followed in the case of rice. There was zero customs duty until 1999 and imports had been subject to QRs and canalisation. Imports were restored only when

---

[5] Milling industries in the south found landed cost of imported wheat lower than the transporting cost domestically from the north, say, Punjab.

[6] Information regarding chronology of wheat trade policy was collected from various media sources along with custom notification of the Directorate General of Foreign Trade (DGFT).

domestic production dropped significantly. However, since 1998–99, trade policy witnessed a major shift when quantitative restrictions on imports were lifted and replaced by tariffs to meet WTO commitments. This resulted in import of 35,000 tonnes of rice in 1999–2000 and 13,000 tonnes during 2000–01. With the decline in international prices[7] of rice during 1999–2000 and 2000–01, imports of low grade rice became attractive, mostly to some of the eastern states of the country. To keep a check on such undesirable imports, in 2002–03, India levied a 70 per cent duty on milled rice import and 80 per cent on paddy, brown rice and broken rice. This import tariff structure was maintained till September 2009, except for the period between 20 March 2008 and 31 March 2009 when the government allowed duty-free import in order to control inflation. In a subsequent move, as the twin impact of drought and floods deepened fears of a dip in output, on 26 October 2009, the government scrapped import duty on 'semi-milled or wholly milled rice, whether or not polished or glazed' till September 2010 to augment domestic supply (*The Hindu Business Line* 2009).

Export restrictions on rice, historically imposed through State trading, quotas, and minimum export prices, have been progressively liberalised. A different policy has been followed for common rice and basmati rice. While there was no restriction on export of basmati rice, export of common rice was restricted through canalisation, minimum export prices and export quotas till 1991 (according to trade policy 1988 to 1991). There were restrictions on stocking rice beyond a limit unless there was an export order in hand (Datta 1996). The devaluation of the Indian rupee in 1991 along with relaxation in export controls on common rice during 1992 changed the situation dramatically. As per the trade policy for 1992–97, though rice was kept in the negative list, its export was freely allowed subject to MEP and registration of contracts with the Agricultural and Processed Food Products Export Development Authority (APEDA). Export controls on all varieties of rice were abolished in October 1994, which further improved possibility of rice export (Bhasin 1996).

In order to liquidate excess stocks, a scheme for export of food grains from the central pool was adopted in the year 2000. As part of that, a decision was taken to offer food grain for export at a price 'equal to the economic cost minus two year carrying cost but not

---

[7] Please refer to the section under 'Trends in Rice Price' in Chapter 4.

lower than the central issue price for BPL'.[8] The scheme, which was extended to rice as well in the subsequent year led to a record growth in India's rice export. The quantities of rice exported and subsidy provided by the government during the years 2000–2004 are presented in Table 5.2. On a review, it was decided to stop fresh allocation from 11 August 2003. After meeting the pending commitments of exports, sale of food grains for commercial exports have been totally stopped w.e.f. 1 October 2004. In October 2007, the government put a ban on non-basmati rice exports to manage rising inflation. However, the government allowed the shipping abroad of about two million tonnes only via diplomatic channels. The government's decision to ban non-basmati exports has brought India down to fourth position, whereas Pakistan has moved up by one place to third rank in the list of top rice exporters in the world in 2008–09 (*Commodity Online* 2009).

Table 5.2: Rice quantities exported and subsidy provided by the Food Corporation of India: 2000–01 to 2004–05

Financial Years	Quantity Lakh tonnes	Rate of Subsidy ₹/Qtl	Amount of Subsidy ₹ lakh
2000–01	0.47	466.04	2,202.40
2001–02	24.69	513.69	126,820.19
2002–03	77.69	570.20	442,989.43
2003–04	27.75	555.70	154,188.72
2004–05	0.65	492.29	3,199.92

Source: Annual report of the Food Corporation of India, various issues.

5.2.3 Oilseeds and Edible Oils

From the 1970s until 1994, India protected its oilseed sector with quantitative restrictions on both imports and exports and annual import and export quantities were determined by an inter-ministerial committee based on domestic demand and supply conditions. Imports were

---

[8] The Cabinet has allowed the Public Distribution Department to enter into counter trade, or extend commodity assistance in the form of food grains to the poor or needy countries on terms decided on a case-by-case basis. The humanitarian assistance in the form of food grains has been extended to Cambodia, Afghanistan, Zambia, Tajikistan, Myanmar, Tanzania, Lesotho, Chad, Iraq, etc., on the recommendations of the Ministry of External Affairs (*Annual Report: Department of Food and Public Distribution, 2005–06*).

particularly restricted during 1989–94, a period corresponding with the Technology Mission on Oilseeds. In a situation of excess domestic demand for edible oils, non-tariff barriers played a crucial role in setting the domestic price level in the oilseed sector. Imports of oilseeds and its products were canalised through the State Trading Corporation (STC) and the Hindustan Vegetable Oils Corporation (HVOC), and were then channelled to state governments for sale through the public distribution system (PDS) at administered prices.

Since 1994, when India began conforming to WTO rules and replacing quantitative trade restrictions with tariffs, oil imports have been placed under Open General License (OGL) allowing imports by private traders subject to applied tariffs. In March 1994, import of palmolein oil was permitted under OGL with a duty rate of 65 per cent for private traders and at a concessional duty of 20 per cent for the state agencies National Dairy Development Board (NDDB) and State Trading Corporation (STC). This was followed by a measure to enlarge the basket of oil under OGL imports on 1 March 1995 when all vegetable oils except coconut, (refined, bleached and deodorised) RBD palm oil and palm stearin were placed under OGL with an import tariff of 30 per cent;[9] STC and NDDB continued to benefit from the 20 per cent concessional tariff rate. But oilseeds import remained under the government's domain. During 1995–98, India started moving towards a liberal and relatively simple tariff structure with a common applied *ad valorem* (percentage) tariff for all oils progressively lowered to a uniform rate of 16.5 per cent by the middle of 1998.[10] In 1998, the government allowed imports of sunflower seed and soybean in cracked and split form at an import duty of 40 per cent. It was realised that cheap imports made production of oilseeds less competitive.

A high import duty and a few restrictions were placed in order to prevent excessive imports. Futures trading in oilseeds got re-introduced from 1999. However, since 1998, the government began making frequent tariff adjustments to protect domestic oilseed producers and processors from imports and to smooth the effect of fluctuating world prices on domestic consumers (Figures 5.1 and 5.2). Though applied tariff rates fell in 1999 after an initial hike in June 1998, the

---

[9] Coconut oil, RBD palm oil and palm stearin remain canalised.

[10] In 1997, a tariff surcharge and a special additional duty were added to the basic duty, but these were applied uniformly across all products and did not affect relative tariffs.

Figure 5.1: India's import tariff on crude oil: 1991–2005

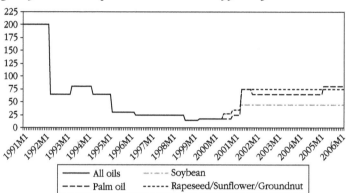

Source: Ministry of Food, Consumer Affairs and Public Distribution, Government of India.

Figure 5.2: India's import tariff on refined oil: 1991–2005

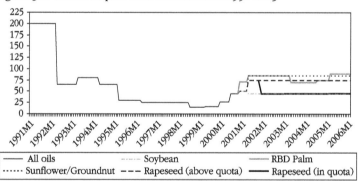

Source: Ministry of Food, Consumer Affairs and Public Distribution, Government of India.

trend after April 2000 was to resort to incremental increases of applied rates for all oils, with adjustments being made to the relative rates on different types of oil.

Table 5.3 gives the detailed chronology of trade policy changes in the Indian edible oil sector since 1994. As can be seen, in December 1999, the government introduced higher tariffs for refined versus crude oils in order to shift imports from refined soft oils to crude oils and improve capacity utilisation in the refining sector. Again in November 2000, tariffs on all oil imports were raised. The change in March 2001 was aimed at reducing the differentials between crude

Table 5.3: Summary of import policy for edible oil: 1994–2007

Date	Policy
April 1994	Import of RBD palmolein placed on OGL with 65% import duty
March 1995	Import of all edible oils (except coconut oil, palm kernel oil, RBD palm oil, RBD palm stearin) placed on OGL with 30% import duty
1996–97 (in regular Budget)	Further reduction in import duty to 20% + 2% (special duty of customs) bringing total import duty to 22%
July 1998	Another special duty of custom @ 3% was later imposed bringing the total import duty to 25%
	Import duty further reduced to 15%
1999–2000 (Budget)	Import duty raised to 15% (basic) + 10% (surcharge) = 16.5%
December 1999	Import duty on refined oils raised to 25% (basic) + 10% (surcharge) = 27.5%. In addition, 4% SAD levied on refined oils
June 2000	Import duty on crude oils raised to 25% (basic) + 10% (surcharge) = 27.5%
	Import duty on refined oils raised to 35% (basic) + 10% (surcharge) + 4% (SAD) = 44.04%
	Import duty on crude palm oil (CPO) for manufacture of vanaspati retained at 15% (basic) + 10% (surcharge) = 16.5%
November 2000	Import duty on CPO for manufacture of vanaspati raised to 25% and on crude vegetable oils raised to 35%
	Import duty on CPO for other than vanaspati manufacture raised to 55%
	Import duty on refined vegetable oils raised to 45% (basic) + 4% (SAD) = 50.8%
	Import duty on refined palm oil and RBD palmolein raised to 65% (basic) + 4% (SAD) = 71.6%
March 2001 (As amended on 26.4.2001)	Import duty on crude oils for manufacture of vanaspati/refined oils by the importers registered with Directorate of VVO&F raised to 75% (for others import duty levied at 85%) except soybean oil, rapeseed oil and CPO at 45%, 75% and 75%, respectively
	The duty on refined oils including RBD palmolein raised to 85% (basic) except in the cases of soybean oil and mustard oil where the duty is placed at 45% (basic) and 75% (basic), respectively, due to WTO binding. In addition, 4% SAD levied on refined oils
October 2001	Import duty on CPO and its fractions, of edible grade, in loose or bulk form reduced from 75% to 65%

Date	Measure
November 2001	Import duty on crude sunflower oil or safflower oil reduced to 50% up to an aggregate of 1,50,000 MTs (Tariff Rate Quota) of total imports of such goods in a financial year subject to certain condition
	Import duty on refined rapeseed, colza or mustard oil reduced to 45% up to an aggregate of 1,50,000 MTs (Tariff Rate Quota) of total imports of such goods in a financial year subject to certain condition
March 2002	Status quo on import duty structure of vegetable oils/edible oils maintained
	Import of vanaspati from Nepal be levied SAD @ 4%
August 2002	SAD is not applicable on vanaspati imported from Nepal under TRQ
March 2003	Status quo on import duty structure of vegetable oils/edible oils maintained
April 2003	Import duty on refined palm oil and RBD palmolein reduced from 85% to 70% and SAD not applicable on edible oils
July 2004	Import duty on refined palm oil and RBD palmolein raised from 70% to 75%
February 2005	Import duty on crude palm oil/crude palmolein raised from 65% to 80%
	Import duty on refined palm oil/RBD palmolein raised from 75% to 90%
2006–2007 (Budget)	With effect from 1 March 2006, edible oils attract a special additional duty of customs @ 4%
	Import duty on vanaspati and similar products raised from 30% to 80%
August 2006	With effect from 8 August 2006, special additional duty of customs not applicable on vanaspati imported from Nepal w.e.f. 11 August 2006
	Import duty on crude palm oil/crude palmolein reduced from 80% to 70%
	Import duty on refined palm oil/RBD palmolein reduced from 90% to 80%
January 2007	From 24 January 2007, import duty on crude palm oil /crude palmolein reduced from 70% to 60%
	Import duty on refined palm oil/RBD palmolein reduced from 80 % to 67.5%
	Import duty on crude sunflower oil reduced from 75% to 65%
	Import duty on refined sunflower oil reduced from 85% to 75%

Source: Ministry of Food, Consumer Affairs and Public Distribution, Government of India.

and refined oil tariffs, and providing limited concessions to vanaspati manufacturers. Because tariffs on soybean oil were bound at 45 per cent, this round of tariff hikes led to large duty differentials between soybean oil and other major imported oils. The tariff adjustments, along with prevailing international prices, led to significant incentives to import soybean oil over other oils.

In August 2001, the government modified the oil tariff regime by setting minimum tariff values (reference prices) to compute import duties. The government established a tariff rate value (TRV) system for palm oil in August 2001 and for soybean oil in September 2002, to prevent under-invoicing, i.e., reporting low import prices to evade tariffs by importers, and establish a government reference price for tariff calculation. Although the tariff values were amended several times to reflect changing market conditions, the system created new potential distortions when actual market prices diverged from the tariff values used by the government (Dohlman, Persaud and Landes 2003).

Until 1995, exports of all edible oilseeds and oils were banned except for hand-picked select (HPS) groundnut, which was placed under OGL. Oil meals were exported without any condition of licence.[11] But exporters were required to take/register export contracts. This registration rule was abolished in 1995. Also in that year, export controls/quantitative ceilings on sunflower seed and rapeseed/mustard seed were removed. However, exports of other oilseeds continued to be controlled and permitted against licence and a registration-cum-allocation certificate issued by APEDA. Later on, export of oilseeds for consumption purposes was made free except for nigerseed, which is canalised through state agencies. Rapeseed/mustard seed exports are also free but subject to quarantine restrictions. From April 2001, export restrictions have been removed on many edible oils such as groundnut oil. But they are permitted only against a licence.

5.2.4 Sugar

Sugar is included under the Essential Commodities Act (ECA) of 1965 and hence, all aspects of the industry including marketing and

---

[11] In fact, exports of oil meals, the production of which exceeded domestic demand, were promoted by a variety of export incentive schemes established by the GoI throughout the 1980s and early 1990s in an effort to generate foreign exchange.

distribution are highly regulated. Until July 2000, ECA was applied to regulate the stocks and turnover of sugar traders, but these controls were lifted in July 2000 and August 2001. However, in June 2003, ECA was invoked as a *de facto* import restriction by obliging importers to obtain permission to resell imported sugar on the grounds that they compete with Indian mills and, therefore, should be subject to the same 'release order' restrictions.

Until the 1980s, sugar imports were canalised and the government held monopoly in sugar import; but subsequently, private firms were allowed subject to import licensing. In March 1994, when world sugar prices were high,[12] import licensing was dropped and tariffs were cut to zero. This policy remained in place for the next four years. Again in 1998 when world sugar prices started declining, the government reversed these policies, and between April 1998 and February 2000 tariffs were increased in steps from zero to 40 per cent. In January 1999, the government again imposed the Essential Commodities Act on sugar imports along with making it mandatory to register all sugar import contracts with APEDA in September 1998, which monitors them to evaluate their impact on the domestic industry. Along with import duties, sugar imports are also subject to countervailing duty (CVD), as is the case with domestically produced sugar (Table 5.4).

Before 1991, sugar exports were canalised, i.e., they were a legal monopoly of the government trading company, STC. During the period of state export monopoly, whenever the government found excess supply in the market, sugar was exported if necessary at a loss in order to maintain a presence in quota markets and the sugar export quotas and losses were allocated between the sugar mills through the Sugar Export Promotion Act of 1958.[13] The 1991–92 trade policy reform de-canalised sugar export by allowing sugar to be exported by the Indian Sugar and General Industry Export Import Corporation (ISGIEIC), now known as Indian Sugar Exim Corporation Ltd. (ISEC), a private association of Indian sugar mills. But, as previously, the quantities exported were controlled by the Ministry of Food and Civil Supplies. Accordingly, export quotas were allocated to sugar mills. In January 1997, individual sugar mills and private traders were allowed

---

[12] Please refer to the section under 'Trends in Sugar Price' in Chapter 4.

[13] The Sugar Export Promotion Act, 1958 gave power to the STC to administer the losses which were shared by the sugar mills in proportion to their production.

Table 5.4: Indian sugar tariffs and QR status: 1991–2008

	Tariffs (Raw Sugar) %	Tariffs (Refined) %	Domestic Taxes ₹/Qtl	QR Status
1991	40	60	64	Restricted
1992	40	60	85	Restricted
1993	40	60	85	Restricted
1994	0	0	85	Restricted
1995	0	0	85	Free
1996	0	0	85	Free
1997	0	0	85	Free
1998	0	0	85	Free
Apr 1998–Jan 1999	5	5	85	Free
Jan 1999–Apr 1999	20	20	85	ECA
Apr 1999–Dec 1999	35	35	85	ECA
Dec 1999–Feb 2000	40	40	85	ECA
Feb 2000–March 2000	60	40	85	ECA
2001	40	40	85	ECA
2002	60	60	85	ECA
2003	60	60	85	ECA
2004	60	60	85	ECA
2005	60	60	85	ECA
2006	60	60	85	ECA
2007	60	60	85	ECA
2008	60	60	85	ECA

Source: Adapted from Pursell (2007).

to export sugar, but the overall level of export was still controlled by the government, and export quotas were allocated by the APEDA. In 1999 and 2000, the export policy was reversed to actively encourage sugar export as a way to reduce excess accumulated stock and assist sugar mills facing severe financial difficulties. This was done in April 2001 by first removing the APEDA's control over export, and by introducing and gradually increasing export subsidies for sugar (Pursell 2007).

In summary, it is evident from the discussion that external trade in agricultural commodities has been liberalised and most of the alterations took place only since 1991 when India opened her markets to world trade. On the whole, the tariffication of farm commodities during the post-liberalisation period resulted in a significant decrease in the level of protection and, hence, a move towards a greater openness. However, despite a decline in the rate of import tariffs, some of the commodities continue to enjoy protection through canalisation and licensing as explained in the preceding sections. The main factors behind these non-tariff barriers were to protect domestic agriculture from world price volatility and import surges and ensure food self-sufficiency.

5.3 AGRICULTURAL TRADE FLOW AND COMMODITY COMPOSITION

India initiated liberalisation of its economy and trade with economic reforms in June 1991. As a part of these reforms, India shifted to a market-determined exchange rate and relaxed restrictions on agricultural exports. This created a favourable environment for agricultural exports. Since 1993–94, agricultural exports started increasing in leaps and bounds. Export earnings doubled in three years between 1992–93 and 1995–96. Imports also increased at almost the same pace and net surplus generated by agriculture trade increased from ₹6,000 crore during 1992–93 to ₹14,500 crore during 1995–96.

The increase in agricultural exports that resulted from domestic liberalisation during 1992–93 to 1994–95 was strengthened during the initial years of the WTO regime and exports touched ₹24,000 crore in 1996–97. However, after 1996–97, the growth in agricultural exports slowed down (Table 5.5) and the value increased only marginally to ₹25,000 crore by the year 1999–2000. This happened despite further liberalisation in agricultural exports announced in the Export–Import policy for 1997–2002. Once again, agricultural exports started rising from the year 2000–01 and reached ₹50,000 crore in 2005–06 which was more than 70 per cent higher than exports during 2000–01. The decline in exports growth during the late 1990s was caused by the sharp fall in global prices (see Chapter 4 for details) and is in keeping with the global trend. However, this dip in prices did not cause a decline in the growth of India's imports during the late 1990s.

The growth in imports and exports after 1990–91 was much higher than the growth in GDP. As a result, the share of imports and exports in GDP increased. Imports which accounted for less than one per cent of India's agricultural GDP during the early 1990s, increased to the level of more than three per cent by 2005–06. Similarly, the share of exports in GDP from agriculture increased from around four per cent in early 1990s to more than 7.5 per cent in 2005–06.

Table 5.5: Agricultural trade and its share in GDP agriculture and total trade

Year	Agricultural Trade ₹ crore		Share in GDP Agriculture %		Share in Total Trade %	
	Import	Export	Import	Export	Import	Export
1990–91	1,205.86	6,012.76	0.75	3.76	2.79	18.49
1991–92	1,478.27	7,838.04	0.80	4.24	3.09	17.80
1992–93	2,876.25	9,040.30	1.38	4.34	4.54	16.84
1993–94	2,327.33	12,586.55	0.96	5.20	3.18	18.05
1994–95	5,937.21	13,222.76	2.13	4.74	6.60	15.99
1995–96	5,890.10	20,397.74	1.94	6.73	4.80	19.18
1996–97	6,612.60	24,161.29	1.82	6.66	4.76	20.33
1997–98	8,784.19	24,832.45	2.27	6.42	5.70	19.09
1998–99	14,566.48	25,510.64	3.29	5.77	8.17	18.25
1999–00	16,066.73	25,313.66	3.48	5.48	7.45	15.91
2000–01	12,086.23	28,657.37	2.58	6.12	5.29	14.23
2001–02	16,256.61	29,728.61	3.11	5.70	6.63	14.22
2002–03	17,608.83	34,653.94	3.94	7.76	5.92	13.58
2003–04	21,972.68	36,415.48	4.13	6.84	6.12	12.70
2004–05	22,811.84	41,602.65	4.13	7.53	4.55	11.08
2005–06	21,499.22	49,216.96	3.44	7.87	3.26	10.78

Source: Computed based on data drawn from *Agricultural Statistics at a Glance,* Ministry of Agriculture, various issues.

These changes indicate that import-affected agriculture (agricultural imports as share of agricultural GDP) has been making a greater impact on domestic agriculture than before. The agricultural trade intensity ratio (agri – trade/agri – GDP ×100) shows that there has been a significant increase in the trade orientation of Indian agriculture after 1990–91, with the ratio increasing from around five per cent in the early 1990s to more than 11 per cent by 2005–06. Despite this increase in agricultural trade, import of agricultural products is relatively small compared to the total import of the country. In most of the recent years, agricultural imports comprised around six per cent of India's total imports. While in the earlier periods, agricultural exports were more than four times that of agricultural imports, more recently, agricultural exports were higher by one-and-a-half times only. Therefore, after 1990–91, there was a decline in the share of agricultural export and an increase in the share of agricultural imports in total exports and imports of the country.

The trends in import and export show that the integration of Indian agriculture with the global economy has increased considerably after 1990–91, though the ratio of trade to GDP is still very low compared to most of the developing Southeast Asian countries. Liberalisation was initially highly favourable for growth of exports and imports, but post-WTO, the situation has turned out to be highly adverse for India's agriculture exports. The following section examines the trade flow of different commodities with a view to identify the items and products where India has lost ground to others, where it has gained and where it has maintained ground.

During the early 1990s, marine products topped the list of agricultural exports closely followed by export of oil meal. Other important items of export were tea, cashew nut, basmati rice, coffee, spices, and tobacco. Liberalisation of non-basmati rice in mid-1990s provided impetus to its export. As a result, rice export figured at the top of the list of exports during 1995–96 and during 1998–99. Out of two grades of rice, basmati rice showed a steady upward trend in its export, but non-basmati rice showed violent year-to-year fluctuations (Table 5.1).

From Table 5.6 we can identify the commodities which explain the fall in agricultural export from 1996–97. The worst affected exports are of oil meal. Exports of oil meal have declined from ₹3,495 crore in 1996–97 to the level of ₹1,638 crorein 1999–2000. Similarly, the export value of cotton has declined from ₹1,575 crore in 1996–97 to a meager ₹77 crore in 1999–2000.

Almost similar has been the case with exports of sugar. Decline in export has also been witnessed in the case of tobacco and pulses till 2001–02. The export of traditional items like tea, cashew, spices, and coffee maintained their status till the early years of the post-WTO period, but started falling since 1998–99 to 1999–2000. Once these commodities picked up, the aggregate agricultural exports also picked up.

The analysis shows that export of horticultural products, dairy and meat products have not been adversely affected by post-WTO trade developments and hold growing prospects for exports.

Changes in India's imports of selected agricultural commodities can be seen from the data presented in Table 5.7. The table shows

Table 5.6: India's export of select agricultural commodities (value in ₹ crore): 1991–2006

	1991	1992	1993	1994	1995	1996	1997	1998	1999	2000	2001	2002	2003	2004	2005	2006
Pulses			53	74	90	132	132	361	223	420	537	369	345	329	603	1,115
Rice (Basmati)	440	499	801	1,061	865	851	1,248	1,686	1,877	1,780	2,155	1,843	2,058	1,993	2,824	3,043
Rice (other than Basmati)		256	175	225	340	3,717	1,925	1,685	4,404	1,346	777	1,331	3,773	2,175	3,945	3,178
Wheat	29	127	10	0	42	367	698	0	1	Neg.	415	1,330	1,760	2,391	1,460	558
Tea	1,075	1,212	977	1,059	975	1,171	1,037	1,876	2,265	1,785	1,789	1,719	1,652	1,637	1,840	1,731
Coffee	253	332	376	546	1,053	1,503	1,427	1,696	1,728	1,435	1,185	1,095	994	1,086	1,069	1,589
Tobacco (manufactured & unmanufactured)	263	377	474	461	255	447	757	1,070	762	1,009	867	808	1,023	1,096	1,255	1,331
Poultry & dairy products					49	59	124	118	97	59	108	208	176	162	459	795
Floriculture products		15	15	19	31	60	63	87	106	117	118	127	181	250	223	301
Spices	233	372	393	569	612	794	1,202	1,410	1,633	1,767	1,618	1,497	1,655	1,544	1,883	2,116
Cashew nuts	447	676	749	1,048	1,247	1,237	1,288	1,407	1,632	2,461	2,053	1,794	2,062	1,705	2,489	2,593
Oil meals	625	921	1,545	2,324	1,798	2,349	3,495	3,435	1,942	1,638	2,045	2,263	1,487	3,250	3,178	4,875
Sugar & mollases	37	157	354	178	62	506	1,078	255	24	40	505	1,782	1,815	1,236	155	598
Fruits/vegetable seeds	217	349	312	414	23	41	42	53	65	80	63	62	98	54	66	93
Fresh fruits					189	230	244	277	266	307	386	417	447	784	862	1,121
Fresh vegetables					248	297	334	313	274	335	457	575	643	954	863	920
Processed fruits & vegetables	62	88	120	156	249	347	326	389	458	558	785	711	831	635	732	1,094
Meat & preparations	141	231	257	345	403	627	709	808	788	819	1,470	1,193	1,377	1,714	1,905	2,750
Marine products	960	1,443	1,743	2,552	3,537	3,381	4,008	4,487	4,369	5,125	6,367	5,898	6,928	6,106	6,469	7,036
Cotton (raw, including waste)	855	306	182	654	140	204	1,575	822	207	77	221	43	50	942	423	2,904
Total Agriculture Export	6,013	7,838	9,040	12,587	13,223	20,398	24,161	24,843	25,511	25,314	28,657	29,729	34,654	36,415	41,603	49,262

Source: Computed based on data drawn from *Agricultural Statistics at a Glance*, Ministry of Agriculture, various issues.

Note: Calendar year 1991 corresponds to the agricultural marketing year 1990–91, and so on.

  Neg. = Negligible

Table 5.7: India's import of select agricultural commodities (value in ₹ crore): 1991–2006

	1991	1992	1993	1994	1995	1996	1997	1998	1999	2000	2001	2002	2003	2004	2005	2006
Pulses	473	255	334	567	593	686	890	1,195	709	355	498	3,160	2,737	2,285	1,778	2,476
Wheat	24	0	710	126	0	10	404	989	1165	774	3	1	–	0	–	–
Rice	39	11	73	55	9	0	0	0	5	30	18	0	1	0	–	0
Cereal preparation	87	162	182	110	83	69	83	94	39	43	51	82	117	87	112	129
Milk & cream	3	8	45	17	6	37	3	5	12	107	7	8	10	90	13	14
Cashew nuts	132	267	376	483	691	760	688	767	969	1,198	961	431	1,236	1,372	1,805	2,089
Fruits & nuts	108	100	189	218	314	331	456	575	670	591	798	757	642	802	1,101	1,390
Sugar	9	1	0	0	2,283	216	3	470	1,111	1,111	31	33	33	63	976	652
Oil seeds	6	10	11	7	5	36	5	2	9	15	7	1	11	14	28	47
Vegetable oils fixed (edible)	322	248	167	167	624	2,262	2,929	2,765	7,589	8,046	5,977	6,465	8,780	11,683	11,077	8,961
Cotton (raw, including waste)	#	#	216	18	507	521	32	81	381	1,254	1,185	2,054	1,238	1,570	1,136	704
Total agriculture imports	1,206	1,478	2,876	2,327	5,937	5,890	6,613	8,784	14,566	16,067	12,086	16,257	17,609	21,973	22,812	21,499

Source. Computed based on data drawn from *Agricultural Statistics at a Glance*, Ministry of Agriculture, various issues.

Note.   Calendar year 1991 corresponds to the agricultural marketing year 1990–91, and so on.

   # = Negligible

that India is no more dependent on rice imports. Despite very high growth in production and claim of self-sufficiency in foodgains, India occasionally imports large quantity of wheat (please refer to section 5.4 for a detailed discussion). Like wheat, India sometimes went for large import of sugar. Import of pulses increased till 1997–98 and started fluctuating thereafter. The other items whose imports were significant are fruits and nuts, cashew nut and cotton. In the case of cashew nut, import is mainly for re-export of processed cashew nuts because India has a labour cost advantage in this commodity. The composition of imports further reveals that most of the increase in agricultural imports was on account of increases in imports of edible oil. Vegetable oils accounted for more than 45 per cent of total agricultural imports in the post-WTO period. The changes in composition of imports that have occurred in the last 15 years is the continuation of the trends originating in the mid-1970s, i.e., decline in the imports of cereals, especially wheat, and increase in the imports of other food items like oil and pulses. The share of edible oil imports has increased massively, while the share of pulses has declined. The imports of these commodities are a matter of concern and have been raised earlier in debates (Chand, Jha and Mittal 2004; Sathe and Agarwal 2004).

To sum up, the discussion on India's agricultural trade flow and commodity composition highlights the fact that trade in agricultural commodities has a greater impact on domestic agriculture since 1991. The initial years of liberalisation were highly favourable for growth of exports and imports, but during the post-WTO years, the situation turned out to be highly adverse for India's agricultural exports.

The situation started improving since 2001 with recovery in world prices; as a result, agricultural exports started growing. The worst affected export items were oil meal, cotton and sugar, whereas export of marine products and groups of livestock and horticultural products maintained the tempo of growth, continuing from early 1990s. The trend in agricultural imports, on the other hand, shows that most of the increase in agriculture imports took place due to increases in import of edible oil, followed by pulses. The following section analyses the trade flow for selected commodities in the light of domestic demand and supply situation, trade policy environment and international prices.

5.4 TRADE FLOWS FOR SELECTED COMMODITIES

5.4.1 Wheat

India was often an importer of wheat prior to the 1990s. During the 1990s, however, India has been a marginal exporter on occasion as well as an importer (Figure 5.3). However, since India is a large market, these marginal quantities can often be significant for the world market. India's wheat trade shows violent year-to-year fluctuation and presents a very interesting pattern. One or two years of good harvest resulted in the piling up of wheat stock, which encouraged the country to opt for large exports. This was immediately followed by huge imports. For instance, India exported 2.75 lakh tonnes of wheat during 1987–88, and in the following year imported as much as 18 lakh tonnes. Again India exported 6.60 lakh tonnes of wheat during 1991–92, which was followed by import of 13.64 lakh tonnes in 1992–93. Wheat export, which was restricted until 1995, was placed in the open category afterwards. Consequently, exports started picking up and for two consecutive years India exported 6.32 lakh tonnes of wheat during 1995–96 and 11.46 lakh tonnes of wheat during 1996–97, at a time when world prices were at a peak. As exports started to pick up there was upward pressure on domestic wheat prices; due to shortfall in supply and depletion of wheat stock with public agencies,[14] the government hastily banned exports of wheat in 1996–97. Simultaneously, it opened up imports of wheat at zero import duty. This was mainly in response to the demand by roller flourmills in the southern part of the country (Hoda and Gulati 2008). Initially, very low levels of import followed, but from 1997–98 the world prices of wheat started coming down (see Chapter 4 for details), encouraging the country to go in for large imports — India imported 15, 18 and 14 lakh tonnes of wheat during 1997–98, 1998–99 and 1999–2000, respectively. A very low level of world prices in 1999–2000 forced the country to impose a varying rate of tariff to regulate wheat importation. The major imports to India were from countries like Australia, France, Belgium, Ukraine, etc.

There was huge build-up of wheat stock with public agencies after 1997–98, and stocks reached a peak of 26 million tonnes in 2002–03. This level of stock was equal to 36 per cent of total wheat produced

---

[14] Only about 3.24 million tonnes of wheat was added to the stock on 1 April 1997.

Figure 5.3: India's export and import volume of wheat ('000 tonnes): 1980–81 to 2007–08

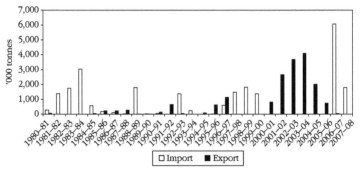

Source: Directorate General of Commercial Intelligence and Statistics (DGCI&S), Kolkata, Ministry of Commerce, Government of India.

in the country in 2002–03 (Appendix, Table A-5.1). The government faced serious difficulty in disposing of these large stocks as domestic demand fell short of supply at ruling prices, which were largely governed by government actions related to the MSP, open market sales and PDS prices (Chand 2007).[15] Consequently, India used the export option to liquidate these stocks at a highly subsidised price[16] through its agencies such as the STC, Mineral and Metals Trading Corporation (MMTC) and Project Equipment Corporation (PEC). India exported 2.65 million tonnes during 2001–02 and 3.67 million tonnes

---

[15] Indian food grain sector was faced with conflicting pressures: procurement prices had been raised substantially between 1996–99; world prices, which were at their peak in 1996, had dropped to the lowest levels by 1999–2000; and domestic production had improved. In 1997, the GoI also reoriented the program of public distribution system (PDS) from being untargeted to one targeted specifically for the poor. This targeting exercise curtailed the PDS demand for foodgrains substantially. As result of this constellation of forces, food grain stocks (including both rice and wheat) with the government accumulated to an unprecedented level, forcing the government to raise import duty to stem the inflow.

[16] Because of the decline in international prices and rise in domestic prices, it became difficult to dispose of the large stock of wheat at a price matching the cost of these food grains to the government. Thus, the government was forced to release wheat for export at a price much lower than the acquisition cost.

during 2002–03. Despite a fall in production to the tune of 7 million tonnes in 2003–04 relative to the previous year, India exported more than 4 million tonnes of wheat during 2003–04. Large scale export continued during 2004–05 and India continued to export wheat till 2005–06. During the period between 2001–02 and 2005–06, India's total wheat export was 13.17 million tonnes constituting around two and a half per cent of the world's total wheat export during the period. India's contribution to the world's total wheat export was highest (around four per cent) during 2003–04 (Figure 5.4). Because of the decline in public procurement due to good open market prices and lower production, there was a decline in wheat stocks with the government agencies, which forced the government to ban wheat export in April 2007.

Figure 5.4: India's wheat export volume and percentage share in the world's total export of wheat: 1980–81 to 2007–08

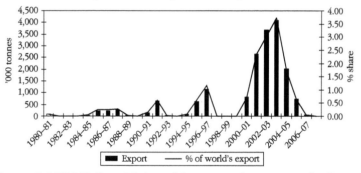

Source: DGCI&S, Kolkata, Ministry of Commerce, Government of India; and FAO STAT.

5.4.2 Rice

India had never been among the major rice exporting countries until it attained self-sufficiency in rice production in the early 1980s. The growing demand for basmati rice in the international market enabled India to increase its export gradually to a level of over four lakh tonnes by 1989–90, constituting around 2.8 per cent of the world's total rice export. In the early 1990s, total rice export trade increased somewhat to reach more than 7 lakh tonnes in 1993–94. Until 1994, India had been exporting comparatively small quantities of fine (basmati) rice, as export only of this variety was permitted, subject to a minimum export price stipulation.

Successive good harvests and increase in rice procurement by public agencies coupled with reduction in offtake due to increase in sales prices resulted in rise in rice stock from the level of 5.07 million tonnes on 1 October 1992 to 10.87 million tonnes on 1 October 1994 (Appendix, Table 5.3). As discussed earlier in the chapter, in order to dispose rice stocks, export of basmati rice was further liberalised in January 1994 by the elimination of minimum export price, and a little later the ban on exports of common rice was removed. These steps led to a dramatic increase in export volumes. The following year, 1995–96, India's exports of rice went up from less than 1 million to about 5 million MT, making India the second largest exporter of rice in that year. India continued to be a major exporter in the next four years, averaging 3.69 million tonnes per year from 1995–96 to 1998–99 (Figure 5.5).

Figure 5.5: India's rice export volume and its share in the world's total rice export: 1980–81 to 2006–07

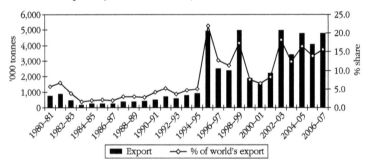

Source: Chart prepared by author using data from Appendix, Table A-5.2.

Rice exports experienced a big setback during 1999–2000 and 2000–01 because of two reasons. One, international prices of rice dropped sharply after 1998–99 (see Chapter 4 for details). Two, domestic prices had been moving up mainly under the pressure of increasing support prices. This reduced the competitiveness and profitability of rice exporters. The net result was the piling up of rice stocks with the government agencies. India's exports picked up again after November 2000 when it began to subsidise internal and international freight and other costs of marketing exports (Table 5.2) in an attempt to neutralise the high subsidisation by OECD countries like the US, and the FCI started selling rice to traders for export at much lower prices compared to open market prices since 2001–02. This attracted a positive response as private traders found it more profitable and resulted in an increase in India's rice exports. Between 2002–03 and 2006–07, India exported on an average around 4.3 million tonnes of rice every year.

The rice trade during the period also witnessed tremendous changes in its composition, particularly after the year 1994–95. Until 1989–90, 90–95 per cent of the rice exported from India was of the basmati variety. But its share and volume started dwindling after that due to a spurt in the export of non-basmati rice (Figure 5.6). The share of basmati exports in total rice exports from India decreased from 94 per cent in 1989–90 to 46 per cent in 1990–91and further to 39 per cent and 8 per cent in 1991–92 and 1995–96, respectively. After 1995–96, exports of non-basmati rice have dominated India's rice trade, constituting around 75 per cent of the total quantity of rice exports during TE 2006–07 (Appendix, Table A-5.2). This sharp decline in basmati rice could be attributed to two factors. First, availability of sufficient stocks with the major buying countries and also to large shipments of superior variety long grain non-basmati rice, and second, stiff competition from cheaper basmati rice produced in Pakistan. In terms of the major markets for India, Saudi Arabia accounted for 39 per cent of the total export value in 2001–02, followed by Nigeria at 8.7 per cent, South Africa at 7.5 per cent, and Kuwait at 6.8 per cent. In terms of quantity as well, Saudi Arabia was the largest importing country with 26.4 per cent in 2001–02, followed by South Africa at 14.4 per cent, Nigeria at 13.7 per cent, and then Indonesia at 6.4 per cent.

India was a marginal importer of rice on occasion, particularly when world prices were on their downward trend. A big drop in world rice prices during the 1980s resulted in import of rice in small quantities in four years, 1983–84, 1984–85, 1988–89, and 1989–90. Again during the 1990s, with a decline in international prices of rice during 1999–2000 and 2000–01, India imported 35,000 tonnes and 13,000 tonnes of rice respectively in those two years (Figure 5.7).

5.4.3 Trade in Oilseed and Products

Trade policy has played an important role in determining the trade volume in India's oilseed economy. India's recent large imports of edible oils have been the result of reduced border protection beginning in 1994. The government made frequent adjustments in its trade

Figure 5.6: India's total rice export and share of Basmati rice in total rice export: 1980–81 to 2006–07

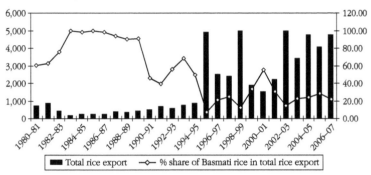

Source: Chart prepared by author using data from Appendix, Table A-5.2.

Figure 5.7: India's rice import volume and its share in the world's total rice import: 1980–81 to 2006–07

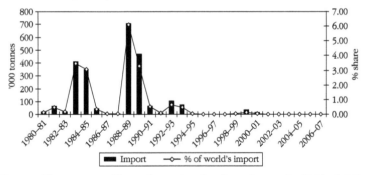

Source: Chart prepared by author using data from Appendix, Table A-5.2.

policy, depending on the domestic demand and supply situation, to protect the interest of oilseed producers and processors, and also to smooth the effect of fluctuating world prices on domestic consumers. The following section discusses the trade pattern in oilseeds and their products.

5.4.3.1 Trade in edible oils

A careful look at the production and consumption levels of vegetable oils shows that beginning with a level of 4.7 kg/capita/annum in 1977–78, consumption of vegetable oils started rising and reached the level of 7 kg/capita/annum by 1987–88. The slow growth in vegetable oil production compared to growing demand for oils has created a gap between domestic supply and demand and necessitated massive imports. As a result, India imported an average of 1.4 million tonnes of vegetable oil every year, constituting around 10 per cent of the world's total vegetable oil import and about 36 per cent of the total supply by 1987–88 (Appendix, Table A-5.4). The gap between domestic consumption and production has narrowed considerably in the early 1990s, and self-sufficiency has been virtually achieved. The achievement in self-sufficiency in edible oils can be attributed to two main factors: a large increase in production, and a virtual stop in the growth of per-capita consumption. The per capita consumption varied slightly between 6.4 kg/annum to 7.3 kg/annum during the period between 1988–89 and 1994–95. However, domestic production of edible oil started falling from 1997–98 due to a steep decline in domestic prices with the liberalisation of edible oil imports. At the same time, consumption started rising due to a consistent increase in per capita income along with low prices of vegetable oils (Figure 5.8). This demand–supply gap has necessitated import of edible oil. Imports of vegetable oils increased rapidly and reached 5 million tonnes, or about 44 per cent of domestic supply during 2003–05. In 2006–07, India was the third largest importer of vegetable oil (5.4 million tonnes) after the European Union (10 million tonnes) and China (8.6 million tonnes), according to *Oil World*. Import growth was most rapid during 1996–2000, when tariffs were

Figure 5.8: Production, consumption and imports of edible oil in India

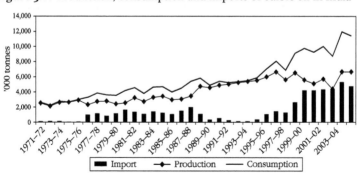

Source: Chart prepared by author using data from Appendix, Table A-5.4.

relatively low (varied between 25 to 27.5 per cent), and were slowed down by higher tariffs, ranging from 45 per cent to 80 per cent for different oils, during 2001–05 (as discussed earlier).

The sensitivity of Indian importers to price was also reflected in the composition of imported oils. Palm oil, generally the lowest priced oil, has dominated Indian imports since the mid-1990s, accounting for about 65 per cent of oil imports during 2000–06. Soybean oil, generally the second cheapest oil in the market, accounted for about 28 per cent of imports during 2000–06. Higher priced oils like sunflower oil and oils traditional to the Indian diet, such as peanut and rapeseed oil, were imported in only small amounts (Figure 5.9).

Figure 5.9: Composition of India's vegetable oil imports: 1979–2006

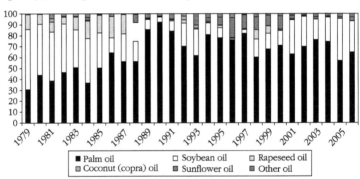

Source: FAO STAT.

The Indian import of palm and soybean oil accounted for 15 per cent and 13 per cent of the world's total import of palm and soybean oil. With the shift of US exports from concessional shipments to commercial sales after the mid-1990s, the US share in the Indian soybean oil market declined sharply. The Indian soybean oil market is dominated by Argentina and Brazil, which offer consistently lower prices than US suppliers (Dohlman, Persaud and Landes 2003).

5.4.3.2 Trade in oilseed cake meal

Oilcake meal exports from India (Figure 5.10) have increased significantly from 1 million tonnes in 1987 to around 5 million tonnes in 1996, accounting for 10.6 per cent of the world's total oil meal export. The rapid diversification of oil meal exports away from

Figure 5.10: India's export of oilseed cake meal and its percentage share in the world's total export of oil meal: 1979–2006

Source: FAO STAT.

groundnut meals, and towards soybean and rapeseed/mustard seed, has played a critical role in this export performance (World Bank 1997). Most of the growth during the period has been driven by soybean and rapeseed oil cake exports and, to a smaller extent, by sunflower exports (Figure 5.11), commodities where there is less of a quality problem. India's oil meal export started declining from 1997 and reached 1.8 million tonnes in 2002. The decline was more in the case of rapeseed as compared to soybean during the period. Rapeseed oil meal export declined by 80 per cent between 1997 and 2002 as against a 52 per cent decline in the case of soybean between 1996 and 2002.

Figure 5.11: Composition of India's oilseed cake meal exports: 1979–2006

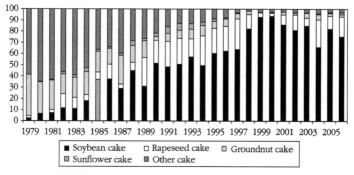

Source: FAO STAT.

India's export of oil meal has slowed due to expanding domestic feed use and slower growth in production. Rapid growth in demand from domestic poultry meat and egg producers along with a decline in production has increased domestic soybean meal prices relative to world prices, reducing their competitiveness in world markets. Oil meal export again started rising since 2003 and reached the highest ever level of 6 million tonnes in 2006, accounting for eight per cent of the world's total oil meal export. An increase in domestic production along with a decline in domestic meal prices relative to world prices has played a critical role in this export performance.

5.4.3.3 Trade in oilseeds

India is not a significant importer of oilseeds for processing. Though the government has allowed imports of oilseeds, there has been virtually no import of oilseeds largely because of the safety measures imposed by the government. India's share in the world's total import of oilseeds varied from 0.01 per cent to 0.05 per cent during 2000 to 2005 (FAO STAT). Oilseed imports are restricted by both a 30 per cent tariff and by non-tariff barriers. Imports of genetically modified oilseeds are not permitted unless approved by the government's Genetic Engineering Approvals Committee (GEAC). In addition, the Plant Quarantine Order of 2002 requires that shipments be certified free of certain pests or that seeds be 'devitalised'. At present, the only permissible means of 'de-vitalisation' is to mechanically split the seed, a process that adds not only considerable cost but also leads to unacceptable deterioration in quality during transit, if done at the point of origin.

In the case of oilseeds export, though India is not a major exporter in the world market, and contributed merely 0.60 per cent to the world's total oilseed export during 2000 to 2005, its share has increased since the early 1990s (Figure 5.12). The composition of oilseeds export basket reveals the fact that, growth in India's oilseeds export comes from groundnut and sesame seed which contribute more than 80 per cent of India's total oilseed export (Figure 5.13). In terms of the world's total export in groundnut and sesame seeds, India's share was 11 per cent and 23 per cent respectively during 2000–2005. India is also the world's second largest exporter of groundnut (in shell) and sesame seed followed by China.

Figure 5.12: India's export volume of oilseeds and its percentage share in the world's total export of oilseeds: 1979–2006

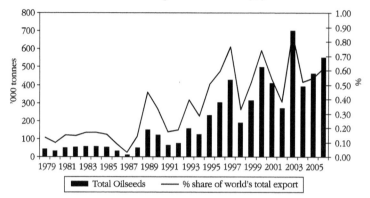

Source: FAO STAT.

Figure 5.13: Composition of India's oilseed exports: 1979–2006

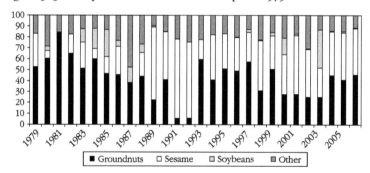

Source: FAO STAT.

5.4.4 Sugar

India's share in the world's sugar trade has always been very small and has been perceived as residual whether we consider imports or exports. When sugar production exceeds demand, stocks build up, and the government has typically removed controls preventing exports, and, if needed, has provided export subsidies to boost exports and help diminish excess sugar stocks. On the other hand, at some point during the downturns in the production cycle when consumption is running ahead of production, it has typically relaxed import controls or reduced tariffs in order to facilitate sugar imports and in this way take some of the pressure off domestic sugar prices. In the case of imports (Figure 5.14), except for a few years, there have been no imports of raw sugar till 1996. Since then, India has imported raw sugar every year in very small quantities for processing into white refined sugar. But there have been sporadic small imports of refined sugar, mostly in very small quantities, with the exception of a period of very low world prices during the mid-1980s when large quantities were imported. In 1985, India imported 1.6 million tonnes of refined sugar which was equivalent to 27 per cent of the domestic white sugar production and 19 per cent of the world's trade in refined sugar. Similarly in 1994, India again imported 1.7 million tonnes of refined sugar to meet domestic demand because of shortfall in sugar production (Appendix, Table A-5.5). As world prices were at a peak during this time, the government typically reduced the applied tariff rate to zero along with withdrawal of import licensing (as discussed earlier in this chapter).

More recently, in response to a large fall in sugar production during 2004 and 2005 (mainly because of a decline in sugarcane production due to bad weather), the government in September 2004 imported Brazilian raw sugar at zero — instead of the normal 60 per cent — import duty, under the 'advance licensing' scheme, which permits duty free imports of inputs used to produce exported products, and allocated it to mills for processing into white refined sugar (Pursell 2007).

However, starting in 1999, sugar production consistently exceeded consumption for five years in a row, leading with a lag to substantial

Figure 5.14: India's import volume of raw and refined sugar: 1980–2006

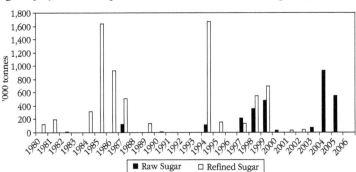

exports beginning in 2001, the cumulative amount of which reached 4.4 million tonnes by 2004 (Figure 5.15). As already discussed, exports during this episode were stimulated by export subsidies that were increased to keep exports profitable as world prices declined. But unlike a few other countries, which produce sugar for exports on a regular basis, Indian exports were mainly to liquidate a part of its surplus stocks. This is because India has a large and growing domestic market. As a result, its export's share in total production varied between six and nine per cent during 2001 to 2003.

Figure 5.15: India's export volume of raw and refined sugar and its share in the world's total sugar export: 1980–2006

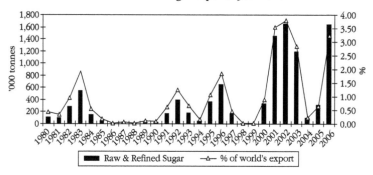

Source: FAO STAT.

In summary, the analysis of trade patterns, in light of the trade policy environment and other factors affecting trade, shows that trade flow in the case of the studied commodities were residual whether we consider imports or exports and reflected the difference between domestic production and domestic consumption. Trade policy instruments were used to manage the trade flow. During the post-WTO period when international prices faced severe downward pressure and stocks at home rose in the case of rice, wheat and sugar, the government typically removed controls preventing exports, and began to provide export subsidies to boost exports and liquidate excess stocks. Among imports, edible oils have shown very high growth in the post-WTO period. With the introduction of liberal policies for edible oil imports, low world prices resulted in a steep decline in domestic prices. As a result, domestic production of edible oil started falling. Therefore, in order to meet growing domestic demand, imports of vegetable oils increased rapidly, constituting about 44 per cent of domestic supply during 2003–05. Growth in edible oil imports, which was most rapid during 1996–2000, has been slowed down by imposing higher tariffs during 2001–05. Whereas in the case of sugar, when consumption exceeded domestic production at the time when world sugar prices were high (say, during 1994 to 1997), the government typically relaxed import controls and reduced tariffs in order to facilitate sugar imports. Again, when world sugar prices started declining (say, after 1998), the government increased tariffs in order to check sugar imports.

5.5 Conclusion

The analysis in the chapter dealt with the role played by trade policy during the post-reform period in terms of imparting stability to domestic prices and influencing the average level of prices. Its conclusions can be summed up as follows:

First, although during the post-reform period a trade policy regime that is more open was being put in place, the approach with respect to agriculture has remained gradual and cautious. While trade restrictions on agricultural products were left mostly untouched in the 1991 reforms, subsequent trade policy changes gradually lifted most of the restrictions on both exports and imports of agricultural products. With the removal of restrictions on imports and exports, trade policy instruments were adjusted from time to time, which helped in ensuring sufficient domestic supply of key products and kept the volatility in domestic prices at relatively low levels compared to earlier decades. An example is the exemption (zero duty) granted for imports of wheat in 2006 to replenish local grain stocks mainly for the public distribution system; the standard tariff rate is currently 50 per cent. Import licences were also issued to support this policy; for example, in 2006, imports of wheat, normally restricted to state trading, were also permitted by private importers. Similarly, in the case of exports, as the vast majority of agricultural exports are unrestricted, the government made notifications from time to time to restrict exports or lift export restrictions in order to maintain domestic supplies and stability in domestic prices. For example, export of sugar was prohibited in 2006 to maintain domestic supplies in order to keep the price at a 'reasonable level'. Whereas in the case of wheat, following a sharp fall in the government's annual food grain procurement because of good open market prices and lower production, India banned exports of wheat and wheat products in April 2007.

Second, trade in agricultural products had a greater impact on the domestic agricultural situation and contributed more than 11 per cent to agricultural GDP. Nonetheless, the post-WTO years turned out to be highly adverse for India's agricultural exports. There were considerable variations in export performance of various commodities. With the liberalisation of export of non-basmati rice, its export picked up during the post-WTO period with a lot of stock being released for export. The commodities which explain the fall in agricultural exports during the post-WTO period include oil meal, cotton, sugar, tobacco, and pulses. Poor export performance during the period was the upshot of a sharp fall in international prices. In case of India's traditional export items, though the initial years of the post-WTO period were quite favourable, their export growth slowed down afterward. The situation started improving since 2001 with recovery in world prices; as a result, agricultural exports started growing. Among imports, edible oils have shown very high growth in the post-WTO period followed by pulses. Thus, agricultural imports are concentrated in these two commodities, where domestic production has not kept pace with the demand.

Third, commodity-specific analysis shows that, during the post-WTO period, when international prices faced severe downward pressure and stocks at home rose in the case of rice, wheat and sugar, the government typically removed controls preventing exports and also started providing export subsidies to boost exports and liquidate excess stocks. Among imports, edible oils have shown very high growth in the post-WTO period. With the introduction of liberal policies for edible oil imports, imports of vegetable oils increased rapidly, constituting about 44 per cent of domestic supply during 2003–05. Growth in edible oil imports, which was most rapid during 1996–2000, has been slowed down by higher tariffs during 2001–05. Whereas, in the case of sugar, when consumption exceeded domestic production at the time when world sugar prices were high (say, during 1994 to 1997), the government relaxed import controls and reduced tariffs in order to facilitate sugar imports. Again, when world sugar prices started declining (say, after 1998), the government increased tariffs in order to check sugar imports and keep the domestic price at a reasonable level.

To sum up, it follows from our analysis that the post-reform period witnessed frequent use of trade policy instruments in order to impart stability to domestic prices compared to the earlier decade by managing trade flow. This not only helped in keeping volatility in domestic prices at a low level, but also ensured sufficient domestic supply. However, the sharp decline in international prices during the post-WTO period adversely affected India's trade competitiveness and resulted in poor export performance.

6

Trade Competitiveness of
Indian Agriculture

A Comparison of Domestic and World Prices

The analyses in previous chapters show that during the post-WTO period the international prices started declining and reached almost 25-year low levels around year 2000. Though there has been some recovery in the price cycle in the recent past, yet the level of prices in 2009 were 15 to 44 per cent lower than the prices prevailing in the beginning of the WTO period. The period also witnessed a decline in Indian export and import of commodities in which India did not have a strong competitive edge or in which international prices registered a sharp decline during the period. Therefore, the behaviour of international prices has a potential consequence that can damage domestic agriculture by price-induced decline in the profitability/ competitiveness of production. In this context, trade policy instruments also acquire greater connotation, and certain crucial questions regarding the role played by them arise. However, as discussed in the previous chapter, the government has made frequent changes in trade policy instruments during the post-WTO period in order to keep the domestic prices at a 'reasonable level'. But the question that remains unanswered is whether these changes in trade policy instruments (tariff rates/subsidy level) were sufficient enough to maintain the profitability/competitiveness of domestic producers.

Towards answering these questions, this chapter makes an attempt to compare the movement of world and domestic agriculture commodity prices. To compare the world prices with domestic prices we should know the price at which our domestic produce competes with the foreign produce. To this end, the types of adjustments made in the world prices to determine the reference price (parity price) are discussed in section 6.1. After discussing the methodology for calculating the reference prices, domestic and world prices are compared in section 6.2. With increasing agriculture trade liberalisation and commitments under WTO for replacing all non-tariff barriers with their tariff-equivalents, it becomes imperative to look at the degree of divergence between domestic and world prices; an attempt is made in section 6.3 to examine the degree of divergence between these sets of prices. As a part of this, the calculated price wedge was then compared with the applied tariff duty/export subsidy rate in order to assess the adequacy of the same. Section 6.4 draws together some conclusions that emerge from the analysis.

6.1 Methodology

Trade competitiveness is a dynamic phenomenon, which depends upon the level of domestic prices relative to international prices. In its simplest form, trade competitiveness, say, in export, assuming the quality of the domestic and foreign product as the same, is a situation when the difference between the domestic supply price and the foreign (market) price is enough to cover a large number of charges. In other words, a commodity is said to be export competitive if a unit of a commodity fetches a price that is considerably higher than what it is sold for in the domestic market. Similarly, in the case of importables, if the domestic price is lower than the international price plus transportation, freight, insurance and other costs involved in bringing produce from the foreign market to the domestic market, then the domestic product is import competitive, otherwise it is not import competitive. The degree of competitiveness (export/import) depends on the extent of divergence between these two prices. However, comparison of Indian agricultural prices with international prices is difficult because we must be sure that the commodities being compared are of similar quality. Also, the prices of similar goods vary considerably across space and over time due to large transportation costs. Therefore, in order to assess trade competitiveness, the domestic prices are compared to an adjusted reference price and, while doing so, we have followed the methodology developed by Gulati, Hanson and Pursell (1990); Goldar and Gulati (1991); Gulati, Sharma and Kohli (1996); and Pursell and Gupta (1998) in their background study papers on effective incentives to Indian agriculture. The types of adjustments made in order to determine the reference price are shown here, both for importables and exportables.

Importable hypothesis

Assuming that the imported commodity would compete with domestic produce in the principal port cities, the reference price under importable hypothesis was calculated both for net surplus as well as net deficit states and aggregated in order to get the reference price at the India level.

For Surplus State:

P^R_S = P^B + Port charges − TC_S − Marketing cost − Traders' margin − PC_S

P^B = (International Price, i.e., FoB price + Freight + Insurance) × Exchange rate

where,

P^R_S = Reference price of the crop for surplus states
P^B = Border price in rupees
TC_S = Transport cost from surplus states to port city
PC_S = Processing cost in surplus state

For Deficit State:

P^R_S = $P^R_{S'}$ + TC_D + Marketing cost + Traders' margin

Where,

$P^R_{S'}$ = Reference price in nearby surplus area
TC_D = Transport cost from surplus area to deficit area

Exportable hypothesis

Under the exportables scenario, only surplus states were included in the analysis. When the commodity was exportable, it was assumed that the point of competition between country's export price and the international price in the world markets would take place at the border of a third country (i.e., the CIF price in the third country). Therefore, the reference price under exportable hypothesis was calculated as:

P^R_S = P^B − Port charges − TC_S − Marketing cost − Traders' margin − PC_S

P^B = (International price, i.e., CIF price − Freight − Insurance) × Exchange rate

where,

P^R_S = Reference price of the crop for surplus states
P^B = Border price in rupees
TC_S = Transport cost from surplus states to port city
PC_S = Processing cost in surplus state

The reference price at the border for export commodities are taken as the export prices of major competitors for an equivalent quality level. This simply assumes that the international freight from the competing export country to a third-country importer and from India to a third-country importer is equal. For example, in case of wheat, it was assumed that the point of competition between Indian wheat and US wheat is Tunis in Tunisia, which is roughly equidistant from India and the US, thus allowing comparison between the FoB price at US and FoB price, say, at Bombay.

Data sources and cost adjustments

Sources for international prices vary by commodity and include sources like USDA, UNCTAD commodity price data set and IMF International Financial Statistics (IFS). Exchange rates were taken from the IFS' market rates. International freight and port charges were taken from the Pursell, Gulati and Gupta (2007) data set.

Data on domestic prices were collected from *Agricultural Prices in India*, published by the Ministry of Agriculture, Government of India (various years) up to the year 2001, and for the later period, it was collected from CACP reports and also from the official website of the Ministry of Agriculture. Regarding the timeframe for domestic prices, we have used average harvest season prices where available, because a majority of the farmers sell their produce during the harvest season. In cases where domestic harvest season prices were used, international prices and exchange rates pertaining to the same timeframe were utilised.

Domestic transportation cost from production site to port city was based on an earlier study by Sharma (1991) and were projected forward and backward by constructing the rail and road transport index (with base 2000 = 100) using the methodology developed in Pursell and Gupta (1998). Marketing costs and traders' margin were taken as certain fixed percentage of domestic price and varied between five to 10 per cent. For commodities that require substantial processing, the prices were taken at wholesale (processed) level, not at farmgate level.

6.2 COMPARISON OF DOMESTIC AND WORLD REFERENCE PRICE

6.2.1 Wheat

In order to analyse the pattern of trade competitiveness of Indian wheat producers, a comparison of the domestic producer's price and world reference price was made under the importable and exportable hypotheses. Competitiveness of domestic cultivators under importable hypothesis was studied for two net surplus states, namely, Haryana and Punjab, and one deficit state (Uttar Pradesh). Reference price for all-India is the weighted average of reference prices of these states (Appendix, Tables A-6.1 and A-6.2). Under exportable scenario, the competitiveness of wheat was studied only for Punjab. The domestic producer price is approximated by procurement price rather than farm harvest price, because procurement price takes care of quality aspects. The international price refers to US Hard Red Winter (HRW) No. 2 with ordinary protein.

Figure 6.1 plots the movements of domestic producer's price and world reference price under importable scenario. These comparisons show that, beginning with the early 1980s, the wheat prices in domestic markets ruled below the world reference price throughout the period under study, indicating that the domestic produce competed well with imports. Two types of trends can be seen in the ratio of domestic to international price, namely, increasing trend from 1981 to 1988, and decreasing trend from 1989 to 1997 (Figure 6.2). During 1981 to 1988, these domestic and international prices were close to each other. Or, in other words, the domestic and border prices were growing at the same rate until the late 1980s (around 1988), and thereafter, the growth of the latter prices was faster than that of the former and resulted in an increasing gap between these two.

Figure 6.1: Domestic and world reference price for wheat under importable hypothesis: 1981–2005

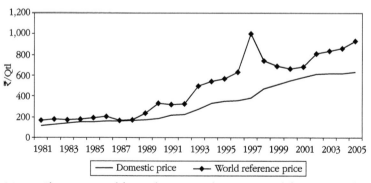

Source: Chart prepared by author using data computed from Appendix, Table A-6.1, columns (8) and (11).

Figure 6.2: Trend in ratio of domestic price to world reference price for wheat under importable scenario: 1981–2005

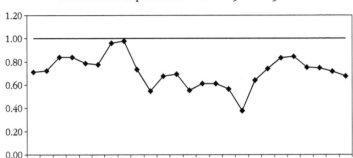

Source: Chart prepared by author using data computed from Appendix, Table A-6.1.

The gap between these reached the maximum in 1997 when world reference prices were at their peak. The situation started changing afterwards, when because of a decline in world prices along with an increase in domestic prices the level of import competitiveness started reducing. And slowly, India started becoming attractive for wheat import. As international prices started improving slowly after 2000, consequently the level of import competitiveness of domestic produce has also started improving.

In sharp contrast to the importable scenario, when wheat was viewed as an exportable, it was found internationally uncompetitive. The Punjab wheat, under the exportable hypothesis, is not internationally competitive, implying that Punjab wheat has been costlier than US HRW wheat all through except for a few years (Figure 6.3).

A comparison of domestic and world prices shows that in most of the years domestic prices are higher than the world reference price. The ratio of domestic to international prices was found below 1 only in a few years when international prices were very high. As seen in Chapter 5, India occasionally exported large quantities of wheat up to 2,000; because of the unfavourable price environment, many times wheat available in government stocks had to be exported at a price lower than the domestic price (Chand and Jha 2001). As discussed later in this chapter, when the combination of declining world prices and higher domestic prices made Indian wheat uncompetitive in world

Figure 6.3: Domestic and world reference price for wheat under exportable hypothesis: 1981–2005

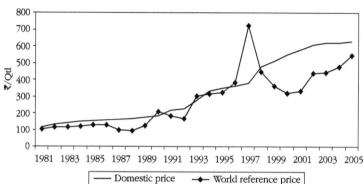

Source: Chart prepared by author using data computed from Appendix, Table A-6.2, columns (7) and (8).

markets, the government decided to provide a subsidy for wheat exports to liquidate the excess stocks with the public agencies.

6.2.2 Rice

Since India was a net exporter of rice for many of the years covered under the study, therefore, a comparison of domestic producers' price with world reference price was made under the exportable hypothesis to analyse the pattern of competitiveness of Indian producers. Export competitiveness of rice was studied for two major producing states, namely, Andhra Pradesh and Punjab. The domestic producer price was approximated by a levy/procurement price of rice of the respective state, whereas the international price refers to 15 per cent broken Thai rice for the months of the Indian harvest season (i.e., October to January).

Figure 6.4 plots the movement of these two prices. This comparison shows that with the exception of three years, namely, 1985, 1986 and 1987, domestic prices were lower than the world reference prices up to the year 1999, implying that India had a comparative advantage in exporting rice during the period. Except for the years 1985 to 1987, the ratio of domestic to international price was also found to be below 1 till the year 1999. Subsequently, the gap between domestic and international prices reduced, and the ratio of

Figure 6.4: Domestic and world reference price for rice under exportable hypothesis: 1981–2005

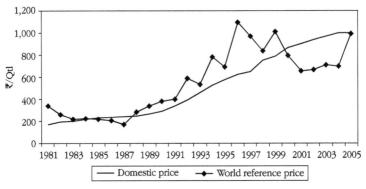

Source: Chart prepared by author using data computed from Appendix, Table A-6.3, columns (7) and (8).

Figure 6.5: Trend in ratio of domestic price to world reference price for rice under exportable scenario: 1981–2005

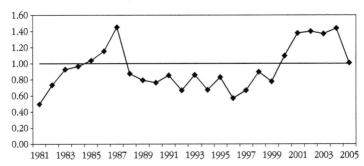

Source: Chart prepared by author using data computed from Appendix, Table A-6.3.

domestic to international price increased to 1 in 2000. As international prices fell sharply, the price advantage of rice for exports got completely eroded by 2000, when world prices started ruling below the domestic prices. Therefore, the competitiveness of rice production has witnessed tremendous changes during the post-WTO period. As mentioned in Chapter 5, the government started providing export subsidies to boost rice export during the period when international prices became adverse for rice export. In the case of Andhra Pradesh and Punjab also, the pattern of protection and competitiveness is more or less the same (Appendix, Table A-6.3).

6.2.3 Groundnut Seed and Oil

Trade competitiveness of Indian groundnut producers has been assessed by making a comparison of domestic producers' price with world reference price under the importable hypothesis. Import competitiveness of groundnut (with shell) was studied for three major producing states, namely, Andhra Pradesh, Gujarat and Tamil Nadu. The world price refers to CIF price of groundnut (kernels) at Rotterdam. The domestic prices were approximated by the averages of month-end wholesale prices during the harvest season of relevant states (Appendix, Table A-6.4).

Figure 6.6 enables a visual grasp of movement of world reference prices and domestic harvest season prices of groundnut (pod or with shell) under the importable hypothesis. These comparisons show that domestic prices were higher than the international prices during the 1980s and early 1990s, making it a fit case for imports. In other words, Indian producers had a competitive disadvantage during the period. However, the level of competitiveness as indicated by the ratio of domestic to world prices started improving after 1988, mainly on account of an increase in world prices, but remained more than 1 (Figure 6.7).

Figure 6.6: Domestic and world reference price for groundnut (pod) under importable hypothesis: 1981–2004

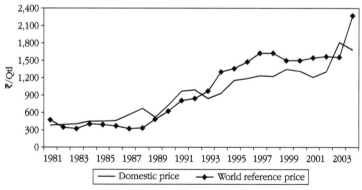

Source: Chart prepared by author using data computed from Appendix, Table A-6.4, columns (22) and (23).

Figure 6.7: Trend in ratio of domestic to world reference price for groundnut under importable scenario: 1981–2004

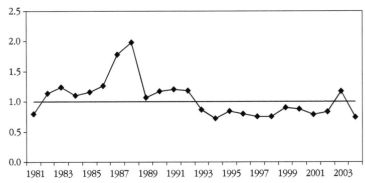

Source: Chart prepared by author using data computed from Appendix, Table A-6.4.

Since the early 1990s, with increased domestic production driving domestic prices down, and with rupee devaluation, the competitiveness of groundnut has improved substantially with domestic prices ruling below world prices. Even during the post-WTO period when world prices for groundnut dropped to the level of the late 1980s, domestic production is found to be less costly compared to imports of groundnut. Therefore, the competitiveness of groundnut improved significantly during the 1990s compared to the 1980s, as supported by the ratio of domestic to world price, which turned out to be less than 1.

In the case of oil, trade competitiveness of Indian producers was evaluated under the importable scenario. Import competitiveness of groundnut oil has been assessed by comparing the wholesale market price[1] at Bombay with international prices at Rotterdam (Appendix, Table A-6.5).

Figure 6.8 shows the movement of these two prices. These comparisons show that, compared to the 1980s and early 1990s, the domestic and international prices were close to each other since the mid-1990s and onwards. It has been observed that groundnut oil had competitive disadvantages during the 1980s and early 1990s

---

[1] Averages of month-end wholesale market prices during the period November to October.

Figure 6.8: Domestic and world reference price for groundnut oil under importable hypothesis: 1981–2005

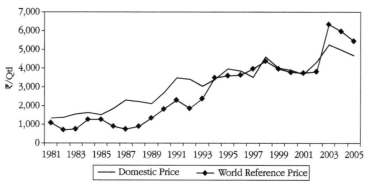

Source: Chart prepared by author using data computed from Appendix, Table A-6.5, columns (10) and (12).

because domestic prices were higher than the international prices. During the post-WTO period, the gap between domestic and world reference prices almost evaporated, as both the prices started moving jointly and competitiveness of groundnut oil improved significantly as indicated by the ratio of domestic to international prices, which turned out to be close to 1 or less than 1 (in some years) during the period (Figure 6.9).

Figure 6.9: Trend in ratio of domestic to world reference price for groundnut oil under importable scenario: 1981–2005

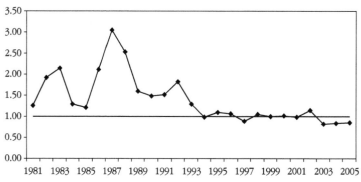

Source: Chart prepared by author using data computed from Appendix, Table A-6.5.

6.2.4 Rapeseed/Mustard Seed and Oil

Trade competitiveness of Indian rapeseed/mustard was analysed under the importable scenario. The comparison between domestic and international prices was made for the largest wholesale domestic market, i.e., Hapur in Uttar Pradesh (deficit state). the domestic price at Hapur was approximated by averages of month-end wholesale market prices during the harvest season, i.e., January to June, whereas international price refers to the CIF Rotterdam price for the same period (Appendix, Table A-6.6).

A comparison between the domestic and world reference prices shows that domestic prices ruled above the international prices during most of the 1980s and early 1990s, implying a competitive disadvantage (Figure 6.10). However, with increased domestic production driving domestic prices down, and rupee devaluation, the competitiveness of domestic production started improving after 1988 but the ratio of domestic to international prices remained more than 1 (Figure 6.11). The situation started reversing itself from 1993 with domestic prices ruling below the international prices, mainly on account of upward movement in international prices. Consequently, the ratio of domestic to international prices also turned out to be less than 1. Therefore, since 1993, the competitiveness of Indian rapeseed improved significantly.

In the case of rapeseed oil, trade competitiveness was evaluated with Kanpur (Uttar Pradesh) as the reference point under the

Figure 6.10: Domestic and world reference price for rapeseed/mustard under importable hypothesis: 1980–2005

Source: Chart prepared by author using data computed from Appendix, Table A-6.6, columns (11) and (13).

Figure 6.11: Trend in ratio of domestic to world reference price for rapeseed under Importable scenario: 1981–2005

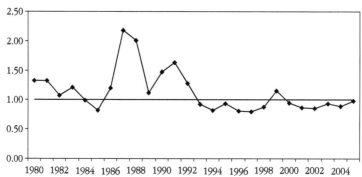

Source: Chart prepared by author using data computed from Appendix, Table A-6.6.

importable scenario. Import competitiveness was assessed by comparing the wholesale market price[2] at Kanpur with international prices at Rotterdam (Appendix, Table A-6.7). These comparisons show that domestic prices were higher than the international prices throughout the period under study, implying that India had competitive disadvantage in the international market (Figure 6.12). Although the ratio of domestic to international prices remained more than 1 throughout the period covered under the study, it points to an improvement in competitiveness after 1992 with the level reaching 1 by 1998 (Figure 6.13). With a sharp decline in international prices during the post-WTO period (1998 onwards), the ratio of domestic to international prices started rising.

6.2.5 Soybean Seed and Oil

Price comparisons for soybean are made under the importable scenario. The international prices are taken in dollars as the CIF price of US No. 2 yellow at Rotterdam, averaged over the Indian harvest season (i.e., October to March). Domestic prices were approximated by month-end wholesale prices of yellow soybean at Indore, Madhya Pradesh (a net deficit state), for the month of October to March (Appendix, Table A-6.8).

---

[2] Averages of month-end wholesale market prices during the period April to March

Figure 6.12: Domestic and world reference price for rapeseed oil under Importable hypothesis: 1981–2005

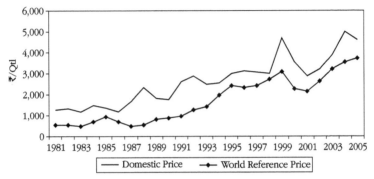

Source: Chart prepared by author using data computed from Appendix, Table A-6.7, columns (10) and (13).

Figure 6.13: Trend in ratio of domestic to world reference price for rapeseed oil under importable scenario

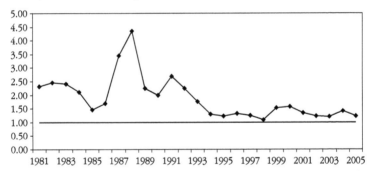

Source: Chart prepared by author using data computed from Appendix, Table A-6.7.

The comparison between domestic and international prices shows that with the exception of two years, namely, 1987 and 1988, domestic prices were lower than international prices throughout the period covered under the study, indicating the competitive advantage of Indian producers (Figure 6.14).

In other words, Indian produce competed well with imported soybean throughout the period covered under the study. The period after 1992 witnessed a further improvement in soybean competitiveness. During the post-WTO period when international prices dropped to

Figure 6.14: Domestic and world reference price for soybean under importable hypothesis: 1981–2005

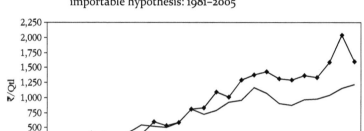

Source: Chart prepared by author using data computed from Appendix, Table A-6.8, columns (10) and (13).

very low levels, domestic production is found to be less costly compared to imports of soybean. The ratio of domestic to international prices reached its lowest level in 2004 with domestic prices ruling more than 40 per cent below the international price (Figure 6.15).

In sharp contrast to the soybean seed prices, domestic prices of soybean oil ruled at higher levels than the international prices. Due to this, import of soybean oil remained an attractive proposition (Figure 6.16).

Figure 6.15: Trend in ratio of domestic to world reference price for soybean under importable scenario

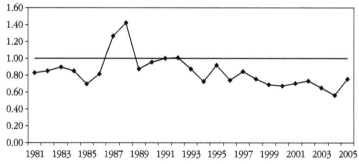

Source: Chart prepared by author using data computed from Appendix, Table A-6.8.

Figure 6.16: Domestic and world reference price for soybean oil under importable hypothesis: 1981–2005

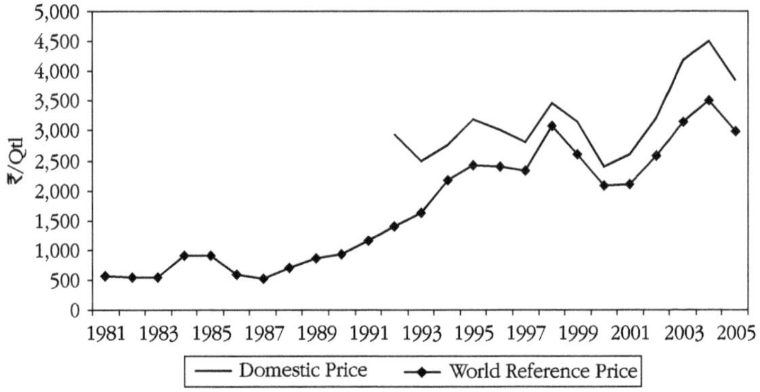

Source: Chart prepared by author using data computed from Appendix, Table A-6.9, columns (10) and (13).

A comparison of month-end domestic wholesale market prices at Madhya Pradesh with international prices at the Dutch port (Appendix, Table A-6.9) shows that with the removal of restriction on imports, domestic prices of soybean oil have moved closer to international prices but their ratio to international prices continue to remain above 1 (Figure 6.17). When edible oil imports into the country were not freely allowed, during the late 1980s and early 1990s for example, the ratio of domestic to international prices for soybean oil was more than three (Chand 2002). The situation started improving since the early 1990s with an increase in import competitiveness of Indian soybean oil.

6.2.6 Price Ratio for Oilseeds v/s Edible Oils

It would be interesting to compare the ratios of domestic to international prices of oilseeds with that of edible oil. This would indicate difference in efficiency of oilseeds and edible oil production. Figures 6.18, 6.19 and 6.20 show the comparison of price ratios of oilseeds with that of edible oils for the above-mentioned crops under the importable hypothesis. As one can see from these figures, the ratio of domestic to international prices in case of edible oils remained higher than the corresponding ratios for the seed prices throughout the period under the study. Therefore, oilseed producers were more efficient than edible oil producers. Though the level

Figure 6.17: Trend in ratio of domestic to world reference price for soybean oil under importable scenario

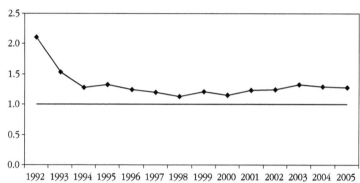

Source: Chart prepared by author using data computed from Appendix, Table A-6.9.

Figure 6.18: Ratio of domestic to international price of groundnut seed and oil

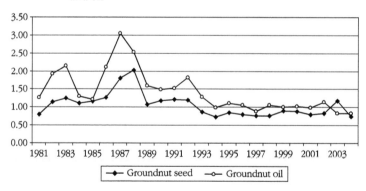

Source: Chart prepared by author.

of import competitiveness started improving since the late 1980s, both in the case of oilseeds and edible oils, the ratio of domestic to international prices in the case of edible oils continued to remain above the ratio of oilseed prices. Thus, these comparisons highlight the fact that since the early 1990s, India is an efficient producer of oilseeds though domestic prices of edible oil are highly attractive for import, as the ratio of domestic to international prices remained more than 1. One plausible explanation of this result seems to be high

Figure 6.19: Ratio of domestic to international price of rapeseed/mustard seed and oil

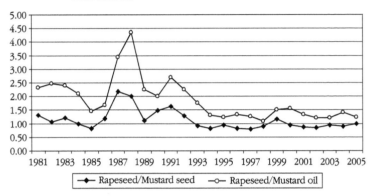

Source: Chart prepared by author.

Figure 6.20: Ratio of domestic to international price of soybean seed and oil

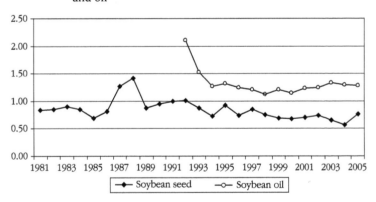

Source: Chart prepared by author.

domestic processing and marketing costs, which make domestic oil prices higher than the international prices.

6.2.7 Sugar

Trade competitiveness of Indian plantation white sugar was analysed under both the importable and exportable scenarios. The price comparisons are averages for the Indian 'sugar year' covering the period from October to September. Competitiveness was estimated for three major producing states, namely, Uttar Pradesh, Maharashtra and Tamil Nadu. Under the importable scenario, the domestic price was approximated by the ex-factory realisation price of sugar mills, whereas the international price refers to the FoB Europe price of plantation white sugar (Appendix, Table A-6.10).[3]

Figure 6.21 illustrates the movement of these two prices. These comparisons show that, during most of 1980s, domestic prices were higher than the world price. This competitive disadvantage has disappeared from the late 1980s when international prices started moving in the upward direction (see Chapter 4) and India became import competitive. As a result, the ratio of domestic to international prices declined to less than 1 (Figure 6.22).

Figure 6.21: Domestic and world reference price for plantation white sugar under Importable hypothesis: 1981–2005

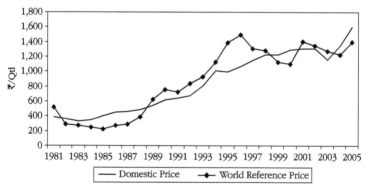

Source: Chart prepared by author using data computed from Appendix, Table A-6.10, columns (30) and (31).

---

[3] Since the world trade is mainly in raw and fully-refined white sugar, and international price data for plantation white sugar is not consistently reported, therefore, based on some limited comparisons of international prices, Goldar and Gulati (1991) and Pursell and Gupta (1998) have assumed that the premium paid for India's plantation sugar over the price of raw sugar is 90 per cent of the premium of international prices of fully-refined sugar over the international prices of raw sugar. Therefore, in order to derive the FoB Europe price of plantation white sugar, we follow the same approach. Or, in other words, the FoB Europe price of plantation white sugar price has been estimated to equal the raw sugar price (CIF Europe) plus 90 per cent of the excess of the price of fully-refined sugar (FoB Europe) over the raw sugar price.

Figure 6.22: Trend in ratio of domestic to world reference price for plantation white sugar under importable scenario: 1981–2005

Source: Chart prepared by author using data computed from Appendix, Table A-6.10.

This situation reverses itself with the sharp decline in international prices during the post-WTO period. The period post-WTO witnessed a decline in import competitiveness of Indian sugar as the gap between domestic and world reference prices started reducing and also the ratio of domestic to world reference prices increased. Therefore, in 1998, the government reversed its import policy by increasing tariff rates and again applying the Essential Commodities Act to sugar imports (see Chapter 5).

Under the exportable hypothesis, Indian plantation white sugar is assumed to compete with sugar from other major exporters in Egypt. This was further simplified by assuming that freight from Europe to Egypt is the same as the freight from India to Egypt. Therefore, the FoB prices in India are taken to be the same as FoB prices in Europe (Pursell and Gupta 1998) (Appendix, Table A-6.11). A comparison of domestic (ex-factory realisation) price and world reference price under exportable hypothesis is shown in Figure 6.23. It can be observed from the figure that Indian sugar had competitive disadvantages in exporting sugar during the 1980s as domestic prices were higher than the export parity prices. This disadvantage started disappearing since the late 1980s with an increase in world prices. During the period between 1989 and 1997, these domestic and world reference prices were close to each other. As a result, the ratio of domestic to world reference price was close to 1 during

Figure 6.23: Domestic and world reference price for plantation white sugar under exportable hypothesis: 1981–2005

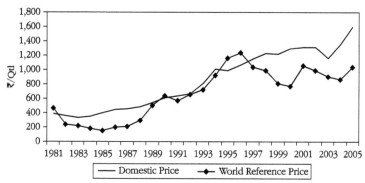

Source: Chart prepared by author using data computed from Appendix, Table A-6.11, columns (30) and (31).

the period (Figure 6.24). After 1997, as world prices fell sharply, the price advantage of sugar for export got completely eroded. Therefore, in most of the years covered under the study, sugar was not found to be export competitive as indicated by the ratio of domestic to world reference prices, which turned out to be less than 1. Because of competitive disadvantages in exporting sugar, the government of India started export promotional measures by introducing and gradually

Figure 6.24: Trend in ratio of domestic to world reference price for plantation white sugar under exportable scenario: 1981–2005

Source: Chart prepared by author using data computed from Appendix, Table A-6.11.

increasing export subsidies for sugar (see Chapter 5) in order to increase sugar export.

In summary, the analysis of trade competitiveness of major agricultural commodities highlights the fact that competitiveness of commodities has undergone significant changes during the last 25 years. This shows that trade competitiveness is a dynamic phenomenon which depends upon changes in international and domestic prices. Under the exportable hypothesis, India has been export competitive in rice since 1981, except during the period when international prices have experienced unusual declines (1985–87 and 2000–2004); whereas there seems not much advantage in exporting wheat, as India was export competitive only for short spells (1990 and 1996–97) when world prices were at their peak. In the case of sugar, India was probably export competitive during the period 1989 to 1997 (as the ratio of domestic to world price was close to 1). After 1997, given the significant levels of distortions in the international market due to domestic and export subsidisation by the European Union (EU), and high protection and support in the US market, Indian sugar exports became uncompetitive in the international market. However, commodities belonging to the group of oilseeds, namely, groundnut and rapeseed/mustard, appear to be efficient import substitutes since the early 1990s, whereas soybean seed has been found to be import substitutable throughout the period under the study (except for a short spell during 1987 and 1988). Compared to oilseeds, edible oils producers were uncompetitive as producers of import substitutes. In the case of cereals, under the importable hypothesis, wheat has been largely competitive with ratios of domestic to international prices below unity throughout the period under study.

6.3 DIVERGENCE BETWEEN DOMESTIC AND WORLD REFERENCE PRICE

The divergence between the compared domestic and world reference prices, i.e., the price wedge, ideally captures the space for policy interventions. For instance, in the case of importables/exportables, the level to which domestic prices are higher than world reference prices gives the indicative level for applied tariff duties/export subsidies on imports/exports. Therefore, in order to understand the implication of trade liberalisation, it is essential to assess the divergence between domestic and adjusted international prices (i.e., world reference price). The price wedge was calculated by taking the difference between domestic and adjusted world prices, expressed as a percentage of the world reference price. The calculated price wedge for each agricultural commodity was then compared with the existing applied tariff duty or export subsidy rate in order to assess the adequacy of the same.

In the case of wheat, the divergence between domestic and world reference price was analysed under the exportable scenario. Figure 6.25 depicts the trend in divergence between these two prices. As discussed earlier, except for the years of unusual increases in international prices, domestic prices ruled above the world reference price throughout the period under study. As a result, the divergence between these two was positive during most of the years.

After 1998, when world prices experienced a sharp decline, the divergence between domestic and world reference prices started increasing and touched a peak in 2001 when domestic prices were 75 per cent higher than the level of world reference prices and the price advantage of Indian wheat for exports was completely eroded. Therefore, the government decided to provide an export subsidy since 2001, when a combination of low world prices and higher domestic prices made Indian wheat uncompetitive in the world markets, to support export of surplus wheat in order to liquidate the excess stocks with the public agencies. As a result, substantial amount of export subsidies were paid to make it worthwhile for private traders to help

Figure 6.25: Divergence between domestic and world reference price for wheat under exportable hypothesis: 1981–2005

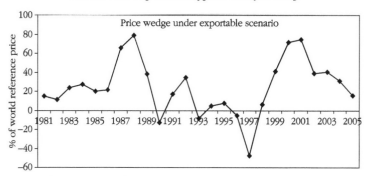

Source: Chart prepared by author using data computed from Appendix, Table A-6.2.

dispose of large excess wheat stocks (see Chapter 5). Figure 6.26 illustrates how the price wedge and the export subsidy rate compare. The wheat export subsidy rate, which varied from 86 per cent to 93 per cent between 2001 and 2003, witnessed a gradual decline afterwards with the recovery in world prices. Since 2005, the government halted export subsidies because of tightening domestic supply and increased Indian competitiveness in the international market.

Figure 6.26: A comparison between price wedge and wheat export subsidy rate (percentage): 1991–2005

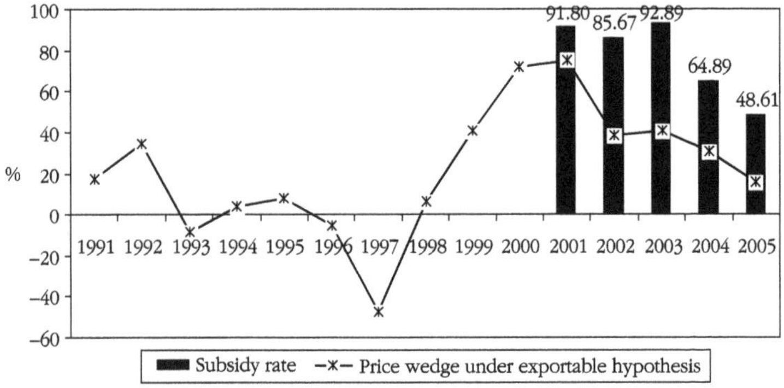

Source: Chart prepared by author.

In the case of rice, India had competitive advantages in exporting rice throughout the study period, with the exception of a period of unusual decline of international prices; therefore, the divergence between these two was negative during most of the years (Figure 6.27). As can be seen from the figure, during the last 25 years, it was only during 1985–87 and 2000–04 when the price wedge between the domestic and world reference price became positive due to sharp declines in international prices. In the recent past, the divergence between these two prices ranged between 37 to 43 per cent during the years 2001–04.

Since 2000, when the price advantage of rice for exports got completely eroded, the government decided to provide export subsidies to maintain the price advantage of Indian rice for exports and also to liquidate the excess stocks with the public agencies (see Chapter 5). The export subsidy rate varied from 24 per cent to 49 per cent during the years 2000 to 2002 (Figure 6.28). As world prices started recovering

Figure 6.27: Divergence between domestic and world reference price for rice under exportable hypothesis: 1981–2005

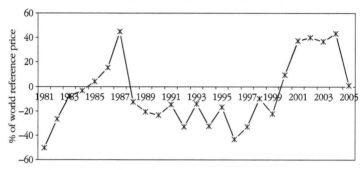

Source: Chart prepared by author using data computed from Appendix, Table A-6.3.

Figure 6.28: A comparison between price wedge and rice export subsidy rate (percentage): 1991–2005

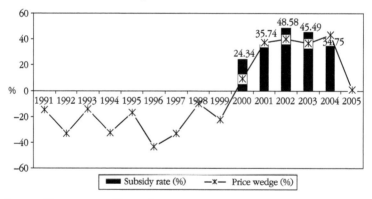

Source: Chart prepared by author.

since 2003, the government started reducing the export subsidy rate and stopped it completely by the year 2005 when the gap between domestic and world reference prices almost became zero.

In the case of edible oils, the divergence between domestic and world reference prices was measured under the importable scenario. Figures 6.29, 6.30 and 6.31 enable a visual grasp of the divergence between these two prices in the case of groundnut oil, rapeseed/mustard oil and soybean oil, respectively. As can be seen from the

Figure 6.29: Divergence between domestic and world reference price for groundnut oil under importable hypothesis: 1981–2005

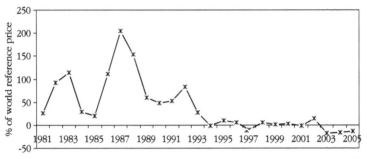

Source: Chart prepared by author using data computed from Appendix, Table A-6.5.

Figure 6.30: Divergence between domestic and world reference price for rapeseed/mustard oil under importable hypothesis: 1981–2005

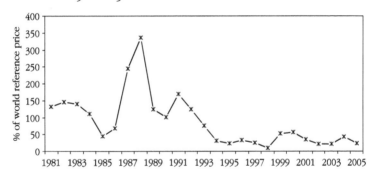

Source: Chart prepared by author using data computed from Appendix, Table A-6.7.

figures, during the 1980s and early 1990s, the divergence between these two prices remained positive, indicating higher value of domestic prices compared to world reference prices. Since the mid-1990s, the price wedge was almost negligible or even negative in the case of groundnut oil, whereas in the case of rapeseed/mustard and soybean oil it remained positive throughout the study period.

As discussed in Chapter 5, in the case of edible oils, since 1994, the government has made frequent adjustments in applied tariff duty rates in the wake of low world prices to protect the interests of

Figure 6.31: Divergence between domestic and world reference price for soybean oil under importable hypothesis: 1992–2005

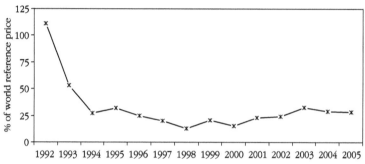

Source: Chart prepared by author using data computed from Appendix, Table A-6.9.

various stakeholders. A comparison of these applied tariff duties with the price wedge gives an idea regarding their adequacy. As shown in Figures 6.32, 6.33 and 6.34, except for groundnut oil, in all other cases, the applied tariff duty rate was close to the required level till 2000. After 2000, the applied tariff duty rates were slightly higher than the required level. In the case of groundnut oil, the applied tariff duty rates were higher than the required level throughout the period.

In the case of sugar, domestic prices were consistently higher than international prices during the 1980s under the importable scenario.

Figure 6.32: A comparison between price wedge and applied tariff rate for groundnut oil: 1991–2005

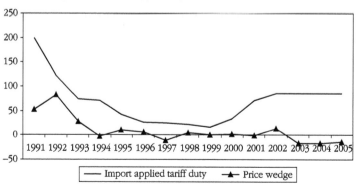

Source: Chart prepared by author.

Figure 6.33: A comparison between price wedge and applied tariff rate for rapeseed/mustard oil: 1992–2005

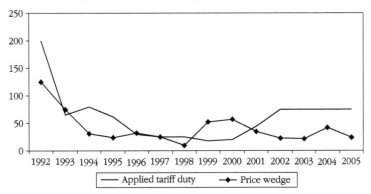

Source: Chart prepared by author.

Figure 6.34: A comparison between price wedge and applied tariff rate for soybean oil: 1992–2005

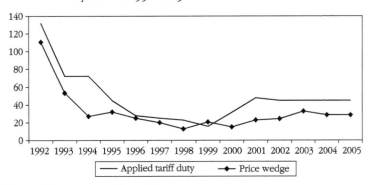

Source: Chart prepared by author.

The highest peak achieved by the domestic prices is about 80 per cent above the international prices in 1985 (Figure 6.35), after which there was a reduction in the price differential. Since the early 1990s, the divergence between domestic and world reference prices turned negative as world reference prices were higher than domestic prices. The sharp decline in world prices during the post-WTO period (after 1996) resulted in a widening of the gap between domestic and world reference prices. The maximum peak achieved during the post-WTO period is about 20 per cent above the international price.

Figure 6.35: Divergence between domestic and world reference price for Indian plantation white sugar under importable hypothesis: 1981–2005

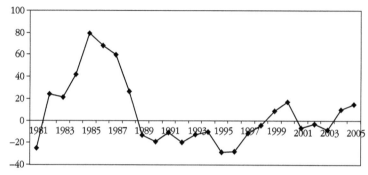

Source: Chart prepared by author using data computed from Appendix, Table A-6.10.

Figure 6.36 gives a comparative picture of applied tariff duty rates and the price wedge observed. As can be seen from the figure, applied tariff duty rates were much higher than the required level throughout the period under study. Three types of trends can be seen in the applied tariff duty rates, namely, a decreasing trend from 1992 to 1995, a constant trend from 1995 to 1998, and an increasing trend from 1998 to 2005. Beginning with 1992, when world prices were on an increasing trend, the government decided to reduce the applied

Figure 6.36: A comparison between price wedge and applied tariff rate for Indian plantation white sugar: 1992–2005

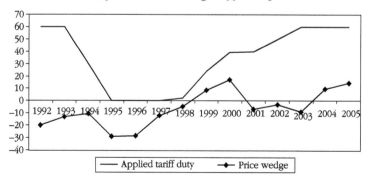

Source: Chart prepared by author.

tariff duty rates on imported sugar, and by March 1994, applied tariffs were cut to zero, which remained in place for the next four years. Again in 1998, when world sugar prices started declining, the government reversed the policy by increasing the tariff duty rates. Increase in tariff rates after 1999 was much higher than the divergence level between the domestic and world reference price. Given the significant levels of distortions in the international market due to domestic and export subsidisation by the EC and USA, coupled with fluctuations in domestic production, which resulted in sizeable imports during some years in the recent past, the present higher tariff bindings may be negotiated till the distortions in international markets are corrected.

To sum up, comparisons between the price wedge, i.e., divergence between domestic and world reference price, and applied tariff duty rates show that applied tariff rates were adequate in the case of edible oils but were higher in the case of sugar. Under the exportables scenario, the export subsidy rates were enough to maintain the competitiveness of Indian produce in international markets in the wake of any unusual decline in world prices as, for example, in the case of rice and wheat.

6.4 CONCLUSION

This chapter sought to analyse the role of international prices in determining the trajectory of agricultural growth since 1991 by price-induced decline in profitability/competitiveness. From the analysis of competitiveness of domestic agriculture, we do not see much ground for granting international prices a significant role in determining the trajectory of agricultural growth during the post-reform period. Analysis of the chapter clearly shows that competitiveness of all the crops covered under the study has improved significantly during the 1990s compared to the 1980s. Since the early 1990s, India is import competitive in most of the crops covered under the study barring some important edible oils. Nonetheless, during the post-WTO period, when international prices of agricultural commodities have witnessed sharp decline, the competitiveness of all the crops studied has declined. For instance, India has been export competitive throughout the period under study in the case of rice, except during the period when international prices have experienced unusual declines during the post-WTO period. Whereas in the case of sugar, with decline in international prices after 1997 due to distortions caused by the policies of support and protection pursued by the major industrial economies, competitiveness was badly affected. If there is substantial reduction in international market distortions, India could emerge as a competitive supplier of sugar as well.

Regarding the role played by trade policy instruments — import tariffs/export subsidies — during the post-WTO period, applied tariff rates were adequate to bridge the price wedge observed between domestic and world reference prices. On the other hand, export subsidy rates were enough to maintain the competitiveness of Indian producers in international markets at the time of unusual decline in world prices, for example, in the case of rice and wheat. Therefore, government intervention has been quite effective in insulating domestic producers from low world prices during the post-WTO period.

7

Decomposing Variability
in Agricultural Prices

As discussed in Chapter 6, during the post-reform period, competitiveness of most of the agricultural commodities had undergone considerable change. It shows a dynamic trend depending upon changes in international and domestic market prices. For example, the competitiveness of most of the agricultural commodities, which improved significantly during the early 1990s, was affected adversely during the post-WTO period with a sharp decline in international prices. The extent to which international prices had influence on domestic prices during the period depends upon the government intervention in the form of policies either at the border or as price support mechanisms which have potential consequence of weakening the link or preventing transmission of the effects of international price movements. Apart from international prices, government policies also affect the domestic prices both directly and indirectly. Typically, indirect effects result from the impact of macroeconomic policies on the exchange rate, whereas direct effects result from impact of government intervention in agriculture in pursuance of its objective of keeping domestic prices at 'reasonable levels'.

A commonly held view among mainstream economists is that any trade policy measure, which partially or totally insulates the domestic market from the rest of the world, increases the amount of price instability in the domestic market compared to situation of free trade. Agricultural policy instruments such as import tariffs, tariff rate quotas and export subsidies, or taxes, intervention mechanisms, as well as exchange rate policies insulate the domestic market and hinder the full transmission of international price signals and increase the amount of price instability compared to free trade by affecting the excess demand or supply schedules in domestic commodity markets. However, our analysis in the previous chapters shows that, during the post-WTO period, government intervention in agriculture was quite successful in terms of maintaining stability in domestic prices while insulating domestic producers from low world prices and maintaining the competitiveness of domestic agriculture. Therefore, the arguments made by the mainstream and the results emerging from our analysis raise certain crucial questions regarding the role played by international prices and different policy variables in terms of maintaining stability in domestic prices. In other words, the question is whether the observed variability, or lack of it, in domestic prices was because of incomplete transmission of international price effects or because government intervention in agriculture has helped in lowering the variability in domestic prices by not allowing the price signals to get fully transmitted. These issues can only be analysed if one can separate the factors responsible for changes in domestic prices and quantify their effects on domestic prices, which, in the Indian context, still remains quite a neglected issue (at least) in analytical studies. In this context, an attempt is made in the present chapter to decompose the changes in domestic prices of agricultural commodities by using a decomposition model with the key variables in the model being trade prices, the exchange rate and agricultural trade policies. This chapter is divided into three sections. The model used to decompose the variability in agricultural prices is discussed in section 7.1. Section 7.2 deals with the decomposition analysis of agriculture commodity price movements, while section 7.3 draws together some conclusions that emerge from the analysis.

7.1 The Decomposition Method

The model used to decompose the variability in prices was adopted from William Liefert (2007, 2011). In this model, domestic price is assumed to be a function of trade prices, the exchange rate and agricultural trade policies, and mathematically can be expressed as:

$$P^d = f(P^w; X; t)$$

where

P^d is domestic agriculture price,

P^w is trade prices, i.e., world prices of agricultural commodities adjusted for transportation and other incidental cost and expressed in foreign currency,

X is the market exchange rate between domestic and foreign currency, and

t represents the *ad valorem* tariff rate.

The decomposition model as described in Appendix II allows one to isolate the effects of complete as well as incomplete transmission on P^d. Incomplete transmission can be caused by domestic policy as well as underdeveloped infrastructure and can reduce the transmission of changes in trade prices and exchange rates to domestic prices. Underdeveloped infrastructure can result in high transaction costs and can also generate market imperfections due to incomplete information (Fackler and Goodwin 2001). The sum of the these two (i.e., complete and incomplete transmission) gives the net effect based on the actual value of Price Transmission Elasticity (PTE) 'e' as estimated in the model by

$$e = \frac{\dot{P}^d}{\left(\overline{P^w \times X (1+t)} \right)}$$

where $[P_t^w X^t (1 + t)]$ is the duty-inclusive landed price. After inserting 'e' in the decomposition equation, one gets two terms: term A for complete transmission and term B for incomplete transmission.

$$\dot{P}^d = (e + k - k \left(\overline{P^w X (1+t)} \right)$$

$$\dot{P}^d = \left(\overline{P^w X (1+t)} \right) - k \left(\overline{P^w X (1+t)} \right)$$
$$\qquad\qquad A \qquad\qquad\qquad B$$

where,

$$k = 1 - e, \quad \text{and} \quad e + k = 1$$

If there is complete transmission of changes in P^w and X on P^d, such that $e = 1$, the term B drops out. The incomplete transmission part measures the degree to which P^d fails to change to the maximum extent possible. Breaking each term A and B further finally yields two terms. The first term measures direct price effects, i.e., change in P^d that occurs from ΔP^w and ΔX. The second term in the equation gives the policy effect (both implicit as well as explicit). The next section gives the results of the decomposition of changes in domestic prices for selected commodities.

7.2 Analysis of Decomposition of Changes in Agricultural Commodity Prices

The commodities selected for the study are wheat, rice, groundnut oil, rapeseed/mustard oil, soybean oil, and sugar. In the case of wheat and rice, domestic price corresponds to the government-announced support price. Therefore, one can argue that decomposition of changes in agricultural prices is not a very relevant issue in the case of these crops. However, the process of macroeconomic stabilisation combined with fiscal adjustment and structural reform aimed at the integration of the domestic economy with the global economy brought the domestic farm prices in line with world market prices. The CACP started considering the international price situation while arriving at the level of the support price and made substantial hikes in support prices during the 1990s to reduce the gap between domestic and international prices.[1] This clearly shows a move towards a policy regime that allows transmission of international price signals (even if not fully).

7.2.1 Decomposing Changes in Wheat Producer's Price: Exportable Scenario

As discussed in Chapter 6, the world reference price for wheat fell sharply after 1997 and the price advantage of Indian wheat for exports got completely eroded by 1998 when world prices started ruling below domestic prices. On the domestic front, the period also corresponded with a decline in demand for wheat along with an increase in supply mainly on account of increases in procurement made by public agencies at higher procurement prices (see Chapter 3 for details). This led to the accumulation of wheat stocks with the public agencies. Wheat stock with public agencies started rising since 1999 and reached a peak of 26 million tonnes in 2003. Consequently, the government lifted quantitative restrictions on wheat exports and started providing budgetary support in the form of export subsidies since 2001 to liquidate the excess wheat stocks from the central pool, when the combination of low world prices and higher domestic prices made Indian wheat uncompetitive in world markets.

The period 2001 to 2004 was chosen to decompose the change in domestic producer prices because of the following reasons:[2] (*i*) the period witnessed an increase in India's wheat export from the level of around one million tonnes in 2001 to more than 4 million tonnes

---

[1] For details on support price, please refer to Chapter 3.

[2] Please refer comparison of domestic and world reference price in the case of wheat in Chapter 6.

in 2004 with no restrictions on wheat export; (*ii*) the period also corresponds to an increase of 34 per cent in the world reference price, which resulted in decline in the divergence between domestic and world reference price from the level of 75 per cent to 31 per cent; and (*iii*) the budgetary support in terms of export subsidies also declined from the level of 92 per cent to 65 per cent of the value of wheat export during this period.

As discussed earlier, the subsidy's purpose was to encourage exports of large accumulated stocks. This makes the situation tricky with respect to decomposition. If the fate and disposition of these stocks have no further effect on India's domestic wheat economy (specifically producers and consumers), then the price relationship to be decomposed is not $P^d = P^w \times X \times (1+s)$ because the export subsidy doesn't affect P^d. Yet, it seems unlikely that a change in stocks would have no effect on current domestic prices and thereby production and consumption. Therefore, we have assumed that the export subsidy affects the domestic wheat market in the conventional manner[3] though this assumption might be exaggerating the policy effect on P^d.

In order to decompose the variability in producer's price, the first step is to compute the price transmission elasticity (PTE), which is nothing but the actual percentage change in the domestic price (P^d) divided by the percentage change in landed price {$P^w X (1+s)$}, where P^w denotes the world reference price expressed in foreign currency. The value of PTE for the period 2001–04 was 30 per cent. After incorporating the value of PTE into the model, the analysis results are presented in Table 7.1. As one can see, in terms of direct price effect, change in trade prices and the exchange rate had an aggregate price effect of increasing domestic price (P^d) by 22 per cent, where increases in P^w and X contribute an increase of 18 per cent and four per cent, respectively. Apart from having direct price effects, these variables have implicit trade policy (i.e., export subsidy) effects as well, while interacting with each other. For instance, increase in P^w and X has an implicit export subsidy policy effect of

---

[3] The budgetary support in the form of export subsidy could have the conventional effect one would expect — that is, they raise domestic producer and consumer prices above the border price (expressed in domestic currency) and, thereby, increase production, decrease consumption, and generate exports.

Table 7.1: Decomposing change in Indian wheat price, 2001–04 (in nominal terms)

Variable (V)	% Change in V	Contribution of % Change in V to % Change in Pd				
		$e + k = 1$			$-k$	Net Effect
		Direct Price Effect	Policy (Subsidy) Effect	Complete Transmission Effect	Incomplete Transmission Effect	e
Wheat, 2001–04; Value of PTE = 30%						
P^w	34	18	14	32	–22	10
X	07	04	03	07	–05	02
s	–29	NA	–17	–17	12	–05
P^d	07	22	–	22	–15	07

Source: Computed by author.

Note: 'NA' means not applicable; '–' means insignificant.

increasing P^d by 14 per cent and three per cent, respectively. Export subsidy policy also has its own explicit policy effect of decreasing P^d by 17 per cent. Therefore, the aggregate export subsidy policy effect (implicit + explicit) on P^d is insignificantly small. The combined effect of these two, i.e., direct price effect plus export subsidy policy effect, is to increase P^d by 22 per cent, if there is full transmission of domestic landed price.

As we have seen, the value of PTE was only 30 per cent, which means that around 70 per cent of effect of change in variables on P^d could not materialise. Therefore, in the presence of incomplete transmission, the change in P^d will always be less then what it would be with complete transmission. The column (–k) measures such effects of incomplete transmission on domestic price (P^d) arising from changes in variables while interacting with incomplete transmission. Because of incomplete transmission, the failure of P^d to increase to its maximum potential due to the increase in P^w, X and s has the attributable effect of reducing P^d by 22 per cent, 5 per cent and 12 per cent, respectively. Therefore, the aggregate effect of the increase in P^w, X and s combining with incomplete transmission is to reduce P^d by 15 per cent.

The column 'e' gives the net effect of changes in P^w, X and s on P^d. The results show that the net effect of the increase in P^w and X and s is to raise P^d by 10 per cent and 2 per cent, whereas, the net effect of decline of s is to reduce P^d by 5 per cent. Therefore, the total net effect is to raise P^d by 7 per cent.

To summarise, the decomposition result shows that incomplete transmission has precluded much of the potential price changes. The policy response to low world prices of providing an export subsidy has cancelled out much of the increase in P^d resulting from rising world prices.

7.2.2 Decomposing Changes in Rice Producer's Price: Exportable Scenario

The comparison of domestic and world reference prices in Chapter 6 showed that the world reference price for rice fell sharply after 1996 and the price advantage of Indian rice exports got completely eroded by 2000, when world prices started ruling below the domestic prices. The period also corresponded with a widening gap between domestic supply and consumption, with domestic supply ruling at a much higher level than the consumption requirement and led to the accumulation of rice stocks with the public agencies on the domestic front. Consequently, in the year 2000, a scheme for the sale of rice for export purposes from the central pool was undertaken to liquidate the excess stocks. In 2000, India began to provide budgetary subsidies to support exports of surplus rice when a combination of declining world prices and higher domestic prices made Indian rice uncompetitive in world markets.

The period 2001 to 2003 was chosen to decompose the change in domestic producer price of rice because it covers the period during which domestic prices were 37–40 per cent higher than the level of world reference prices indicating price disadvantages for rice export. The period also witnessed an increase in India's rice export from the level of 1.53 million tonnes in 2001 to 4.97 million tonnes in 2003, with an increase in budgetary support in the form of export subsidy from the level of 35.74 per cent to 45.49 per cent of value of rice export during the period. The decomposition of domestic price was done with the key variables in the model being trade prices, the exchange rate, and export subsidy, with the assumption that the export subsidy affects the domestic rice market in the conventional manner as it was in the case of wheat.

The price transmission elasticity (PTE) between domestic price (P^d) and landed price $\{P^w\,X\,(1+s)\}$, for the period 2001–03 was 51 per cent. After incorporating the value of PTE into the model, the analysis results are presented in Table 7.2. As presented in the table, in terms of direct price effect, change in trade prices and exchange rate has an aggregate price effect of increasing P^d by 7 per cent, where increase in P^w and X contributes to an increase of 4 per cent and 3 per cent, respectively. Apart from having direct price effect, these variables have implicit trade policy (i.e., export subsidy policy) effects as well, while interacting with each other. For instance, increase in P^w and X has an implicit export subsidy policy effect of increasing P^d by 1 per cent by each. The export subsidy policy also has its own explicit policy effect of increasing P^d by 7 per cent. Therefore, the aggregate export subsidy policy effect (implicit + explicit) is to increase P^d by 9 per cent. The combined effect of these two, i.e., direct price effect plus export subsidy policy effect, is to increase P^d by 16 per cent, if there is full transmission of domestic landed price.

As mentioned earlier, the value of PTE was only 51 per cent, which means that around 49 per cent of effect of change in variables on P^d could not materialise. Therefore, in presence of incomplete

Table 7.2: Decomposing change in Indian rice price, 2001–03 (in nominal terms)

		Contribution of % Change in V to % Change in Pd				
			e + k = 1		*–k*	*Net Effect*
Variable (V)	% Change in V	Direct Price Effect	Policy (Subsidy) Effect	Complete Transmission Effect	Incomplete Transmission Effect	*e*
Rice, 2001–03; Value of PTE = 51%						
P^w	5	4	3	5	–3	2
X	3	3	1	4	–2	2
s	25	NA	7	7	–3	4
P^d	8	7	9	16	–8	8

Source: Computed by author.

Note: 'NA' means not applicable.

transmission, the change in P^d will always be less than what it would be with complete transmission. The column -k measures such effects of incomplete transmission on domestic price (P^d), arising from changes in variables while interacting with incomplete transmission. Because of incomplete transmission, the failure of P^d to increase its maximum potential due to increase in P^w, X and s has the attributable effect of reducing P^d by 3 per cent, 2 per cent and 3 per cent, respectively. Therefore, the aggregate effect of the increase in P^w, X and s combining with incomplete transmission is to reduce P^d by 8 per cent.

The column 'e' gives the net effect of changes in P^w, X and s on P^d. The results show that the net effect of the increase in P^w, X and s is to raise P^d by 2 per cent, 2 per cent and 4 per cent, respectively. Therefore, the total net effect is to raise P^d by 8 per cent.

To sum up, the decomposition result shows that the policy response to lower world prices during the period by raising export subsidy has contributed to 50 per cent of change in domestic prices despite the fact that the low transmission negates much of the potential price changes arising from increase in export subsidy.

7.2.3 Decomposition of Changes in Indian Edible Oil Prices: Importable Scenario

The period selected to decompose the changes in domestic prices of edible oils corresponds to the post-WTO period, when world prices of edible oils were on a downward trend and reached their minimum level. For example, in the case of groundnut oil, the period 1997 to 2002 witnessed a decline of 29 per cent in world reference prices, whereas in the case of rapeseed and soybean oil, the world reference price witnessed a decline of 36 per cent and 41 per cent respectively during the period 1998 and 2001. These periods also witnessed a sharp increase in Indian import tariff rates, in response to low world prices. For instance, the applied tariff duty rates on imported rapeseed oil was increased by 240 per cent (from 25 per cent to 85 per cent) between 1997 and 2002, whereas in the case of rapeseed and soybean oil, it increased by 76 per cent (from 25 per cent to 44 per cent) and 110 per cent (from 23 per cent to 47 per cent), respectively.

The decomposition analysis begins with calculating the price transmission elasticity between domestic price (P^d) and the landed price $\{P^w X(1+t)\}$, where P^w denotes the world reference price expressed in foreign currency. The value of PTE for groundnut and rapeseed oil shows a poor transmission of price signals between landed and domestic price (Table 7.3), whereas in the case of soybean oil, the value of PTE was more than 1, which reveals that, because of either policies or poor market conditions, there was little or no relationship between the border and domestic prices, or if there is some relationship, other factors dominate it.

After incorporating the values of PTE into the model, the analysis results for groundnut, rapeseed/mustard and soybean oils are presented in Table 7.3. The actual percentage change in P^d and the variables that determine P^d are presented in the column under 'percentage change in V'. The next two columns measure the degree to which changes in these variables change P^d, under the assumption of full transmission of changes in landed price to domestic price. For example, in the case of groundnut oil, in terms of direct price effect, changes in trade prices and the exchange rate have an aggregate price effect of decreasing P^d by 3 per cent, where drop in P^w decreases P^d by 27 per cent and rise in X increases P^d by 24 per cent.

Apart from having direct price effect, these variables have implicit policy effect on P^d, while interacting with tariff. The column under 'tariff policy effect' measures such effects. For instance, in groundnut oil, the drop in P^w has an implicit policy effect of decreasing P^d by 15 per cent and the rise in X has an effect of increasing P^d by 13 per cent. Tariff policy also has its own explicit policy effect of increasing P^d by 48 per cent. Therefore, the aggregate policy (tariff) effect (implicit + explicit) is to increase P^d by 46 per cent. The combined effect of these two — i.e., direct price effect plus tariff policy effect — is to increase P^d by 43 per cent, if there is full transmission of changes in landed price to domestic price.

In the presence of incomplete transmission, the change in P^d will always be less than what it would be with complete transmission. The column '−k' measures such effects of incomplete transmission on P^d, arising from changes in variables while interacting with incomplete transmission. In the case of groundnut oil, because of incomplete transmission, the failure of P^d to drop its maximum potential due to decrease in P^w has the attributable effect of increasing P^d by 19 per cent. Likewise, rise in X and t has the attributable effect of decreasing P^d by 17 per cent and 22 per cent, respectively. Therefore, the aggregate effect of changes in P^w, X and t combining with incomplete transmission is to reduce P^d by 20 per cent.

Table 7.3: Decomposition result for changes in Indian edible oil prices (in nominal terms)

| | | | Contribution of % Change in V to % Change in Pd | | | |
| | | | *e + k = 1* | | *-k* | *Net Effect* |
Variable (V)	*% Change in V*	*Direct Price Effect*	*Policy (Tariff) Effect*	*Complete Transmission Effect*	*Incomplete Transmission Effect*	*e*
Groundnut oil, 1997–2002; Value of PTE = 55%						
p^w	-29	-27	-15	-42	19	-23
X	35	24	13	37	-17	20
t	240	NA	48	48	-22	26
p^d	23	-3	46	43	-20	23
Rapeseed/mustard oil, 1998–2001; Value of PTE = 35%						
p^w	-36	-33	-11	-44	29	-15
X	23	15	05	20	-13	07
t	76	NA	14	14	-09	05
p^d	-03	-18	08	-10	07	-03
Soybean oil, 1998–2001; Value of PTE = 144%						
p^w	-41	-36	-13	-49	-22	-71
X	17	11	04	15	06	21
t	110	NA	17	17	08	25
p^d	-25	-25	08	-17	-08	-25

Source: Computed by author.
Note: 'NA' means not applicable.

The column 'e' gives the net effect of changes in P^w, X and t on P^d and is equal to the sum of the values in the complete and incomplete transmission effect columns. In the case of groundnut oil, the net attributable effect of changes in P^w, X and t on P^d is -23 per cent, 20 per cent and 26 per cent, respectively. Therefore, the total net effect is to raise P^d by 23 per cent.

In the case of rapeseed oil, the net effect of changes in P^w, X and t on P^d shows that the fall in P^w has the net attributable effect to decrease P^d by 15 per cent, the rise in X has the net attributable effect to increase P^d by 7 per cent, while the net attributable effect of the rise in t is to increase P^d by 5 per cent. The aggregate net effect is to decrease P^d by 3 per cent.

In the case of soybean oil, the column 'e' shows that the net attributable effect of the drop in P^w is to decrease P^d by 71 per cent, the net attributable effect of the rise in X is to increase P^d by 21 per cent, while the net attributable effect of the rise in t is to increase P^d by 25 per cent. The aggregate net effect is to decrease P^d by 25 per cent.

To sum up, the results of the decomposition analysis of domestic edible oil prices reveals the following facts: first, there was a fair amount of movement in world prices and the exchange rate for these commodities over the periods in question. However, currency depreciation and rising import tariff cancelled out much of the downward effect on P^d from falling world prices, such as in the case of rapeseed/mustard and soybean oil; second, the policy response to falling world prices of raising import tariffs also had a strong impact on prices, such that for groundnut oil the combined effects of the policy response and currency depreciation results in net price increases of 23 per cent in domestic price; and lastly, with the exception of soybean oil, low transmission precluded much of the potential price changes.

7.2.4 Decomposing Changes in Domestic Price of Sugar: Importable Scenario

The period selected to decompose the change in domestic sugar price corresponds to the post-WTO period when world sugar prices were on downward trend and reached their minimum level. As seen in Chapter 6, the world reference price for sugar fell sharply after 1996 and reached their minimum in the year 2000. The period also witnessed a sharp increase in Indian import tariff rates in response to low world prices. For instance, during the year 1998 when world sugar prices were on a downward trend, the government started increasing applied tariff duty rates on imported sugar, and between April 1998 and February 2000, tariffs were increased in steps from zero to 40 per cent. Since 1997, India started importing sugar every year up to the year 1999.

The price transmission elasticity between domestic price (P^d) and the landed price $\{P^w X(1+t)\}$, where P^w denotes the world reference price expressed in foreign currency, shows a poor transmission of price signals, i.e., 34 per cent between landed and domestic price. After incorporating the value of PTE into the model, the analysis results are presented in Table 7.4. As presented in the table, in terms of direct price effect, changes in trade prices and the exchange rate have an aggregate price effect of decreasing P^d by 13 per cent, the drop in P^w decreases P^d by 22 per cent and rise in X increases P^d by 9 per cent. Apart from having direct price effects, these variables have an implicit policy effect on P^d while interacting with tariffs. The column under 'tariff policy effect' measures such effects. For instance, drop in P^w has implicit policy effect of decreasing P^d by 5 per cent, and rise in X has an effect of increasing P^d by 2 per cent. The tariff policy also has its own explicit policy effect of increasing P^d by 32 per cent. Therefore, the aggregate policy (tariff) effect (implicit + explicit) is to increase P^d by 29 per cent. Under the assumption of full transmission of changes in landed price to domestic price, the combined effect of these two — i.e., direct price effect plus tariff policy effect — is to increase P^d by 16 per cent.

As mentioned earlier, the value of PTE was only 34 per cent, which means that around two-thirds of the effect of change in variables on P^d could not materialise. Therefore, in the presence of incomplete transmission, the change in P^d will always be less than what it would be with complete transmission. The column '$-k$' measures such effects of incomplete transmission on the domestic price, arising from changes in variables while interacting with incomplete transmission. Because of incomplete transmission, the failure of P^d to drop its maximum potential due to decrease in P^w has the attributable effect of increasing P^d by 18 per cent. Likewise, rise in X and t has the attributable effect of decreasing P^d by 7 per cent and 21 per cent, respectively. Therefore, the aggregate effect of changes in P^w, X and t combining with incomplete transmission is to reduce P^d by 10 per cent.

The column 'e' gives the net effect of changes in P^w, X and t on P^d and is equal to the sum of the values in the complete and incomplete transmission effect columns. The net attributable effect of changes in

Table 7.4: Decomposition result for changes in Indian sugar price, 1998–2000 (in nominal terms)

| Variable (V) | % Change in V | Contribution of % Change in V to % Change in Pd | | | | Net Effect |
| | | e + k = 1 | | | −k | |
		Direct Price Effect	Policy (Tariff) Effect	Complete Transmission Effect	Incomplete Transmission Effect	e
Sugar, 1998–2000; Value of PTE = 34%						
p^w	−22	−22	−5	−27	18	−9
X	10	9	2	11	−7	4
t	1200	NA	32	32	−21	11
p^d	6	−13	29	16	−10	6

Source: Computed by author.
Note: 'NA' means not applicable.

P^u, X and t on P^d is -9 per cent, 4 per cent and 11 per cent, respectively. Therefore, the total net effect is to raise P^d by 6 per cent.

Therefore, the result of decomposition analysis of domestic sugar price shows that there was poor transmission of movement in world prices and the exchange rate over the periods in question. The policy response to low world prices by raising import tariffs has cancelled out much of the downward effect on P^d from falling world prices. The combined effect of policy response and currency depreciation resulted in net increases of 6 per cent in domestic price.

7.3 Conclusion

The decomposition analysis of changes in domestic prices of major agricultural commodities into the effects of trade prices, the exchange rate and agricultural trade policies highlights the fact that in a majority of the cases, poor transmission of changes in trade prices and exchange rates on domestic prices has precluded much of the potential price changes. The value of price transmission elasticity between domestic price and the landed price varied between 30 to 50 per cent in a majority of the cases over the periods in question. The trade policy response to low world price, either by raising import tariffs or by providing export subsidies, has cancelled out much of the downward effect on domestic prices from falling world prices. The incomplete transmission of changes in trade prices and exchange rates to domestic prices results from both government policies as well as an underdeveloped market infrastructure. Domestic price support policies, such as stock policy and price floors, along with frequent use of non-tariff barriers like export restrictions, import licensing, state trading corporation, and so on, to ensure sufficient domestic supply and maintaining stability in domestic prices, has weakened the link between trade prices and exchange rate on domestic price.

8

Evaluation and Conclusion

In Indian agriculture, which continues to provide livelihood to more than half of the population, price policy plays an important role in achieving growth and equity. The green revolution of the 1960s and 1970s, which helped in overcoming a 'ship-to-mouth' existence and achieving self-sufficiency in production, was built on a platform of state support — these included price, subsidy, credit, and marketing supports. The interventionist role of the state in the 1970s and 1980s led to the creation of a network of institutional support structures in rural areas. However, the initiation of economic reforms in India in 1991 brought about major changes in the macroeconomic policy framework of the planned economy that existed in India during 1950–51 to 1990–91. Although no direct reference was made to agriculture, it was argued that the new macroeconomic policy framework would benefit tradable agriculture by ending discrimination against it and by turning the terms of trade in its favour. The package of reforms in agriculture was based on the diagnosis that while the sector remained net disprotected, the subsidies arising out of the inappropriate pricing of the inputs and outputs led to the inefficient use of resources and eroded the capacity of the government to finance public investment in the agricultural sector. For correcting these so-called distortions, the reform package revolved around setting prices right and included the withdrawal of subsidies on inputs, targeting the public distribution system to only the poor, abolition of the food management system and its attendant costs, and the liberalisation of the trade in agricultural commodities. As a result, the post-reform period witnessed a dilution of the supportive mechanisms that were built up, in stages, in the post-Independence period to protect the farmers from the uncertainties of the market. However, contrary to expectations and anticipation, the agricultural sector in India neither experienced any significant growth subsequent to the initiation of economic reforms in 1991 nor did it derive the expected benefits from trade liberalisation. As a matter of fact, when compared with the decade just before liberalisation, agricultural growth in India recorded a visible deceleration during the post-liberalisation period. This happened at a time when the rest of the economy was growing at an unprecedented rate. In this context, the analysis in the book was an attempt to examine the observed slowdown in Indian agricultural growth with a view to assessing the effect of the market-based reform project.

The specific objectives of our studies were as follows:

(*i*) To analyse the agricultural growth performance and document the movement of the factors that have been recognised as being the determinants of agricultural growth with a view to identifying the proximate causes of the slowdown.

(*ii*) To document and analyse the impact of the past and the current agriculture price policy on farm profitability with a view to identifying the causes of the slowdown in agricultural production.

(*iii*) To analyse the potential consequences of the behaviour of international prices in terms of their level and variability on domestic agriculture with a view to their possible role in determining the trajectory of agricultural growth since 1991.

(*iv*) To analyse whether the observed variability in domestic prices was shaped by the incomplete transmission of the price signals to domestic prices due to government intervention in agriculture or whether government intervention helped lower the variability in domestic prices.

The major findings of the analysis are summarised and some inferences having bearing on agricultural policy are discussed here.

The analysis of the growth of agricultural output over the last 25 years highlights the fact that the decade of the 1980s witnessed an unprecedented annual growth rate of crop output with a significant change in the cropping pattern away from coarse cereals towards more valuable oilseed crops. An interesting feature of the 1980s was that agricultural growth permeated to all agricultural commodity groups in India. The spread of new agricultural technology to other regions and crops resulted in a notable increase in the levels and growth rates of yields and output during the 1980s. But the post-reform period was characterised by a serious retrogression in both the levels and growth rates of yields and output in almost all crops/ crop groups and a slowdown in diversification towards oilseeds.

The disquieting aspect of the post-reform growth process was that the agricultural and non-agricultural sectors were on a disparate growth path. There are different reasons for slowdown of growth of yield and output. The analysis of factors related to agricultural growth during the period 1980–81 to 2005–06 shows that both price and non-price factors played a positive role in determining agricultural output. However, in comparison to price factors, non-price factors played a dominant role in influencing output growth at the all-India level. The analysis shows that a slowdown/stagnation or even decline in growth of fertiliser use, irrigation and net sown area, and a decline in the capital stock in agriculture have had an adverse impact on agricultural growth during the post-reform period. The predicted positive impact of trade liberalisation on agriculture's terms of trade could not materialise. Also, no unidirectional link between agricultural growth and relative prices was observed, indicating that there was no significant relationship between these two. The evidence of price shifts is too marginal to account for the observed slowing of growth during the post-reform period.

Historically, agricultural price policy evolved to take care of any undue rise in prices, while maintaining a balance between the interests of consumers and producers. Nevertheless, the limits of price policy in achieving these goals were recognised by the government and as a result other non-price interventions were used primarily for the purpose. While a large public distribution system network ensured access to cheap food to the needy, with appropriate levels of subsidy from time to time, a slew of policy initiatives were put in place to make farming profitable enough to induce investment in technology for improving productivity per unit of land. The policy aimed at encouraging higher production and the resultant food produce was to be made available at lower prices. The higher emphasis and reliance on price policy in the 1990s and relative exclusion of non-price interventions in the form of public investment shifted the earlier policy regime of 'low-input and low-output' to a 'high-input and high-output' price policy regime. Public investments on irrigation, research, extension, and other related infrastructure went down from 3.4 per cent of agricultural GDP in the early 1980s to 1.9 per cent during 2001–03. On the other hand, private investment, while increasing initially, stopped flowing by the late 1990s due to the operation of complementarity between public and private investments. Technology development, dissemination and adoption received a major setback due to this.

As a part of the reform strategy, the government not only slashed the subsidies on major inputs in order to discourage environmentally unsustainable practices but also absolved itself of the responsibility to produce or procure and distribute these inputs at farm gates. As a result of this policy shift, growth rates in yields have gone down and eventually costs of production started rising. The cost of production in nominal terms in the case of both rice and wheat, during the one and a half decades of the reform period, increased three times faster than in the 1980s. Increasing costs of production along with a desire to link domestic prices with international prices with the aim of integrating the domestic economy with the global economy necessitated higher support prices. The trend analysis of MSPs shows this phenomenon clearly. There has been a systematic attempt to cover cost of production, and in the case of wheat and paddy, procurement prices have remained well above the cost of production. The agricultural price policy, on an average, has been largely successful in playing a major role in regard to providing reasonable levels of margins over total costs to the farmers of both rice and wheat. Nonetheless, the margin over total cost and variable cost has declined since the late 1990s in the case of both wheat and rice. Both the level of the margin and the net income in absolute terms has declined since the late-1990s in the case of both wheat and rice. The net income from the cultivation of wheat witnessed a sharp decline from the level of ₹6,161 per hectare to ₹3,215 per hectare during the period between 1999–2000 and 2004–05, whereas in the case of rice, it started declining from the level of ₹3,513 per hectare in 1998–99 and reached an insignificant level in 2002–03 leading to distress for cultivators. The decline in profitability has discouraged the farmers from increasing spending on yield augmenting technology, which resulted in poor yield growth rates and, in turn, a decline in production growth rates.

The economic reform initiated in the year 1991 gave a big boost to agricultural export. The main factor for this impressive export growth was that international prices of several agricultural commodities were well above the domestic prices and liberalisation provided the opportunity to exploit this advantage. The achievements in agricultural exports led to the belief among academicians and policy makers that Indian agriculture was highly export competitive and generated a favourable environment for freeing agricultural trade. This happened at the time when the URAA was being finalised. It was anticipated that implementation of the new agreement would benefit Indian agriculture. Consequently, the decade of the 1990s witnessed increased integration of the domestic agricultural economy with the world economy by switching to a more liberal and open trade regime. And the liberalisation of the agricultural trade was put forward as an important step towards imparting efficiency to Indian agriculture. However, this has brought new challenges for Indian agriculture as well, where the behaviour of international prices has assumed greater significance for domestic food prices and production than before. For example, a decline in international prices implies relatively cheaper imports, and if the domestic prices are higher than the imported commodity's prices, it would result in more imports into the domestic market. An increase in imports enhances supplies, and for agricultural commodities — the prices of which are determined by supply and demand — may be expected to lower the price relative to the counterfactual equilibrium and can damage domestic agriculture production by making it unprofitable. The analysis of the behaviour of international market prices of agricultural commodities clearly shows that a country like India cannot afford to excessively rely on the international market; doing so would make domestic agriculture vulnerable to the developments in and policies of the major exporting countries. Though the world demand and supply situation determines the movements in world prices, however, the output and stockholding policies of major exporting countries still holds large implications for world price movement and stability. To elaborate, in the case of rice, just after the Asian crisis, the international price of rice started declining. Low demand from some big importers of rice from Asia and Latin America was one of the reasons behind this decline. On the supply side, India and China's entry as exporters in the international rice market and domestic policies undertaken by developed countries increased the supply–demand gap. The consequent decline in international prices of rice was accentuated by heavy subsidisation of rice farmers in the US. The increased direct support to US rice producers by way of counter-cyclical payments to absorb the shock of low prices and maintain their high trading volumes resulted in oversupply of rice in the international market and exacerbated the decline in international rice prices.

The increased alignment of domestic prices with world prices also has a potential consequence that can damage agricultural growth independent of its influence on the level of domestic prices, as it can increase the volatility of domestic prices. However, the analysis of price volatility points to lower inter-year variability in domestic market prices compared to international market prices. On the other hand, the higher intra-year variability in domestic markets (except sugar) than in the international markets highlights the fact that Indian market prices are more prone to within-the-year fluctuations. The decadal analysis of intra-year variability shows that domestic market prices have witnessed a continuous decline in volatility. The only exception to this was groundnut seed and oil where volatility has increased slightly during the most recent sub-period. In contrast to domestic markets, international market prices showed cyclical movement in intra-year volatility. The decade of the 1990s turned out to be a relatively stable period compared to the 1980s in the case of international market prices for most of the commodities except for rice and wheat. After the 1990s, international market prices again witnessed an increase in volatility with the exception of rice and wheat where volatility has declined relative to the decade of the 1990s. The results from the GARCH model confirm the results obtained by using the standard deviation method and shows similar patterns of intra-year variability across commodities as observed using the standard deviation method. Therefore, the analysis does not provide much ground for granting price volatility a significant role in determining the trajectory of agricultural growth by making it more risky because of continuous decline in within-the-year fluctuations in domestic market prices.

Nonetheless, in sharp contrast to the initial years of liberalisation, which were highly favourable for growth of agricultural exports, the post-WTO years turned out to be highly adverse for India's agricultural exports. However, there were considerable variations in export performance of various commodities. For example, with the liberalisation of export of non-basmati rice, its export picked up during the post-WTO period with a lot of stock being released for export. The commodities which explain the fall in agricultural exports during the post-WTO period include oilmeal, cotton, sugar, tobacco, and pulses. Poor export performance during the period was the upshot of a sharp fall in international prices. In the case of India's traditional export items, their export growth slowed down during the post-WTO period. The situation started improving since 2001 with recovery in world prices; as a result, agricultural exports started growing. Among imports, edible oils have shown very high growth in the post-WTO period, followed by pulses. Thus, agricultural imports are concentrated in these two commodities, where domestic production has not kept pace with the demand.

Our analysis of trade competitiveness of major agricultural commodities also highlights the fact that the competitiveness of commodities has undergone significant changes during the study period. This shows that trade competitiveness is a dynamic phenomenon that depends upon changes in international and domestic prices. Under the exportable hypothesis, India has been export competitive in rice since 1981, except during the period when international prices have experienced unusual declines (1985–87 and 2000–04). On the other hand, there does not seem to be much advantage in exporting wheat, as India was export competitive only for short spells (1990 and 1996–97) when world prices were at their peak. In the case of sugar, India was probably export competitive during the period 1989 to 1997 (as the ratio of domestic to world price was close to 1). After 1997, given the significant levels of distortions in the international market due to domestic and export subsidisation by the EC and high protection and support in the US market, Indian sugar exports became uncompetitive in the international market. However, commodities belonging to the group of oilseeds, namely groundnut and rapeseed/mustard, appear to be efficient import substitutes since the early 1990s, whereas soybean seed has been found to be import substitutable throughout the period under study (except for a short spell during 1987 and 1988). Compared to oilseeds, edible oil producers were uncompetitive as producers of import substitutes. In the case of cereals, under the importable hypothesis, wheat has been largely competitive, with ratios of domestic to international prices below unity throughout the period under study.

Moreover, the divergence between the domestic and world prices, which ideally captures the space for policy interventions, shows that trade policy instruments — import tariffs/export subsidies — during the post-WTO period, especially applied tariff rates, were adequate to bridge the price wedge observed between domestic and world reference prices. On the other hand, export subsidy rates were enough to maintain the competitiveness of Indian producers in international markets at the time of unusual decline in world prices, for example, of rice and wheat.

Therefore, what emerges from our analysis is that the government intervention has been quite effective in insulating domestic producers from low world prices as well as from the effect of instability in international prices during the post-reform period. As our study clearly brings out, although during the post-reform period a trade policy regime which is more open was being put in place, the approach with respect to agriculture has remained gradual and cautious. While trade restrictions on agricultural products were left mostly untouched in the 1991 reforms, subsequent trade policy changes gradually lifted most of the restrictions on both exports and imports of agricultural products. With the removal of restrictions on imports and exports, trade policy instruments were adjusted from time to time, which helped in ensuring sufficient domestic supply of key products and kept the volatility in domestic prices at relatively low levels compared to earlier decades. An example is the exemption (zero duty) granted for imports of wheat in 2006 to replenish local grain stocks mainly for the public distribution system; the standard tariff rate is currently 50 per cent. Import licences were also issued to support this policy; for example, in 2006, imports of wheat, normally restricted to state trading, were also permitted by private importers. Similarly, in the case of exports, as the vast majority of agricultural exports are unrestricted, the government made notifications from time to time to restrict exports or lift export restrictions in order to maintain domestic supplies and stability in domestic prices. For example, in 2006, export of sugar was prohibited to maintain domestic supplies in order to keep the price at a 'reasonable level'; whereas in the case of wheat, following a sharp fall in the government's annual food grain procurement because of good open market prices and lower production, India banned exports of wheat and wheat products in April 2007.

The analysis decomposing changes in domestic prices of major agricultural commodities also substantiates our argument regarding the role played by the government in insulating domestic producers. The decomposition of changes in domestic prices of major agricultural commodities into the effects of trade prices, the exchange rate and agricultural trade policies highlights the fact that in a majority of the cases, poor transmission of changes in trade prices and exchange rate on domestic prices has precluded much of the potential price changes. The value of price transmission elasticity between domestic price and the landed price varied between 30 to 50 per cent in a majority of the cases over the periods in question. The trade policy response to low world price, either by raising import tariffs or by providing export subsidies, has cancelled out much of the downward effect on domestic prices from falling world prices. The incomplete transmission of changes in trade prices and exchange rates to domestic prices results from both government policies as well as underdeveloped market infrastructure. Domestic price support policies, such as stock policy and price floors, along with frequent use of non-tariff barriers like export restrictions, import licensing, state trading corporation and so on, to ensure sufficient domestic supply and maintain stability in domestic prices, has weakened the link between trade prices and exchange rate, on the one hand, and the domestic price, on the other.

To conclude, higher emphasis has to be placed on non-price interventions through public investments to supplement price policy measures. This can help in increasing yields and reducing the exclusive reliance on prices for farm profitability. The behaviour of international prices in terms of level and fluctuations shows that output and stockholding policies of major exporters have a crucial bearing on the world prices. Therefore, a country like India cannot afford to excessively rely on the international market. This implies that unregulated and freer trade would impart instability to domestic prices and there is a strong case to regulate trade to maintain domestic price stability.

Appendix I
Methodology for Measuring Price Volatility

The basic framework that was followed to quantify the volatility in the price series by using the GARCH model is presented as a flowchart in Figure A-1.

Figure A-1: Flowchart of methodology to compute conditional volatility

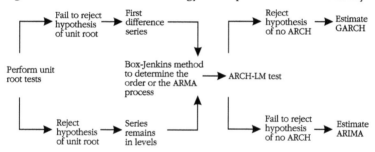

Source: Moledina, Roe and Shane (2003).

Before testing for stationarity of the time series using the unit root test, the predictable components (such as the effects of inflation, trend and seasonality) of the price process should be removed leaving only the unpredictable or stochastic component for further analysis (Moledina, Roe and Shane 2003). The steps that were followed in order to remove the predictable components from the data process are as follows:

First, in the analysis, the effect of inflation was removed by deflating the nominal prices with the consumer price index (CPI for industrial workers with base 2000 = 100).[1] Second, the seasonality component from the series was removed by using seasonal dummy variables. And for that purpose, 11 seasonal dummy variables were included for the 12 months in a year.[2]

---

[1] The CPI for industrial workers of India was used to deflate the domestic prices, while international prices were deflated by using the CPI of the United States. (Source: IFS, IMF data CD, April 2007)

[2] The reason for including only 11 dummy variables is to avoid falling into the dummy variable trap, which is a situation of perfect collinearity.

The 12th month was used as the base category to which the effects of the different months were compared. Since the month chosen as the base category month does not influence the overall explanatory power of the estimated model, therefore, the month used as base category was chosen arbitrarily. To check the presence of seasonality, the null hypothesis to be tested is that the coefficients of all dummy variables in the equation are equal. If they are equal, there are no seasonal effects, and vice versa. If the seasonality was found, the residual of the regression was used as the de-seasonalised prices data in further analysis.

Third, in order to remove the trend component from the data process, the Dicky–Fuller test and augmented Dicky–Fuller tests were carried out to determine whether data contains a trend and whether the trend is deterministic or stochastic. The usual methods for eliminating the trends are differencing and detrending. If the data process contains a stochastic trend (i.e., difference stationary series), then we use the differencing method to remove the trend, or if it was deterministic (i.e., trend stationary series), then we use the detrending method.

Fourth, after performing the unit root tests and testing for the presence of trend and drift terms, the Box–Jenkins approach, along with the Akaike and Schwartz information criteria, was applied to the differenced (respectively, undifferenced) series to select the values of p and q in the ARIMA(p,d,q) process (Box and Jenkins 1976).

The ARIMA process is represented by the following equation (ibid.):

$$y_t = \alpha_0 + \sum_{p}^{p\,max} \phi_p y_{(t-p)} + \sum_{q}^{q\,max} \theta_q \varepsilon_{(t-q)} + \sum_{n}^{n\,max} \eta_n d_t \tag{1}$$

Theoretically, the point where the highest value of either the Akaike information criterion (AIC) or the Schwarz-Bayes Criterion (SBC) lies is seen to determine the values of p and q. The standard error of regression (1) is taken as the measure of unconditional volatility.

The next step is to test whether or not the volatility is time varying through the identification of significant ARCH effect by performing ARCH-LM test suggested by Engle (1982). For those series that reject the null hypothesis of no ARCH effect, we estimate the GARCH model.

The univariate GARCH (1, 1) model is presented as

$$\sigma_t^2 = \gamma_0 + \gamma_1 \varepsilon_{(t-1)}^2 + \gamma_2 \sigma_{(t-1)}^2$$

where σt^2 is the variance of ε conditional upon information up to period t.

When using the GARCH approach, the conditional standard deviation is the measure of volatility, and is given by the square root of each of the fitted values of σt^2. Unlike the volatility in the absence of ARCH effect, the conditional standard deviation varies over time which makes it impossible to present in a single value. Therefore, we have taken the *median of the conditional volatility* in order to compare the conditional volatility with unconditional volatility. The standard error of equation (1) and median of the conditional volatility over the whole time series was used to show the long-run volatility, whereas the medians of the conditional standard deviations of the prices with varying volatility for each of the years was used as short-run volatility.

Appendix II
The Decomposition Model

The model used to decompose the variability in prices was adopted from William Liefert (2007, 2011). In this model, domestic price is assumed to be function of trade prices, exchange rate and agricultural trade policies, and mathematically can be expressed as:

$$P^d = f(P^w; X; t)$$

Where, P^d is domestic agriculture price, P^w is trade prices, i.e., world prices of agricultural commodities adjusted for transportation and other incidental cost and expressed in foreign currency, X is the market exchange rate between domestic and foreign currency and t represents the tariff rate. The derivation of the decomposition model begins with;

$$P_t^d = P_t^d$$

Where, P_t^d is the country's domestic price for a commodity in time t

$$\text{Multiplying RHS by } 1 = \left\{ \frac{P_t^w X_t (1+t)}{P_t^w X_t (1+t)} \right\}^1$$

where

X_t = market exchange rate between domestic and foreign currency in time t.

$[P_t^w X_t (1+t)]$ = Duty included landed price and gives the value of the imported good immediately after it clears customs, and thereby equals the CIF (Cost, Insurance and Freight) value plus the tariff.

$$P_t^d = P_t^d \left\{ \frac{P_t^w X (1+t)}{P_t^w X (1+t)} \right\} \tag{1}$$

---

[1] When tariff is a fixed per unit tax, then one should multiply $\dot{P}^d$ on the right side by $1 = \left\{ \dfrac{P_t^w X_t + T}{P_t^w X_t + T} \right\}$, where landed price of good is $[P_t^w X_t + T]$ and T is the per unit tariff.

The next step in the decomposition derivation is to put equation (1) into natural logs and then differentiate with respect to time, which yields the equation

$$\dot{P}^d = \dot{P}^d \left[\frac{\left(\overline{\dot{P^w X(1+t)}} \right)}{\left(\overline{P^w X(1+t)} \right)} \right] \tag{2}$$

Isolating the sub term $\dfrac{\dot{P}^d}{\left(\overline{P^w \times X(1+t)} \right)}$ from the right hand side of equation

(2) gives the price transmission elasticity (PTE) between landed price and domestic price. The price transmission elasticity e is

$$e = \frac{\dot{P}^d}{\left(\overline{P^w \times X \, (1+t)} \right)} \tag{3}$$

This gives

$$\dot{P}^d = e \left(\overline{P^w \times X \, (1+t)} \right) \tag{4}$$

The next step in decomposition is to isolate the effect of incomplete transmission from equation (4),

$$\dot{P}^d = (e+k-k) \left(\overline{P^w \, X(1+t)} \right) \tag{5}$$

$$\dot{P}^d = \underbrace{\left(\overline{P^w \, X(1+t)} \right)}_{A} - k \underbrace{\left(\overline{P^w \, X(1+t)} \right)}_{B} \tag{6}$$

where,

$$k = 1 - e, \quad \text{and} \quad e + k = 1 \tag{7}$$

To measure the shares of $\dot{P}_d$, which are caused by, and therefore can be attributed to, $\dot{P}_w$, $\dot{X}$, $\dot{t}$ requires in the final form of the equation that no terms should contain the percentage change of either a sum or product of two or more of these variables. Therefore, one can break the terms A and B

in equation (6) into two additive parts by using the result that 'the percent change of a sum of two numbers equals the sum of the percent change in each number, weighted by each number's share in their sum'. This gives the following equation:

$$\dot{P}^d = \frac{P^w X \overrightarrow{P^w X}}{P^w X (1+t)} + \frac{P^w X t \overrightarrow{P^w X t}}{P^w X (1+t)} - \frac{k P^w X \overrightarrow{P^w X}}{P^w X (1+t)} - \frac{k P^w X t \overrightarrow{P^w X}}{P^w X (1+t)} \qquad (8)$$
$$\quad\quad C \quad\quad\quad\quad D \quad\quad\quad\quad E \quad\quad\quad\quad F$$

By using the OECD (2002) approach, we compute the change in $P^w X \overrightarrow{P^w X}$ attributable to P^w as $P^w \dot{P}^w \dfrac{X_1 + X_2}{2}$, where X_1 and X_2 are the values of X in the beginning and end years of the period of measurement. Likewise, we compute the change in $P^w X \overrightarrow{P^w X}$ attributable to $\dot{X}$ as $X \dot{X} \dfrac{P_1^w + P_2^w}{2}$, where, P_1^w and P_2^w are the values of P^w in the beginning and the end years of measurement. Therefore, the term C of equation (8) will be of the following form:

$$C = \frac{P^w \dot{P}^w (X_1 + X_2)}{2 (P^w X (1+t))} + \frac{X \dot{X} (P_1^w + P_2^w)}{2 (P^w X (1+t))} \qquad (9)$$

It measures the change in P^d from the direct price effect that occurs from ΔP^w and ΔX.

Similarly, the term D of equation (8) will be of the following form:

$$D = \frac{t \dot{t} \left(P_1^w + P_2^w\right)(X_1 + X_2)}{2 \times 2 \times \left(P^w X (1+t)\right)} + \frac{P \dot{P} (t_1 + t_2)(X_1 + X_2)}{2 \times 2 \times \left(P^w X (1+t)\right)} + \frac{X \dot{X} (P_1^w + P_2^w)(t_1 + t_2)}{2 \times 2 \times \left(P^w X (1+t)\right)}$$

The first term in this equation measures the change in P^d from the explicit policy effect, while the last two terms measure the change in P^d from implicit policy effects (resulting from ΔP^w and ΔX interacting with the tariff).

In terms E and F, in equation (8), the sub-terms associated with $\dot{P}^w$, $\dot{X}$ and $\dot{t}$ measure the change in P^d from the incomplete transmission effect, which results from changes in P^w, X and t being only partially transmitted to P^d.

The derivation of the decomposition equation when a country gives export subsidies to boost export of domestic produce is similar to the decomposition equation when tariff is used. For instance, if export subsidy is *ad valorem*, the port price of exported goods is now equal to $\{P^w X (1+S)\}$ or $\{P^w X + S\}$ if the subsidy is fixed per unit.

Appendix III
Tables

Table A-2.1: GDP of agriculture and allied sector and its percentage share in total GDP: 1980–81 to 2005–06 (at current prices)

Year	GDP of Agriculture and Allied sector	GDP Total	% Share of Agriculture GDP to Total GDP
1980–81	47,312	132,520	35.70
1981–82	53,327	155,158	34.37
1982–83	57,496	173,337	33.17
1983–84	68,613	202,750	33.84
1984–85	73,989	227,694	32.49
1985–86	79,294	254,427	31.17
1986–87	85,108	283,681	30.00
1987–88	94,677	321,589	29.44
1988–89	116,925	383,790	30.47
1989–90	129,222	442,134	29.23
1990–91	150,800	515,032	29.28
1991–92	176,166	594,168	29.65
1992–93	197,569	681,517	28.99
1993–94	229,172	792,150	28.93
1994–95	263,895	925,239	28.52
1995–96	286,946	1,083,289	26.49
1996–97	345,020	1,260,710	27.37
1997–98	366,125	1,401,934	26.12
1998–99	420,486	1,616,082	26.02
1999–00	446,515	1,786,525	24.99
2000–01	449,565	1,925,017	23.35
2001–02	486,617	2,097,726	23.20
2002–03	472,060	2,261,415	20.87
2003–04	532,342	2,538,171	20.97
2004–05	552,422	2,877,706	19.20
2005–06	615,845	3,275,670	18.80

Source: National Accounts Statistics, various issues, Central Statistical Organization, Government of India, New Delhi.

Table A-2.2: Index of Terms of Trade (TOT) between agriculture and non-agriculture sector: 1982–83 to 2005–06

Year	Index of Prices Received	Index of Prices Paid (IPP) for			Combined Index	Index to Terms of Trade (ITT)
		Final Consumption	Intermediate Consumption	Capital Formation		
Weight		73.54	21.63	4.83	100	
1982–83	60.3	58.8	91.1	62.6	66.0	91.4
1983–84	64.2	64.2	91.0	67.4	70.1	91.6
1984–85	68.0	66.6	92.3	72.5	72.4	93.9
1985–86	70.4	69.5	94.3	76.4	75.2	93.6
1986–87	76.7	74.8	98.7	78.8	80.2	95.7
1987–88	86.0	84.6	102.3	82.5	88.3	97.4
1988–89	90.3	90.4	96.9	90.9	91.8	98.3
1989–90	97.5	97.6	99.2	100.6	98.1	99.4
1990–91	112.3	112.1	104.0	108.5	110.2	101.9
1991–92	130.8	124.9	119.4	127.2	123.8	105.6
1992–93	138.7	131.5	139.5	137.5	133.5	103.9
1993–94	151.4	143.9	152.9	147.3	146.1	103.6
1994–95	171.1	159.0	166.1	158.4	160.5	106.6
1995–96	182.9	173.4	174.2	176.1	173.7	105.3

1996–97	190.6	185.6	181.5	188.8	184.8	103.1
1997–98	205.9	195.7	192.0	196.7	194.9	105.6
1998–99	220.8	213.8	197.1	206.8	209.9	105.2
1999–2000	219.8	217.1	203.9	212.6	214.0	102.7
2000–01	225.0	220.5	230.4	227.0	223.0	100.9
2001–02	235.3	226.4	235.2	240.4	229.0	102.8
2002–03	247.9	234.9	252.7	245.2	239.3	103.6
2003–04	251.2	245.2	259.1	255.7	248.7	101.0
2004–05	258.2	252.3	264.5	305.6	257.5	100.3
2005–06	275.8	266.0	277.1	310.5	270.6	101.9

Source: Agricultural Statistics at a Glance, various issues, Directorate of Economics and Statistics, Ministry of Agriculture (MoA), Government of India.

Table A-3.1: Levy rates for procurement of rice in India (percentage)

State	Category	1983–84	1991–92	1992–93	1997–98	1999–2000	2004–05	2005–06	2007–08
Andhra Pradesh	Millers/Dealers	50	50	50	50	50	100	75	75
Haryana	Millers/Dealers	75 to 90	75	75	75	75	75	75	75
Madhya Pradesh	Millers				50 / 25 (special mill)	50	30 (raw rice)	30 (raw rice)	30
Orissa	Millers	50	50	50	50	75	75	75	75
Punjab	Millers/Dealers	75 to 90	75	75	75	75	75	75	75
Tamil Nadu	Millers/Dealers	50	50	50	50	50	50	50	50
Uttar Pradesh	Millers/Dealers	60	40	60	40 (East UP) 60 (West UP)	40 (East UP) 60 (West UP)	40 (East UP) 60 (West UP)	60	60 to 75
West Bengal	Millers	40	50	30	30	50	70	50	50

Source: Data for up to 1997–98 figures are from World Bank (1999) report, and thereafter from Annual reports of the Ministry of Consumer Affairs, Department of Food and Public Distribution, Government of India.

Table A-5.1: Total supply and use of wheat in India (quantity in 'ooo tonnes): 1984–85 to 2007–08

	Production	Beginning Stock	Import	Export	Consumption			Ending Stock
					Total	Food	Feed/Seed/Waste	
1984–85	45,480	9,620	564.37	39.51	43,155	37,470	5,685	12,470
1985–86	44,070	12,470	183.14	229.61	46,284	40,775	5,509	10,210
1986–87	47,050	10,210	119.25	221.78	47,717	41,836	5,881	9,440
1987–88	44,320	9,440	21.48	274.97	50,167	44,627	5,540	3,340
1988–89	46,170	3,340	1,792.40	15.80	48,977	43,205	5,771	2,310
1989–90	54,110	2,310	32.63	11.79	52,981	46,217	6,764	3,460
1990–91	49,850	3,460	63.61	139.54	47,634	41,403	6,231	5,600
1991–92	55,140	5,600	0.00	660.43	57,870	50,977	6,893	2,210
1992–93	55,690	2,210	1,363.70	36.75	56,487	49,526	6,961	2,740
1993–94	57,210	2,740	241.70	0.39	53,191	46,040	7,151	7,000
1994–95	59,840	7,000	0.57	86.63	58,034	50,554	7,480	8,720
1995–96	65,770	8,720	8.69	632.47	66,106	57,885	8,221	7,760
1996–97	62,100	7,760	616.17	1,145.90	66,090	58,328	7,763	3,240
1997–98	69,350	3,240	1,485.78	1.52	68,994	60,326	8,669	5,080
1998–99	66,350	5,080	1,803.70	1.76	63,572	55,278	8,294	9,660
1999–00	71,290	9,660	1,365.97	0.00	69,126	60,215	8,911	13,190
2000–01	76,370	13,190	4.22	813.49	67,251	57,704	9,546	21,500

Table A-5.1: (Continued)

Table A-5.1: (*Continued*)

	Production	Beginning Stock	Import	Export	Consumption			Ending Stock
					Total	Food	Feed/Seed/Waste	
2001–02	69,680	21,500	1.35	2,649.38	62,492	53,782	8,710	26,040
2002–03	72,770	26,040	0.00	3,671.25	79,489	70,393	9,096	15,650
2003–04	65,760	15,650	0.46	4,093.08	70,387	62,167	8,220	6,930
2004–05	72,160	6,930	0.00	2,009.35	73,015	63,995	9,020	4,066
2005–06	68,640	4,066	0.00	746.18	69,951	61,371	8,580	2,009
2006–07	69,350	2,009	6,079.56	46.64	72,689	64,020	8,669	4,703
2007–08	75,800	4,703	1,793.21	0.23	76,493	67,018	9,475	5,803

Source: Basic data retrieved from Ministry of Food, Consumer Affairs and Public Distribution; Directorate General of Commercial Intelligence and Statistics (DGCI&S), Kolkata, Ministry of Commerce; and *Agricultural Statistics at a Glance*, various issues, Directorate of Economics and Statistics, Ministry of Agriculture, Government of India.

Table A-5.2: India and world rice trade: 1982–83 to 2006–07

Marketing Years	Import Quantity ('000 tonnes)			Export Quantity ('000 tonnes)						Share of Basmati in Total Rice Export
	India	World⁺	% Share	Basmati	Non-Basmati	Total	World +	% Share		
1982–83	19.33	11,438.80	0.17	343.50	110.00	453.50	12,065.80	3.76		75.74
1983–84	408.74	11,885.25	3.44	175.60	0.00	175.60	11,540.72	1.52		100.00
1984–85	348.60	11,398.46	3.06	243.50	4.10	247.60	12,768.19	1.94		98.34
1985–86	43.83	12,460.55	0.35	244.80	0.70	245.50	11,546.42	2.13		99.71
1986–87	6.89	12,695.69	0.05	244.30	3.90	248.20	13,325.30	1.86		98.43
1987–88	5.38	12,217.99	0.04	366.10	22.80	388.90	13,012.57	2.99		94.14
1988–89	705.94	11,620.91	6.07	314.05	35.52	349.57	12,234.95	2.86		89.84
1989–90	468.63	14,317.25	3.27	384.12	37.64	421.76	15,203.24	2.77		91.08
1990–91	66.04	12,274.94	0.54	232.30	272.69	504.99	12,458.42	4.05		46.00
1991–92	12.12	12,938.88	0.09	266.53	411.94	678.47	13,141.99	5.16		39.28
1992–93	102.38	15,576.01	0.66	324.79	255.62	580.41	16,074.03	3.61		55.96
1993–94	75.52	15,940.70	0.47	527.23	240.44	767.67	16,830.37	4.56		68.68
1994–95	6.99	17,734.64	0.04	442.13	448.50	890.63	17,974.19	4.96		49.64
1995–96	0.08	21,604.98	0.00	373.31	4,540.70	4,914.01	22,494.41	21.85		7.60
1996–97	0.00	21,665.58	0.00	523.16	1,989.04	2,512.20	19,737.39	12.73		20.82

Table A-5.2: (Continued)

Table A-5.2: (Continued)

Marketing Years	Import Quantity ('000 tonnes)			Export Quantity ('000 tonnes)					Share of Basmati in Total Rice Export
	India	World$^+$	% Share	Basmati	Non-Basmati	Total	World +	% Share	
1997–98	0.05	19,132.15	0.00	593.32	1,795.74	2,389.06	21,017.98	11.37	24.83
1998–99	6.63	24,571.18	0.03	597.79	4,365.89	4,963.68	28,842.78	17.21	12.04
1999–00	34.99	27,300.57	0.13	638.38	1,257.79	1,896.17	25,277.46	7.50	33.67
2000–01	13.20	22,821.08	0.06	849.02	682.27	1,531.29	23,545.81	6.50	55.44
2001–02	0.06	23,444.49	0.00	667.07	1,541.49	2,208.56	26,685.41	8.28	30.20
2002–03	0.87	26,812.05	0.00	708.79	4,259.08	4,967.87	27,350.20	18.16	14.27
2003–04	0.54	27,358.03	0.00	771.49	2,640.57	3,412.06	27,858.67	12.25	22.61
2004–05	0.00	27,385.21	0.00	1,163.00	3,615.10	4,778.10	29,051.40	16.45	24.34
2005–06	0.26	26,428.46	0.00	1,166.57	2,921.60	4,088.17	29,492.44	13.86	28.54
2006–07	0.16	28,557.16	0.00	1,045.73	3,702.22	4,747.95	30,553.68	15.54	22.02

Source: Data retrieved from DGCI&S, Kolkata, Ministry of Commerce; and *Agricultural Statistics at a Glance*, various issues, Ministry of Agriculture, Government of India; and FAO trade statistics.

Table A-5.3: Total supply and use of rice in India (quantity in '000 tonnes): 1992–93 to 2007–08 (marketing years)

Marketing Years	Production	Beginning Stock as on 1 October	Import	Export	Consumption			Ending Stock as on 30 September	Total Supply
					Total	Food	Feed/Seed/Waste		
1992–93	74,680	5,070	102.38	580.40	72,052	62,717	9,335	7,220	79,852
1993–94	72,860	7,220	75.52	767.67	68,518	59,410	9,108	10,870	80,156
1994–95	80,300	10,870	6.99	890.57	77,286	67,249	10,038	13,000	91,177
1995–96	81,810	13,000	0.08	4,914.01	80,556	70,330	10,226	9,340	94,810
1996–97	76,980	9,340	0.00	2,511.98	76,768	67,146	9,623	7,040	86,320
1997–98	81,740	7,040	0.05	2,389.86	77,430	67,213	10,218	8,960	88,780
1998–99	82,530	8,960	6.63	4,963.59	78,793	68,477	10,316	7,740	91,497
1999–00	86,080	7,740	34.99	1,896.12	78,749	67,989	10,760	13,210	93,855
2000–01	89,680	13,210	13.20	1,534.48	79,919	68,709	11,210	21,450	102,903
2001–02	84,980	21,450	0.06	2,208.56	88,452	77,829	10,623	15,770	106,430
2002–03	93,340	15,770	0.87	4,967.87	98,903	87,236	11,668	5,240	109,111
2003–04	71,820	5,240	0.54	3,412.06	67,558	58,581	8,978	6,090	77,061
2004–05	88,530	6,090	0.00	4,778.10	84,993	73,927	11,066	4,849	94,620
2005–06	83,130	4,849	0.26	4,088.17	77,921	67,530	10,391	5,970	87,979
2006–07	91,790	5,970	0.16	4,747.95	87,523	76,049	11,474	5,489	97,760
2007–08	93,350	5,489	0.15	6,495.84	84,480	72,812	11,669	7,863	98,839

Source: Data retrieved from Ministry of Food, Consumer Affairs and Public Distribution; DGCI&S, Kolkata, Ministry of Commerce; and *Agricultural Statistics at a Glance*, various issues, Directorate of Economics and Statistics, Ministry of Agriculture, Government of India.

Table A-5.4: Availability of edible oil for human consumption: 1971–72 to 2004–05

Years	Domestic Production of Oilseeds	Domestic Production of Edible Oil*	Import of Edible Oil	Total Availability	Import as % of Total Availability
	thousand tonnes				
1971–72	9,080	2,543	86	2,629	3.27
1972–73	7,140	2,126	104	2,230	4.66
1973–74	9,390	2,634	126	2,760	4.57
1974–75	9,150	2,648	26	2,674	0.97
1975–76	10,610	2,922	67	2,989	2.24
1976–77	8,430	2,340	959	3,299	29.07
1977–78	9,660	2,732	1,123	3,855	29.13
1978–79	10,100	2,799	821	3,620	22.68
1979–80	8,740	2,411	1,149	3,560	32.28
1980–81	9,370	2,560	1,633	4,193	38.95
1981–82	12,080	3,219	1,350	4,569	29.55
1982–83	10,000	2,728	1,090	3,818	28.55
1983–84	12,690	3,282	1,383	4,665	29.65
1984–85	12,950	3,446	1,227	4,673	26.26
1985–86	10,830	2,964	1,036	4,000	25.90
1986–87	11,270	3,049	1,474	4,523	32.59
1987–88	12,650	3,463	1,945	5,408	35.97
1988–89	18,030	4,735	1,083	5,818	18.61
1989–90	16,920	4,567	324	4,891	6.62
1990–91	18,610	4,877	526	5,403	9.74
1991–92	18,600	5,022	226	5,248	4.31
1992–93	20,110	5,247	103	5,350	1.93
1993–94	21,500	5,397	114	5,511	2.07
1994–95	21,340	5,531	347	5,878	5.90
1995–96	22,110	5,989	1,062	7,051	15.06
1996–97	24,380	6,634	1,417	8,051	17.60
1997–98	21,320	5,605	1,266	6,871	18.43
1998–99	24,750	6,525	2,622	9,147	28.67
1999–00	20,720	5,586	4,196	9,782	42.90
2000–01	18,440	5,107	4,177	9,284	44.99
2001–02	20,660	5,711	4,322	10,033	43.08
2002–03	14,840	4,381	4,365	8,746	49.91
2003–04	25,190	6,672	5,290	11,962	44.22
2004–05	24,350	6,679	4,751	11,430	41.57

Source: Ministry of Food, Consumer Affairs and Public Distribution; *Agricultural Statistics at a Glance*, Directorate of Economics and Statistics, Ministry of Agriculture, Government of India.

Note: * Domestic edible oil includes groundnut, rapeseed/mustard, seasum, safflower, nigerseed, soybean, sunflower, cotton seed, and coconut oil.

Table A-5.5: Production, consumption and trade of sugar in India (quantity in 'ooo tonnes): 1982–2006

Sugar Year	Production	Export	Import	Consumption	Surplus over Production	Export as % of Production	Import as % of Production
			thousand tonnes				
1982	8,437	287.87	12.00	5,743	2,694	3.41	0.14
1983	8,229	556.32	0.00	6,488	1,741	6.76	0.00
1984	5,917	152.32	321.68	7,565	-1,648	2.57	5.44
1985	6,144	47.10	1,638.70	8,093	-1,949	0.77	26.67
1986	7,016	7.60	930.69	8,272	-1,256	0.11	13.27
1987	8,502	18.69	638.42	8,687	-185	0.22	7.51
1988	9,110	6.65	0.32	9,385	-275	0.07	0.00
1989	8,752	31.36	134.32	9,936	-1,184	0.36	1.53
1990	10,990	26.63	12.00	10,215	775	0.24	0.11
1991	12,047	176.50	2.59	10,714	1,333	1.47	0.02
1992	13,405	393.78	1.34	11,270	2,135	2.94	0.01
1993	10,609	187.11	0.45	11,875	-1,266	1.76	0.00
1994	9,833	49.48	1,780.78	11,960	-2,127	0.50	18.11
1995	14,643	365.85	150.63	12,270	2,373	2.50	1.03
1996	16,453	653.13	2.13	13,121	3,332	3.97	0.01
1997	12,905	171.71	346.89	13,792	-887	1.33	2.69

Table A-5.5: (*Continued*)

Table A-5.5: (*Continued*)

Sugar Year	Production	Export	Import	Consumption	Surplus over Production	Export as % of Production	Import as % of Production
			thousand tonnes				
1998	12,852	12.21	901.17	14,717	-1,865	0.10	7.01
1999	15,539	11.91	1,180.95	15,224	315	0.08	7.60
2000	18,200	337.78	30.96	16,101	2,099	1.86	0.17
2001	18,519	1,447.83	26.58	16,201	2,318	7.82	0.14
2002	18,527	1,661.62	41.43	16,781	1,746	8.97	0.22
2003	20,140	1,198.31	74.40	18,384	1,756	5.95	0.37
2004	13,560	105.96	932.44	17,285	-3,725	0.78	6.88
2005	12,691	320.61	558.77	18,500	-5,809	2.53	4.40
2006	19,267	1,642.26	1.05	18,500	767	8.52	0.01

Source: DGCI&S, Ministry of Commerce; *Agricultural Statistics at a Glance*, Directorate of Economics and Statistics, Ministry of Agriculture, Government of India.

Table A-6.1: Comparison of world reference price and domestic prices for wheat under importable hypothesis: 1981–2005

	FoB Price 1	Freight US GULF–India 2	CIF Import Price 3=(1+2)	Exchange Rate 4	Border Price Importable 5=(3 4)/10	Port Charges 6	Port Price for Importable 7=(5+6)	Price Received by Farmer (MSP) 8	Marketing Cost and Traders' Margin 9=(8 0/0.06)	Reference Price for Surplus State 10=(7−9)	Weighted Reference Price 11
	US$/MT	US$/MT	US$/MT	LC/US$	LC/Qtl	LC/Qtl	LC/Qtl	LC/Qtl	LC/Qtl	LC/Qtl	LC/Qtl
1981	160	53.86	214.19	7.9	169.64	6.7	176.38	117	7.02	169.36	164.46
1982	175	46.42	221.42	8.4	186.21	7.6	193.85	130	7.80	186.05	179.97
1983	161	29.54	190.21	9.4	177.97	8.5	186.50	142	8.52	177.98	169.15
1984	159	30.00	188.67	10.0	188.79	10.2	198.97	151	9.06	189.91	180.16
1985	154	30.00	184.00	11.0	201.85	11.5	213.34	152	9.12	204.22	193.93
1986	139	30.00	169.33	12.5	211.67	12.2	223.89	157	9.42	214.47	202.76
1987	114	25.33	139.33	12.5	174.12	13.6	187.74	162	9.72	178.02	168.29
1988	115	25.75	140.42	12.8	179.45	15.4	194.83	166	9.96	184.87	170.11
1989	138	43.58	181.25	13.4	243.35	18.7	262.01	173	10.38	251.63	235.40
1990	172	42.00	213.67	16.1	344.07	20.5	364.60	183	10.98	353.62	334.30
1991	148	41.00	189.33	17.3	328.37	22.6	350.94	215	12.90	338.04	317.21
1992	121	41.00	162.33	20.5	333.22	26.7	359.91	225	13.50	346.41	324.33
1993	153	42.29	195.06	25.9	505.00	30.7	535.70	275	16.50	519.20	495.11
1994	135	42.08	177.41	31.3	556.13	34.1	590.22	330	19.80	570.42	542.09
1995	142	45.00	186.60	31.4	585.36	38.7	624.02	350	21.00	603.02	570.99
1996	162	44.00	205.70	31.4	646.10	42.4	688.50	360	21.60	666.90	634.69

Table A-6.1: (Continued)

Table A-6.1: (Continued)

	FoB Price GULF-India	Freight US GULF-India	CIF Import Price	Exchange Rate	Border Price Importable	Port Charges	Port Price for Importable	Price Received by Farmer (MSP)	Marketing Cost and Traders' Margin	Reference Price for Surplus State	Weighted Reference Price
	1	2	3=(1+2)	4	5=(3·4)/10	6	7=(5+6)	8	9=(8·0.06)	10=(7−9)	11
	US$/MT	US$/MT	US$/MT	LC/US$	LC/Qtl	LC/Qtl	LC/Qtl	LC/Qtl	LC/Qtl	LC/Qtl	LC/Qtl
1997	248	44.00	291.70	34.7	1,013.37	46.3	1,059.69	380	22.80	1,036.89	1,002.96
1998	168	44.42	212.19	35.8	759.91	49.6	809.49	475	28.50	780.99	742.61
1999	129	42.42	171.82	40.8	700.28	56.1	756.36	510	30.60	725.76	688.37
2000	115	42.73	157.42	42.9	675.01	58.0	732.98	550	33.00	699.98	661.04
2001	116	43.05	158.55	44.1	699.21	60.1	759.35	580	34.80	724.55	685.71
2002	133	43.05	175.63	46.9	823.84	62.6	886.42	610	36.60	849.82	811.94
2003	128	43.90	172.11	49.0	842.63	65.3	907.92	620	37.20	870.72	833.10
2004	141	43.90	184.63	47.1	868.85	67.7	936.58	620	37.20	899.38	863.04
2005	165	43.90	208.47	44.9	935.96	70.4	1,006.40	630	37.80	968.60	931.07

Table A-6.1: (*Continued*)

Year	TC: Bombay to Karnal 12 LC/Qtl	RP for Haryana 13=(10–12) LC/Qtl	Value Weight 14 %	TC: Bombay to Ludhiana 15 LC/Qtl	RP for Punjab 16=(10–15) LC/Qtl	Value weight 17 %	TC: Ludhiana to Lucknow 18 LC/Qtl	RP for Uttar Pradesh 19=(9+16+18) LC/Qtl	Value Weight 20 %	Weighted Reference Price 21 LC/Qtl
1981	10.70	158.66	0.16	11.49	157.87	0.37	6.76	171.65	0.47	164.46
1982	13.96	172.09	0.14	14.99	171.06	0.31	8.28	187.14	0.55	179.97
1983	17.13	160.85	0.15	18.40	159.58	0.34	9.86	177.97	0.51	169.15
1984	19.28	170.63	0.15	20.71	169.20	0.32	11.18	189.44	0.53	180.16
1985	20.38	183.84	0.15	21.89	182.34	0.31	12.03	203.49	0.54	193.93
1986	21.92	192.54	0.15	23.54	190.93	0.34	12.98	213.33	0.52	202.76
1987	19.91	158.10	0.16	21.38	156.63	0.33	12.91	179.26	0.50	168.29
1988	26.62	158.26	0.16	28.58	156.29	0.31	15.60	181.86	0.53	170.11
1989	28.47	223.16	0.15	30.57	221.05	0.34	16.98	248.41	0.51	235.40
1990	32.91	320.71	0.17	35.34	318.28	0.31	18.80	348.06	0.52	334.30
1991	35.80	302.24	0.17	38.44	299.60	0.33	21.35	333.85	0.50	317.21
1992	38.47	307.94	0.17	41.32	305.10	0.33	23.97	342.57	0.50	324.33
1993	44.03	475.17	0.17	47.28	471.92	0.32	27.19	515.61	0.52	495.11
1994	50.46	519.96	0.18	54.19	516.23	0.31	30.09	566.12	0.50	542.09
1995	55.67	547.35	0.17	59.78	543.24	0.32	32.80	597.04	0.50	570.99
1996	57.70	609.21	0.17	61.96	604.95	0.31	34.24	660.79	0.52	634.69

Table A-6.1: (*Continued*)

Table A-6.1: (Continued)

	TC: Bombay to Karnal 12 LC/Qtl	RP for Haryana 13=(10–12) LC/Qtl	Value Weight 14 %	TC: Bombay to Ludhiana 15 LC/Qtl	RP for Punjab 16=(10–15) LC/Qtl	Value weight 17 %	TC: Ludhiana to Lucknow 18 LC/Qtl	RP for Uttar Pradesh 19=(9+16+18) LC/Qtl	Value Weight 20 %	Weighted Reference Price 21 LC/Qtl
1997	61.78	975.11	0.18	66.35	970.55	0.30	37.52	1,030.86	0.52	1,002.96
1998	71.57	709.42	0.17	76.85	704.13	0.30	42.66	775.29	0.53	742.61
1999	73.36	652.40	0.18	78.78	646.98	0.29	45.73	723.32	0.53	688.37
2000	75.24	624.75	0.18	80.79	619.19	0.31	47.89	700.09	0.50	661.04
2001	76.70	647.85	0.19	82.36	642.18	0.31	49.46	726.44	0.50	685.71
2002	76.87	772.94	0.19	82.55	767.27	0.31	50.66	854.53	0.50	811.94
2003	78.13	792.60	0.19	83.89	786.83	0.31	52.18	876.21	0.51	833.10
2004	77.02	822.36	0.20	82.71	816.67	0.30	52.83	906.70	0.50	863.04
2005	81.13	887.47	0.19	87.11	881.48	0.29	55.42	974.70	0.52	931.07

Notes and Basic Data Sources:

Calendar years correspond to Indian wheat marketing year, where year 1981 corresponds to April 1980 to March 1981

Column (1) Refers to US Hard Red Winter No.2, FoB US Gulf price for peak Indian marketing season, i.e., April–June (Source: UNCTAD world commodity price data set)

Column (2) Freight charges from US–Gulf to India (at Mumbai port), from Pursell, Gulati and Gupta (2007)

Column (4) Exchange rate for period April to June1980/81 (corresponds to wheat marketing year April-March 1980/81) is under 1981 (Source: IMF, IFS data set, 2007)

Column (6)	Port charges from Pursell, Gulati and Gupta (2007) data set
Column (8)	Minimum Support Price (Source: Commission on Agricultural Costs and Prices reports, Government of India)
Column (9)	Marketing cost and trader's margin is assumed to be 6 per cent of price received by farmers
Column (10)	Refers to reference price for surplus state excluding domestic transportation cost
Column (11)	Weighted reference price for all India from column (21)
Columns (12), (15) and (18)	Refers to transportation cost (TC) from Bombay to Karnal, Bombay to Ludhiana (Punjab) and Ludhiana to Lucknow (Uttar Pradesh). TC was calculated by constructing rail and road transport index by following the methodology developed by Pursell and Gupta (1998) (Source: CSO report, GoI)
Columns (13), (16) and (19)	Reference price under importable hypothesis was calculated for three major producing states, namely, Haryana (surplus sate), Punjab (surplus state) and Uttar Pradesh (deficit state) as per the methodology discussed in the chapter.
Columns (14), (17) and (20)	Refers to percentage share of state in total value of wheat output (Source: CSO report, GoI)
Column (21)	Refers to weighted average of reference price (RP) for the state of Haryana, Punjab and Uttar Pradesh; weight refers to percentage share of the state in total value of wheat output

Table A-6.2: Comparison of world reference price and domestic prices for wheat under exportable hypothesis: 1981–2005

	FoB Price at Bombay 1 US$/MT	Exchange Rate 2 LC/US$	FoB Price at Bombay Port 3=(1*2)/10 LC/Qtl	Port Charges 4 LC/Qtl	TC: Bombay to Ludhiana 5 LC/Qtl	Marketing Cost and Traders' Margin 6 LC/Qtl	Reference Price at Ludhiana 7=(3-4-5-6) LC/Qtl	Price Received by Farmer (MSP) 8 LC/Qtl
1981	160	7.9	126.98	6.74	11.49	7.02	101.73	117
1982	175	8.4	147.18	7.63	14.99	7.80	116.75	130
1983	161	9.4	150.33	8.53	18.40	8.52	114.88	142
1984	159	10.0	158.77	10.18	20.71	9.06	118.82	151
1985	154	11.0	168.94	11.49	21.89	9.12	126.44	152
1986	139	12.5	174.17	12.22	23.54	9.42	128.98	157
1987	114	12.5	142.46	13.62	21.38	9.72	97.74	162
1988	115	12.8	146.54	15.38	28.58	9.96	92.62	166
1989	138	13.4	184.84	18.65	30.57	10.38	125.23	173
1990	172	16.1	276.44	20.53	35.34	10.98	209.59	183
1991	148	17.3	257.26	22.57	38.44	12.90	183.35	215
1992	121	20.5	249.06	26.69	41.32	13.50	167.55	225
1993	153	25.9	395.51	30.70	47.28	16.50	301.03	275
1994	135	31.3	424.22	34.08	54.19	19.80	316.15	330
1995	142	31.4	444.20	38.66	59.78	21.00	324.76	350
1996	162	31.4	507.90	42.40	61.96	21.60	381.95	360
1997	248	34.7	860.51	46.33	66.35	22.80	725.04	380
1998	168	35.8	600.83	49.58	76.85	28.50	445.90	475

1999	129	40.8	527.39	56.08	78.78	30.60	361.93	510
2000	115	42.9	491.78	57.98	80.79	33.00	320.01	550
2001	116	44.1	509.36	60.14	82.36	34.80	332.05	580
2002	133	46.9	621.90	62.58	82.55	36.60	440.17	610
2003	128	49.0	627.70	65.29	83.89	37.20	441.32	620
2004	141	47.1	662.26	67.73	82.71	37.20	474.62	620
2005	165	44.9	738.86	70.44	87.11	37.80	543.51	630

Notes and Basic Data Sources:

Under exportable hypothesis following the methodology of Gulati, Hanson and Pursell (1990), it was assumed that point of competition of Indian Wheat with wheat from other countries is Tunis in Tunisia, which is roughly at equal distance from India and US, therefore FoB price at Bombay, is equal to the FoB US price (Source: UNCTAD world commodity price data set)

Columns (2), (4), (5), (6), and (8) Sources are same for these columns as in Table A-6.1 for the corresponding information

Column (7) Reference price under exportable hypothesis was calculated only for one surplus state, i.e., Punjab

Table A-6.3: Comparison of world reference price and domestic prices for rice under exportable hypothesis: 1981–2005

1	FoB Price at Indian Ports 2 US$/MT	Exchange Rate (Oct–Jan) 3 LC/US$	Border Price Exportable 4=(2*3)/10 LC/Qtl	Port Charges 5 LC/Qtl	Port Price for Exportable 6=4-5 LC/Qtl	Weighted Producers Price 7=19 LC/Qtl	Weighted Reference Price 8=20 LC/Qtl
1981	462	7.8	362	6.74	354.9	168	340
1982	313	9.1	285	7.63	277.8	192	260
1983	255	9.7	248	8.53	239.2	203	219
1984	248	10.4	259	10.18	248.4	218	227
1985	209	12.3	256	11.49	244.5	229	220
1986	200	12.1	243	12.22	230.3	237	205
1987	159	13.0	207	13.62	193.4	243	168
1988	254	13.0	331	15.38	315.5	251	286
1989	258	15.0	386	18.65	367.0	267	338
1990	257	16.9	435	20.53	414.3	291	380
1991	254	18.1	461	22.57	438.3	340	399
1992	253	25.9	656	26.69	629.4	391	585
1993	236	26.0	615	30.70	584.2	458	533
1994	278	31.4	872	34.08	838.1	527	779

1995	253	31.4	794	38.66	755.5	575	691
1996	345	35.0	1,209	42.40	1,166.6	624	1,099
1997	304	35.8	1,087	46.33	1,040.6	647	970
1998	255	38.0	968	49.58	918.7	749	834
1999	272	42.4	1,153	56.08	1,096.5	785	1,011
2000	218	43.5	946	57.98	887.8	869	795
2001	174	46.6	810	60.14	750.1	901	656
2002	172	48.1	829	62.58	766.2	937	669
2003	183	48.2	881	65.29	816.0	972	710
2004	192	45.5	871	67.73	803.4	1,001	698
2005	263	44.7	1,175	70.44	1,104.1	1,001	996

Table A-6.3: (*Continued*)

Table A-6.3: (*Continued*)

	Andhra Pradesh (Vijayawada) ₹/Qtl					Punjab (Ludhiana) ₹/Qtl					All India ₹/Qtl	
	Producer's Price	Marketing Cost and Traders' Margin	TC to Madras	Reference price	Value weight	Producer's price	Marketing Cost and Traders' Margin	TC to Calcutta	Reference Price	Value weight	Weighted Producers Price	Weighted Reference Price
	9	10=9 0.05	11	12=6–10–11	13	14	15=14 0.05	16	17=6–15–16	18	19	20
1981	166	8.3	4.0	343	0.69	175	8.7	10.8	335	0.31	168.3	340.4
1982	191	9.5	4.8	263	0.68	194	9.7	14.1	254	0.32	191.6	260.4
1983	202	10.1	5.7	223	0.66	205	10.2	17.3	212	0.34	202.7	219.3
1984	217	10.9	6.5	231	0.67	221	11.0	19.5	218	0.33	218.4	226.6
1985	227	11.4	7.0	226	0.59	231	11.5	20.6	212	0.41	228.8	220.3
1986	235	11.8	7.5	211	0.60	239	11.9	22.2	196	0.40	236.7	204.9
1987	242	12.1	7.6	174	0.54	245	12.3	20.1	161	0.46	243.2	167.7
1988	250	12.5	9.0	294	0.58	251	12.6	26.9	276	0.42	250.6	286.2
1989	266	13.3	9.8	344	0.70	270	13.5	28.8	325	0.30	267.1	337.8
1990	288	14.4	10.8	389	0.61	295	14.7	33.3	366	0.39	290.9	379.9
1991	336	16.8	12.4	409	0.61	347	17.4	36.2	385	0.39	340.4	399.3
1992	388	19.4	14.0	596	0.59	396	19.8	38.9	571	0.41	391.4	585.3
1993	454	22.7	15.8	546	0.57	463	23.2	44.5	517	0.43	458.0	532.8
1994	521	26.1	17.4	795	0.57	535	26.8	51.0	760	0.43	527.2	779.4
1995	567	28.4	19.0	708	0.56	585	29.3	56.3	670	0.44	575.2	690.9
1996	623	31.2	19.8	1,116	0.58	624	31.2	58.3	1,077	0.42	623.7	1,099.1
1997	626	31.3	21.8	987	0.60	678	33.9	62.5	944	0.40	647.2	969.9
1998	735	36.8	24.7	857	0.53	764	38.2	72.4	808	0.47	748.8	833.6
1999	783	39.2	26.7	1,031	0.61	788	39.4	74.2	983	0.39	785.4	1,011.5
2000	867	43.4	28.0	816	0.56	871	43.5	76.1	768	0.44	868.9	794.7
2001	900	45.0	29.0	676	0.59	904	45.2	77.6	627	0.41	901.4	655.5

2002	935	46.8	29.8	690	0.58	939	47.0	77.7	642	0.42	936.8	668.7
2003	970	48.5	30.7	737	0.47	974	48.7	79.0	688	0.53	972.5	710.2
2004	999	50.0	31.2	722	0.50	1,003	50.2	77.9	675	0.50	1,001.1	697.9
2005	999	50.0	32.7	1,021	0.49	1,003	50.2	82.0	972	0.51	1,001.1	995.7

Notes and Basic Data Sources:

Column (2)	Calendar years correspond to Indian rice marketing year, i.e., October–September; October–September 1980/81 is under 1981 Indian states covered under exportable hypothesis include Andhra Pradesh (surplus state) and Punjab (surplus state) Average price from October–January for 15 per cent broken Thai rice (Source: ERS USDA); Under exportable hypothesis following the methodology of Gulati, Hanson and Pursell (1990), it was assumed that the point of competition of domestic rice with Thai rice is Malacca, which is roughly equidistant from Bangkok and Indian ports. Therefore, the FoB price at Bangkok and Indian ports are the same.
Column (3)	Refers market exchange rate for period October–January; IMF, IFS data set, 2007
Column (5)	Port charges from Pursell, Gulati and Gupta (2007) data set
Columns (7) and (8)	Refers to columns (19) and (20)
Columns (9) and (14)	Refers to the procurement price of rice of the respective state (Source: Annual reports of the Food Corporation of India)
Columns (10) and (15)	Refers to marketing cost and trader's margin. Marketing cost and trader's margin is assumed to be 5 per cent of the procurement price of the respective state
Columns (11) and (16)	Refers to transportation cost (TC) from Vijayawada (Andhra Pradesh) to Madras (Tamil Nadu) and Ludhiana (Punjab) to Calcutta (West Bengal). TC was calculated by constructing rail and road transport index by following the methodology developed by Pursell and Gupta (1998) (Source: CSO report, GoI)
Columns (13) and (18)	Refers to the weighted share of corresponding state in the total value of output
Columns (19) and (20)	Refers to weighted average of domestic producer's price and world reference price for the state of Andhra Pradesh and Punjab; weight refers to values given in columns (13) and (18) for the states of Andhra Pradesh and Punjab, respectively.

Table A-6.4: Comparison of world reference price and domestic price for groundnut (pod) under importable hypothesis: 1981–2004

Year	CIF Price Kernels 1 US$/MT	Freight Rott-US Gulf 2 US$/MT	FoB US Export Price 3=1-2 US$/MT	Freight US GULF-India 4 US$/MT	CIF Import Price Pod 5=(3+4) 0.70 US$/MT	Exchange Rate 6 LC/US$	Border Price (Pods) for Importable 7=5 6/10 LC/Qtl	Port Charges 8 LC/Qtl	Port Price for Importable 9=7+8 LC/Qtl	Marketing Cost and Traders' Margin 10=9 0.10 LC/Qtl	Reference Price for Deficit State 11=9+10 LC/Qtl
1981	662.00	29.63	632.37	86.18	502.98	8.32	418.65	5.26	423.91	42.39	466.3
1982	409.00	20.16	388.84	74.27	324.18	9.31	301.92	5.96	307.87	30.79	338.7
1983	379.00	17.07	361.93	47.26	286.43	9.94	284.60	6.65	291.25	29.13	320.4
1984	441.00	18.80	422.20	48.00	329.14	10.91	359.09	7.94	367.03	36.70	403.7
1985	368.00	20.19	347.81	48.00	277.07	12.39	343.19	8.97	352.16	35.22	387.4
1986	338.00	17.54	320.46	48.00	257.92	12.37	319.16	9.53	328.69	32.87	361.6
1987	283.00	18.50	264.50	40.53	213.52	12.97	276.96	10.63	287.58	28.76	316.3
1988	289.00	25.41	263.59	41.20	213.35	13.44	286.68	12.00	298.68	29.87	328.5
1989	342.00	28.34	313.66	69.73	268.37	15.73	422.09	14.55	436.64	43.66	480.3
1990	420.75	35.50	385.25	67.20	316.71	17.21	545.09	16.01	561.10	56.11	617.2
1991	449.01	30.40	418.61	65.60	338.95	20.79	704.82	17.61	722.42	72.24	794.7
1992	367.17	27.07	340.10	65.60	283.99	25.89	735.34	20.83	756.17	75.62	831.8
1993	377.98	29.87	348.10	67.66	291.04	29.15	848.25	23.95	872.20	87.22	959.4

1994	481.40	27.77	453.62	67.33	364.67	31.37	1,143.96	26.59	1,170.55	117.06	1,287.6
1995	502.89	30.37	472.52	72.00	381.17	31.58	1,203.88	30.16	1,234.04	123.40	1,357.4
1996	493.13	34.80	458.33	70.40	370.11	35.19	1,302.32	33.08	1,335.40	133.54	1,468.9
1997	530.91	29.81	501.10	70.40	400.05	35.87	1,434.78	36.14	1,470.92	147.09	1,618.0
1998	459.88	19.76	440.12	70.40	357.36	40.04	1,430.72	38.68	1,469.40	146.94	1,616.3
1999	388.90	18.74	370.17	67.87	306.63	42.80	1,312.41	43.75	1,356.16	135.62	1,491.8
2000	373.95	18.74	355.22	67.87	296.16	44.15	1,307.41	45.23	1,352.64	135.26	1,487.9
2001	360.31	18.74	341.57	67.87	286.61	46.85	1,342.77	46.92	1,389.69	138.97	1,528.7
2002	352.92	18.74	334.18	67.87	281.44	48.53	1,365.87	48.93	1,414.80	141.48	1,556.3
2003	358.74	18.74	340.01	67.87	285.51	47.28	1,350.01	50.94	1,400.94	140.09	1,541.0
2004	580.82	18.7	562.08	67.87	440.97	45.45	2,004.27	52.84	2,057.11	205.71	2,262.8

Table A-6.4: (*Continued*)

Table A-6.4: (Continued)

	Domestic Price Gujarat	Reference Price Gujarat	Production Weight	Domestic Price T.N.	Reference Price T.N.	Production Weight	Domestic Price A.P.	TC: Madras to Nandyal	Reference Price at A.P.	Production Weight	Weighbed Domestic Price	Weighbed Reference Price
	12	13=11	14	15	16=11	17	18	19	20=11+19	21	22	23
	LC/Qtl	LC/Qtl	%	LC/Qtl	LC/Qtl	%	LC/Qtl	LC/Qtl	LC/Qtl	%	LC/Qtl	LC/Qtl
1981	364.5	466.3	0.5	396.60	466.3	0.21	379.7	5.1	471.4	0.3	375.46	467.67
1982	390.0	338.7	0.5	400.60	338.7	0.25	376.9	6.0	344.7	0.3	388.84	340.44
1983	390.8	320.4	0.4	419.51	320.4	0.26	397.8	7.0	327.4	0.3	400.62	322.79
1984	458.8	403.7	0.4	466.08	403.7	0.22	431.7	8.0	411.7	0.4	450.04	406.78
1985	453.1	387.4	0.4	451.42	387.4	0.26	449.2	8.7	396.1	0.3	451.38	390.25
1986	470.5	361.6	0.2	458.19	361.6	0.40	458.1	9.4	371.0	0.4	460.03	365.80
1987	503.3	316.3	0.3	604.68	316.3	0.30	600.0	9.9	326.2	0.4	567.57	319.84
1988	758.8	328.5	0.0	646.53	328.5	0.38	670.0	11.3	339.8	0.6	664.82	335.03
1989	480.8	480.3	0.5	547.48	480.3	0.18	548.1	12.4	492.7	0.4	516.68	484.71
1990	718.5	617.2	0.3	698.91	617.2	0.25	751.7	13.3	630.5	0.4	727.41	622.74
1991	1,029.2	794.7	0.2	929.21	794.7	0.26	956.1	15.6	810.2	0.5	966.15	802.51
1992	1,052.0	831.8	0.2	957.68	831.8	0.35	1003.4	17.9	849.7	0.5	995.29	840.62
1993	843.7	959.4	0.4	795.36	959.4	0.30	866.7	20.2	979.7	0.3	836.75	966.28
1994	1,001.7	1,287.6	0.1	925.32	1,287.6	0.37	935.0	21.9	1,309.5	0.5	940.32	1,298.58
1995	1,164.2	1,357.4	0.4	1,134.62	1,357.4	0.30	1,172.2	23.7	1,381.2	0.3	1,157.52	1,364.26
1996	1,264.3	1,468.9	0.2	1,179.34	1,468.9	0.29	1,153.1	24.9	1,493.8	0.5	1,182.93	1,481.57
1997	1,191.7	1,618.0	0.4	1,199.26	1,618.0	0.24	1,316.7	27.7	1,645.7	0.3	1,236.60	1,627.55

Year												
1998	1,200.3	1,616.3	0.5	1,206.18	1,616.3	0.27	1,302.8	31.1	1,647.4	0.2	1,224.78	1,623.28
1999	1,337.8	1,491.8	0.4	1,274.86	1,491.8	0.25	1,427.3	34.2	1,526.0	0.3	1,352.75	1,503.48
2000	1,320.0	1,487.9	0.2	1,270.03	1,487.9	0.43	1,363.9	36.3	1,524.2	0.3	1,313.30	1,500.29
2001	1,245.0	1,528.7	0.2	1,175.69	1,528.7	0.32	1,225.6	37.7	1,566.4	0.5	1,212.58	1,547.97
2002	1,214.2	1,556.3	0.5	1,438.03	1,556.3	0.24	1,360.0	39.1	1,595.4	0.2	1,303.95	1,565.78
2003	1,844.2	1,541.0	0.4	1,903.84	1,541.0	0.27	1,702.2	40.6	1,581.6	0.3	1,816.21	1,553.68
2004	1,695.0	2,262.8	0.7	1,712.04	2,262.8	0.14	1,576.2	41.65	2,304.5	0.2	1,679.10	2,269.26

Notes and Basic Data Sources:

Column (1)	Calendar years corresponds to Indian groundnut marketing year, i.e., October–September, October–September 1980/81 is under 1981; Indian states covered under importable hypothesis include Andhra Pradesh (deficit state), Gujarat (deficit state) and Tamil Nadu (deficit state)
Column (1)	Refers to world price, i.e., CIF Europe (shelled) for period October–September; Up to 1990 prices were taken from oil world for shelled groundnut (CIF, Europe). Prices from 1991 and onwards were estimated from regression of crush kernel prices on oil and meal prices (Source: Oil world)
Columns (2) and (4)	Refers to freight charges from Rotterdam to US gulf and US gulf to India and were taken from Pursell, Gulati and Gupta (2007)
Column (5)	Conversion factor for kernels to pod=kernels * 0.70
Column (6)	Refers to market exchange rate for period October–September (corresponds to Indian groundnut marketing year); IMF, IFS data set, 2007

Table A-6.4: (*Continued*)

Table A-6.4: (*Continued*)

Column (8)	Port charges from Pursell, Gulati and Gupta (2007) data set
Column (10)	Marketing cost and trader's margin is assumed to be 10 per cent of landed price/port price of importable
Column (11)	Refers to reference price for deficit state excluding domestic transportation cost
Columns (12), (15) and (18)	Refers to domestic market price of groundnut (pods) for Gujarat (Rajkot, October–March), Tamil Nadu (Madras, Oct–June) and Andhra Pradesh (Nandyal, October–June) during harvest seasons (Source: *Agricultural Prices in India*, Ministry of Agriculture, GoI)
Columns (13), (16) and (20)	Refers to reference price for states under importable hypothesis; Following the methodology of Gulati, Hanson and Pursell (1990), it was assumed that domestic groundnut would compete with imported groundnut (from USA) at port city in the west (Kandla, Gujarat) or in the south (Madras, Tamil Nadu).
Columns (14), (17) and (21)	Refers to percentage share of state in total groundnut production of three states
Column (19)	Refers to transportation cost (TC) from Nandyal (Andhra Pradesh) to Madras (Tamil Nadu), was calculated by constructing rail and road transport index by following the methodology developed by Pursell and Gupta (1998); CSO report, GoI
Columns (22) and (23)	Refers to weighted average of domestic price and reference price (RP) for the states of Gujarat, Tamil Nadu and Andhra Pradesh; weight refers to percentage share of the state in total output.

Table A-6.5: Comparison of world reference price and domestic price for groundnut oil under importable hypothesis: 1981–2005

Year	CIF Rotterdam 1 US$/MT	Freight Rott-US Gulf 2 US$/MT	FoB at US Gulf 3=1-2 US$/MT	Freight US Gulf-India 4 US$/MT	CIF Import Price 5=3+4 US$/MT	Exchange Rate 6 LC/US$	Border Price for Importable 7=5 6/10 LC/Qtl	Port Charges 8 LC/Qtl	Port Price for Importable 9=7+8 LC/Qtl	Price Bombay Market 10 LC/Qtl	Marketing Cost and Traders' Margin 11=9 0.06 LC/Qtl	Reference Price 12=9+11 LC/Qtl
1981	1,105.08	37.04	1,068.04	107.72	1,175.76	8.44	992.83	6.74	999.58	1,339.49	59.97	1,059.55
1982	633.92	25.20	608.72	92.84	701.56	9.36	656.36	7.64	664.00	1,353.07	39.84	703.84
1983	637.00	21.34	615.66	59.08	674.74	9.98	673.50	8.53	682.03	1,549.63	40.92	722.96
1984	1,017.50	23.50	994.00	60.00	1,054.00	11.07	1,166.25	10.18	1,176.43	1,612.87	70.59	1,247.02
1985	911.83	25.24	886.59	60.00	946.59	12.38	1,172.12	11.50	1,183.62	1,514.20	71.02	1,254.63
1986	624.25	21.92	602.33	60.00	662.33	12.44	824.10	12.22	836.33	1,866.58	50.18	886.51
1987	505.50	23.12	482.38	50.66	533.04	12.99	692.33	13.62	705.95	2,282.43	42.36	748.31
1988	580.83	31.76	549.07	51.50	600.57	13.58	815.38	15.38	830.76	2,228.80	49.85	880.61
1989	723.25	35.42	687.83	87.16	774.99	15.90	1,232.56	18.66	1,251.21	2,125.00	75.07	1,326.29
1990	935.92	44.38	891.54	84.00	975.54	17.31	1,688.65	20.53	1,709.18	2,694.83	102.55	1,811.74
1991	957.00	38.00	919.00	82.00	1,001.00	21.45	2,146.73	22.57	2,169.30	3,498.75	130.16	2,299.46
1992	620.92	33.84	587.08	82.00	669.08	25.90	1,732.57	26.70	1,759.27	3,406.25	105.56	1,864.83
1993	694.50	37.34	657.16	84.58	741.74	29.60	2,195.74	30.70	2,226.44	3,027.50	133.59	2,360.03
1994	989.60	34.72	954.88	84.16	1,039.04	31.37	3,259.47	34.09	3,293.56	3,418.00	197.61	3,491.17
1995	1,001.75	37.96	963.79	90.00	1,053.79	31.85	3,356.31	38.66	3,394.97	3,975.83	203.70	3,598.67
1996	917.92	43.50	874.42	88.00	962.42	35.28	3,395.17	42.40	3,437.57	3,860.00	206.25	3,643.82
1997	976.08	37.26	938.82	88.00	1,026.82	35.91	3,687.75	46.33	3,734.08	3,517.50	224.05	3,958.13
1998	944.13	24.70	919.43	88.00	1,007.43	40.55	4,084.69	49.58	4,134.27	4,600.00	248.06	4,382.33
1999	795.79	23.42	772.37	84.84	857.21	42.89	3,676.87	56.09	3,732.95	3,983.20	223.98	3,956.93
2000	731.66	23.42	708.24	84.84	793.08	44.39	3,520.23	57.98	3,578.21	3,873.40	214.69	3,792.91

Table A-6.5: (*Continued*)

Table A-6.5: (*Continued*)

Year	CIF Rotterdam Rott-US Gulf 1 US$/MT	Freight Rott-US Gulf 2 US$/MT	FoB at US Gulf 3=1-2 US$/MT	Freight US Gulf-India 4 US$/MT	CIF Import Price 5=3+4 US$/MT	Exchange Rate 6 LC/US$	Border Price for Importable 7=5 6/10 LC/Qtl	Port Charges 8 LC/Qtl	Port Price for Importable 9=7+8 LC/Qtl	Price Bombay Market 10 LC/Qtl	Marketing Cost and Traders' Margin 11=9 0.06 LC/Qtl	Reference Price 12=9+11 LC/Qtl
2001	675.58	23.42	652.16	84.84	737.00	46.99	3,463.11	60.15	3,523.26	3,681.00	211.40	3,734.65
2002	664.19	23.42	640.77	84.84	725.61	48.56	3,523.61	62.73	3,586.34	4,333.80	215.18	3,801.52
2003	1,194.32	23.42	1,170.90	84.84	1,255.74	47.04	5,906.35	65.30	5,971.65	5,247.50	358.30	6,329.95
2004	1,163.67	23.42	1,140.25	84.84	1,225.09	45.48	5,572.20	67.74	5,639.94	4,976.80	338.40	5,978.34
2005	1,088.69	23.42	1,065.27	84.84	1,150.11	43.91	5,050.33	70.45	5,120.78	4,679.50	307.25	5,428.03

Notes and Basic Data Sources:

Calendar year corresponds to Indian groundnut oil marketing year, i.e., November–October; November–October 1980/81 is under 1981

Indian state covered under importable hypothesis includes Maharashtra (deficit state)

Column (1)   Refers to world price i.e. CIF Rotterdam for period Nov-Oct. Source, IMF, IFS data set 2007

Columns (2) and (4)   Refers to freight charges from Rotterdam to US Gulf and US Gulf to Bombay port; Freight charges for oil is assumed to be 125 per cent of those between Rotterdam to US gulf and US gulf to India for groundnut (Source: columns 2 and 4 of Table A-6.4)

Column (6)   Refers to market exchange rate for period November–October (corresponds to Indian groundnut oil marketing year (Source: IMF, IFS data set, 2007)

Column (8)   Refers to port charges and assumed to be 125 per cent of those for groundnuts (Source: column 8 of Table A-6.4)

Column (10)   Refers to domestic wholesale price of groundnut oil at Bombay market for the period November–October (Source: The Solvent Extractors' Association of India)

Column (11)   Marketing cost and trader's margin is assumed to be 6 per cent of port price of importable

Column (12)   Refers to reference price for groundnut oil under importable hypothesis for Maharashtra

Table A-6.6: Comparison of world reference price and domestic price for rapeseed/mustard seed under importable hypothesis: 1981–2005

Years	CIF Rott. Price 1 US$/MT	Freight Rott-Canada 2 US$/MT	FoB Canada 3=1–2 US$/MT	Freight Canada-India 4 US$/MT	CIF Import Price 5=3+4 US$/MT	Exchange Rate 6 LC/US$	Border Price Importable 7=5 6/10 LC/Qtl	Port Charges 8 LC/Qtl	Port Price Importable 9=7+8 LC/Qtl	Marketing Cost Traders' Margin 10=9 0.06 LC/Qtl	Domestic Price Hapur 11 LC/Qtl	TC: Hapur to Bombay 12 LC/Qtl	Reference Price 13=9+10+12 LC/Qtl
1981	305	29.63	275.4	86.18	361.5	8.26	298.64	5.26	303.9	18.23	442.5	13.4	335.5
1982	300	20.16	280.0	74.27	354.3	9.28	328.65	5.96	334.6	20.08	398.8	17.2	371.9
1983	297	17.07	280.3	47.26	327.5	9.95	325.78	6.65	332.4	19.95	453.7	21.0	373.4
1984	380	18.80	361.4	48.00	409.4	10.86	444.44	7.94	452.4	27.14	501.7	23.7	503.2
1985	314	20.19	293.8	48.00	341.8	12.67	433.07	8.97	442.0	26.52	405.7	25.1	493.7
1986	233	17.54	215.8	48.00	263.8	12.41	327.24	9.53	336.8	20.21	458.3	27.1	384.0
1987	182	18.50	163.5	40.53	204.0	12.90	263.17	10.63	273.8	16.43	689.2	25.1	315.3
1988	211	25.41	185.1	41.20	226.3	13.24	299.50	12.00	311.5	18.69	727.5	32.8	363.0
1989	239	28.34	210.7	69.73	280.4	15.69	439.98	14.55	454.5	27.27	580.8	35.2	517.0
1990	219	35.50	183.7	67.20	250.9	17.19	431.15	16.01	447.2	26.83	760.0	40.3	514.3
1991	204	30.40	173.3	65.60	238.9	19.67	469.77	17.61	487.4	29.24	916.3	44.2	560.9
1992	199	27.07	171.9	65.60	237.5	25.90	615.24	20.83	636.1	38.16	922.5	48.0	722.2
1993	243	29.87	212.8	67.66	280.5	29.62	830.63	23.95	854.6	51.27	889.2	54.8	960.7
1994	297	27.77	269.1	67.33	336.4	31.37	1,055.25	26.59	1,081.8	64.91	995.0	62.4	1,209.1
1995	292	30.37	261.5	72.00	333.5	31.44	1,048.35	30.16	1,078.5	64.71	1,140.0	68.6	1,211.9
1996	295	34.80	260.0	70.40	330.4	35.18	1,162.30	33.08	1,195.4	71.72	1,091.7	71.2	1,338.3
1997	290	29.81	260.2	70.40	330.6	35.85	1,185.01	36.14	1,221.1	73.27	1,097.5	76.7	1,371.1
1998	314	19.76	294.2	70.40	364.6	40.01	1,458.80	38.68	1,497.5	89.85	1,480.8	88.5	1,675.8
1999	220	18.74	200.9	67.87	268.8	42.68	1,147.12	43.75	1,190.9	71.45	1,566.7	91.5	1,353.9
2000	191	18.74	172.1	67.87	240.0	43.84	1,052.07	45.23	1,097.3	65.84	1,188.3	94.3	1,257.4

Table A-6.6: (*Continued*)

Table A-6.6: (Continued)

Years	CIF Rott. Price 1 US$/MT	Freight Rott-Canada 2 US$/MT	FoB Canada 3=1-2 US$/MT	Freight Canada-India 4 US$/MT	CIF Import Price 5=3+4 US$/MT	Exchange Rate 6 LC/US$	Border Price Importable 7=5 6/10 LC/Qtl	Port Charges 8 LC/Qtl	Port Price Importable 9=7+8 LC/Qtl	Marketing Cost Traders' Margin 10=9 0.06 LC/Qtl	Domestic Price Hapur 11 LC/Qtl	TC: Hapur to Bombay 12 LC/Qtl	Reference Price 13=9+10+12 LC/Qtl
2001	197	18.74	178.3	67.87	246.1	46.73	1,150.28	46.92	1,197.2	71.83	1,191.7	96.4	1,365.4
2002	208	18.74	189.4	67.87	257.3	48.78	1,254.99	48.93	1,303.9	78.24	1,260.8	97.1	1,479.3
2003	290	18.74	271.3	67.87	339.1	47.42	1,608.07	50.94	1,659.0	99.54	1,740.8	99.0	1,857.5
2004	341	18.74	321.9	67.87	389.8	45.07	1,756.97	52.84	1,809.8	108.59	1,800.0	98.2	2,016.6
2005	258	18.74	239.1	67.87	307.0	43.66	1,340.07	54.95	1,395.0	83.70	1,558.3	103.3	1,582.1

Notes and Basic Data Sources:

Calendar years corresponds to Indian rapeseed/mustard seed marketing year, i.e., January–December; January–December 1981 is under 1981;

Indian state covered under importable hypothesis includes Uttar Pradesh (deficit state)

Column (1)   Refers to world price, i.e., CIF Hamburg for Indian harvest season, i.e., January–June (Source, USDA)

Columns (2) and (4)   Refers to freight charges from Hamburg to Canada and Canada to Bombay port; Freight charges is assumed to be same for those between Rotterdam to US gulf and US gulf to India for groundnut (Source: columns 2 and 4 of Table A-6.4)

Column (6)   Refers to market exchange rate for period January–June (Source: IMF, IFS data set, 2007)

Column (8)   Port charges from Pursell, Gulati and Gupta (2007)

Column (10)   Marketing cost and trader's margin is assumed to be 6 per cent of landed price/port price of importable

Column (11)   Refers to domestic wholesale price of rapeseed/mustard seed at Hapur market (Uttar Pradesh) during harvest season, i.e., January–June (Source: *Agricultural Prices in India*, Ministry of Agriculture, GoI)

Column (12)   Refers to transportation cost (TC) from Hapur (Uttar Pradesh) to Bombay (Maharashtra), was calculated by constructing rail and road transport index by following the methodology developed by Pursell and Gupta (1998); CSO report, GoI

Column (13)   Refers to reference price under importable hypothesis

Years	CIF Price 1 US$/MT	Freight Rott-US Gulf 2 US$/MT	FoB price US Gulf 3=1-2 US$/MT	Freight US Gulf-India 4 US$/MT	CIF Import Price 5=3+4 US$/MT	Exchange Rate 6 LC/US$	Border Price Importable 7=5 6/10 LC/Qtl	Port Charges 8 LC/Qtl	Port Price Importable 9=7+8 LC/Qtl	Wholesale Price Kanpur 10 LC/Qtl	Marketing Cost Traders' Margin 11=9 0.06 LC/Qtl	TC: Bombay to Kanpur 12 LC/Qtl	Reference Price 13=9+11+12 LC/Qtl
1981	551	37.04	514.4	107.72	622.10	7.9	491.0	6.74	497.73	1,261	29.86	16.74	544.33
1982	467	25.20	441.5	92.84	534.31	8.9	477.1	7.64	484.77	1,319	29.09	21.55	535.41
1983	406	21.34	384.5	59.08	443.57	9.6	427.1	8.53	435.66	1,170	26.14	26.28	488.08
1984	572	23.50	548.3	60.00	608.25	10.3	627.2	10.18	637.39	1,485	38.24	29.63	705.26
1985	674	25.24	648.7	60.00	708.68	11.9	842.3	11.50	853.82	1,358	51.23	31.43	936.48
1986	473	21.92	450.9	60.00	510.91	12.2	625.3	12.22	637.54	1,196	38.25	33.83	709.62
1987	292	23.12	269.1	50.66	319.79	12.8	408.9	13.62	422.50	1,654	25.35	31.33	479.18
1988	328	31.76	296.4	51.50	347.91	13.0	451.2	15.38	466.56	2,333	27.99	40.99	535.54
1989	433	35.42	397.8	87.16	484.99	14.5	702.1	18.66	720.76	1,815	43.25	44.00	808.00
1990	415	44.38	370.8	84.00	454.79	16.7	757.8	20.53	778.32	1,752	46.70	50.41	875.42
1991	424	38.00	385.5	82.00	467.50	17.9	839.1	22.57	861.66	2,602	51.70	55.32	968.67
1992	410	33.84	375.7	82.00	457.74	24.5	1,122.3	26.70	1,149.05	2,877	68.94	60.01	1,278.00
1993	425	37.34	387.5	84.58	472.08	26.4	1,246.8	30.70	1,277.53	2,490	76.65	68.55	1,422.73
1994	505	34.72	470.0	84.16	554.11	31.4	1,737.9	34.09	1,772.02	2,558	106.32	77.98	1,956.31
1995	637	37.96	598.8	90.00	688.79	31.4	2,162.6	38.66	2,201.28	2,995	132.08	85.82	2,419.18
1996	579	43.50	535.6	88.00	623.58	33.5	2,086.7	42.40	2,129.07	3,110	127.74	89.07	2,345.88
1997	557	37.26	520.0	88.00	607.99	35.5	2,158.4	46.33	2,204.75	3,047	132.28	95.84	2,432.87
1998	591	24.70	566.5	88.00	654.47	37.2	2,431.9	49.58	2,481.47	2,986	148.89	110.59	2,740.95
1999	590	23.42	566.5	84.84	651.34	42.1	2,739.7	56.09	2,795.77	4,685	167.75	114.44	3,077.96
2000	391	23.42	367.8	84.84	452.67	43.3	1,961.6	57.98	2,019.59	3,550	121.18	117.90	2,258.67

Table A-6.7: (Continued)

Table A-6.7: (Continued)

Years	CIF Price 1 US$/MT	Freight Rott-US Gulf 2 US$/MT	FoB price US Gulf 3=1-2 US$/MT	Freight US Gulf-India 4 US$/MT	CIF Import Price 5=3+4 US$/MT	Exchange Rate 6 LC/US$	Border Price Importable 7=5 6/10 LC/Qtl	Port Charges 8 LC/Qtl	Port Price Importable 9=7+8 LC/Qtl	Wholesale Price Kanpur 10 LC/Qtl	Marketing Cost Traders' Margin 11=9 0.06 LC/Qtl	TC: Bombay to Kanpur 12 LC/Qtl	Reference Price 13=9+11+12 LC/Qtl
2001	343	23.42	319.6	84.84	404.42	45.7	1,847.6	60.15	1,907.74	2,883	114.46	120.54	2,142.75
2002	422	23.42	398.5	84.84	483.34	47.7	2,305.3	62.73	2,368.04	3,213	142.08	121.40	2,631.53
2003	525	23.42	501.9	84.84	586.75	48.4	2,840.3	65.30	2,905.58	3,884	174.33	123.75	3,203.66
2004	624	23.42	600.3	84.84	685.17	46.0	3,148.6	67.74	3,216.32	5,007	192.98	122.76	3,532.06
2005	679	23.42	655.7	84.84	740.50	44.9	3,327.2	70.45	3,397.65	4,597	203.86	129.18	3,730.69

Notes and Basic Data Sources:

Calendar years corresponds to the Indian rapeseed/mustard oil marketing year, i.e., April–March; April–March 1980/81 is under 1981;

Indian state covered under importable hypothesis include Uttar Pradesh (deficit state)

Column (1)	Refers to world price, i.e., Dutch FoB ex-mill for Indian rapeseed/mustard oil marketing year (April–March) (Source: USDA)
Columns (2) and (4)	Refers to freight charges from Rotterdam to US Gulf and US Gulf to Bombay port (Source: columns 2 and 4 of Table A-6.5)
Column (6)	Refers to market exchange rate for period April–March; Source, IMF, IFS data set 2007
Column (8)	Port charges from Pursell, Gulati and Gupta (2007) data set
Column (10)	Refers to domestic wholesale price of Rapeseed/Mustard oil at Kanpur market (Uttar Pradesh) during April–March, Source, Agriculture prices in India
Column (11)	Marketing cost and trader's margin is assumed to be 6 percent of landed price/port price of importable
Column (12)	Refers to transportation cost (TC) from Kanpur (Uttar Pradesh) to Bombay (Maharashtra), was calculated by constructing rail and road transport Index by following the methodology developed by Pursell and Gupta (1998); CSO report, GoI;
Column (13)	Refers to reference price under importable hypothesis

Table A-6.8: Comparison of world reference price and domestic price for soybean seed under importable hypothesis: 1981–2005

Years	CIF Price 1 US$/MT	Freight Rott-US Gulf 2 US$/MT	FoB Price US Gulf 3=1-2 US$/MT	Freight US Gulf-India 4 US$/MT	CIF Import Price 5=3+4 US$/MT	Exchange Rate 6 LC/US$	Border Price Importable 7=5 6/10 LC/Qtl	Port Charges 8 LC/Qtl	Port Price Importable 9=7+8 LC/Qtl	MP Wholesale Market Price 10 LC/Qtl	Marketing Cost Trader's Margin 11=9 0.06 LC/Qtl	TC: Bombay to Bhopal 12 LC/Qtl	Reference Price 13=9+11+12 LC/Qtl
1981	328	29.6	298	86.2	384	8.0	305	5.3	311	281	18.6	8.3	338
1982	257	20.2	237	74.3	311	9.2	285	6.0	291	273	17.5	10.2	319
1983	232	17.1	215	47.3	262	9.8	257	6.7	264	262	15.8	12.1	292
1984	313	18.8	294	48.0	342	10.5	361	7.9	368	345	22.1	13.7	404
1985	243	20.2	223	48.0	271	12.5	339	9.0	348	267	20.9	14.8	383
1986	214	17.5	196	48.0	244	12.2	298	9.5	307	279	18.4	15.9	342
1987	200	18.5	181	40.5	222	13.0	289	10.6	299	421	18.0	15.9	333
1988	242	25.4	216	41.2	257	13.0	335	12.0	347	551	20.8	19.2	387
1989	313	28.3	284	69.7	354	15.1	535	14.6	549	529	33.0	20.9	603
1990	243	35.5	207	67.2	274	17.0	466	16.0	482	509	28.9	23.1	534
1991	242	30.4	212	65.6	278	18.4	512	17.6	530	586	31.8	26.2	588
1992	237	27.1	210	65.6	275	25.9	713	20.8	734	813	44.0	29.5	807
1993	233	29.9	203	67.7	271	26.9	729	23.9	753	730	45.2	33.5	832
1994	270	27.8	242	67.3	310	31.4	972	26.6	998	791	59.9	37.0	1,095
1995	239	30.4	209	72.0	281	31.4	883	30.2	913	926	54.8	40.3	1,008
1996	291	34.8	257	70.4	327	35.2	1,150	33.1	1,183	960	71.0	42.1	1,296
1997	301	29.8	271	70.4	342	35.8	1,223	36.1	1,259	1,169	75.6	46.1	1,381
1998	277	19.8	257	70.4	327	38.4	1,257	38.7	1,296	1,078	77.8	52.4	1,426
1999	220	18.7	201	67.9	269	42.4	1,141	43.8	1,185	902	71.1	56.3	1,312
2000	207	18.7	188	67.9	256	43.5	1,115	45.2	1,160	868	69.6	59.0	1,289
2001	205	18.7	186	67.9	254	46.6	1,185	46.9	1,232	966	73.9	61.0	1,367

Table A-6.8: (*Continued*)

Table A-6.8: (*Continued*)

Years	CIF Price 1 US$/MT	Freight Rott-US Gulf 2 US$/MT	FoB Price US Gulf 3=1-2 US$/MT	Freight US Gulf-India 4 US$/MT	CIF Import Price 5=3+4 US$/MT	Exchange Rate 6 LC/US$	Border Price Importable 7=5 6/10 LC/Qtl	Port Charges 8 LC/Qtl	Port Price Importable 9=7+8 LC/Qtl	MP Wholesale Market Price 10 LC/Qtl	Marketing Cost Trader's Margin 11=9 0.06 LC/Qtl	TC: Bombay to Bhopal 12 LC/Qtl	Reference Price 13=9+11+12 LC/Qtl
2002	189	18.7	170	67.9	238	48.3	1,147	48.9	1,196	978	71.8	62.5	1,331
2003	240	18.7	221	67.9	289	48.0	1,390	50.9	1,441	1,040	86.4	64.4	1,591
2004	350	18.7	331	67.9	399	45.4	1,811	52.8	1,864	1,151	111.8	65.3	2,041
2005	265	18.7	246	67.9	314	44.3	1,391	55.0	1,445	1,215	86.7	68.5	1,601

Notes and Basic Data Sources:

	Calendar years corresponds to the Indian soybean marketing year, i.e., October–September; October–September 1980/81 is under 1981;
	Indian states covered under importable hypothesis include Madhya Pradesh (deficit state)
Column (1)	Refers to world price, i.e., Soybean, US No. 2, yellow, CIF Rotterdam for Indian harvest season, i.e., October–March (Source: UNCATD commodity price data set, 2007)
Columns (2) and (4)	Refers to freight charges from Rotterdam to US gulf and US gulf to India and were taken from Pursell, Gulati and Gupta (2007)
Column (6)	Refers to market exchange rate for period October–March (corresponds to Indian soybean harvest season); IMF, IFS data set, 2007
Column (8)	Port charges from Pursell, Gulati and Gupta (2007) data set
Column (10)	Refers to harvest season, i.e., Oct–March; wholesale domestic market price of yellow soybean at Indore (Madhya Pradesh) (Source: Agriculture Prices in India)
Column (11)	Marketing cost and trader's margin is assumed to be 6 per cent of landed price/port price of importable
Column (12)	Refers to transportation cost (TC) from Bombay (Maharashtra) to Bhopal (Madhya Pradesh), calculated by constructing rail and road transport index by following the methodology developed by Pursell and Gupta (1998); CSO report, GoI
Column (13)	Refers to reference price under importable hypothesis

Table A-6.9: Comparison of world reference price and domestic price for soybean oil under importable hypothesis: 1981–2005

Year	Dutch FoB ex-Mill 1 US$/MT	Freight Rott-US Gulf 2 US$/MT	FoB price US Gulf 3=1-2 US$/MT	Freight US Gulf-India 4 US$/MT	CIF Import Price 5=3+4 US$/MT	Exchange Rate 6 LC/US$	Border Price Importable 7=5 6/10 LC/Qtl	Port Charges 8 LC/Qtl	Port Price Importable 9=7+8 LC/Qtl	Wholesale Market Price 10 LC/Qtl	Marketing Cost Traders' Margin 11=9 0.06 LC/Qtl	TC: Bombay to Bbopal 12 LC/Qtl	Reference Price 13=9+11+12 LC/Qtl
1981	540.17	37.04	503.13	107.72	610.85	8.32	508.43	6.74	515.17		30.91	10.41	556.49
1982	463.33	25.20	438.13	92.84	530.97	9.31	494.51	7.64	502.15		30.13	12.72	545.00
1983	463.42	21.34	442.08	59.08	501.16	9.94	497.94	8.53	506.47		30.39	15.13	551.99
1984	722.00	23.50	698.50	60.00	758.50	10.91	827.52	10.18	837.70		50.26	17.15	905.12
1985	624.83	25.24	599.59	60.00	659.59	12.39	817.02	11.50	828.51		49.71	18.48	896.70
1986	376.83	21.92	354.91	60.00	414.91	12.37	513.42	12.22	525.64		31.54	19.94	577.12
1987	324.67	23.12	301.55	50.66	352.21	12.97	456.84	13.62	470.46		28.23	19.90	518.60
1988	443.00	31.76	411.24	51.50	462.74	13.44	621.77	15.38	637.15		38.23	23.95	699.34
1989	435.08	35.42	399.66	87.16	486.82	15.73	765.65	18.66	784.31		47.06	26.08	857.45
1990	437.50	44.38	393.12	84.00	477.12	17.21	821.16	20.53	841.69		50.50	28.82	921.02
1991	454.42	38.00	416.42	82.00	498.42	20.79	1,036.42	22.57	1,058.99		63.54	32.80	1,155.33
1992	437.42	33.84	403.58	82.00	485.58	25.89	1,257.32	26.70	1,284.02	2,949	77.04	36.91	1,397.97
1993	453.33	37.34	416.00	84.58	500.58	29.15	1,458.97	30.70	1,489.67	2,484	89.38	41.84	1,620.89
1994	580.17	34.72	545.45	84.16	629.61	31.37	1,975.09	34.09	2,009.18	2,771	120.55	46.23	2,175.96
1995	641.83	37.96	603.87	90.00	693.87	31.58	2,191.53	38.66	2,230.19	3,186	133.81	50.37	2,414.38
1996	574.92	43.50	531.42	88.00	619.42	35.19	2,179.57	42.40	2,221.98	3,008	133.32	52.59	2,407.89
1997	535.58	37.26	498.32	88.00	586.32	35.87	2,102.85	46.33	2,149.18	2,808	128.95	57.68	2,335.82
1998	633.42	24.70	608.72	88.00	696.72	40.04	2,789.36	49.58	2,838.95	3,465	170.34	65.54	3,074.82
1999	482.92	23.42	459.50	84.84	544.34	42.80	2,329.85	56.09	2,385.94	3,138	143.16	70.40	2,599.50
2000	354.92	23.42	331.50	84.84	416.34	44.15	1,837.92	57.98	1,895.90	2,395	113.75	73.80	2,083.45
2001	335.92	23.42	312.50	84.84	397.34	46.85	1,861.52	60.15	1,921.67	2,601	115.30	76.25	2,113.22

Table A-6.9: (Continued)

Table A-6.9: (Continued)

Year	Dutch FoB ex-Mill 1 US$/MT	Freight Rott-US Gulf 2 US$/MT	FoB price US Gulf 3=1–2 US$/MT	Freight US Gulf-India 4 US$/MT	CIF Import Price 5=3+4 US$/MT	Exchange Rate 6 LC/US$	Border Price Importable 7=5 6/10 LC/Qtl	Port Charges 8 LC/Qtl	Port Price Importable 9=7+8 LC/Qtl	Wholesale Market Price 10 LC/Qtl	Marketing Cost Traders' Margin 11=9 0.06 LC/Qtl	TC: Bombay to Bhopal 12 LC/Qtl	Reference Price 13=9+11+12 LC/Qtl
2002	411.58	23.42	388.16	84.84	473.00	48.53	2,295.56	62.73	2,358.29	3,205	141.50	78.17	2,577.96
2003	536.58	23.42	513.16	84.84	598.00	47.28	2,827.56	65.30	2,892.86	4,182	173.57	80.56	3,146.99
2004	633.42	23.42	610.00	84.84	694.84	45.45	3,158.15	67.74	3,225.89	4,508	193.55	81.65	3,501.09
2005	545.08	23.42	521.66	84.84	606.50	43.99	2,668.11	70.45	2,738.56	3,836	164.31	85.64	2,988.52

Notes and Basic Data Sources:

Calendar years correspond to Indian soybean oil marketing year, i.e., October–September; October–September 1980/81 is under 1981;

Indian state covered under importable hypothesis includes Madhya Pradesh (deficit state)

Column (1) Refers to world price, i.e., the Dutch, FoB ex-mill for period October–September (Source: UNCTAD commodity price data set, 2007)

Columns (2) and (4) Refers to freight charges from Rotterdam to US Gulf and US Gulf to Bombay port (Source: columns 2 and 4 of Table A-6.5)

Column (6) Refers to market exchange rate for period October–September; corresponds to Indian soybean oil marketing year (Source: IMF, IFS data set, 2007)

Column (8) Port charges from Pursell, Gulati and Gupta (2007) data set

Column (10) Refers to domestic wholesale price of soybean refined oil at Madhya Pradesh for the period October–September (Source: The Soybean Processors Association of India [SOPA] Madhya Pradesh)

Column (11) Marketing cost and trader's margin is assumed to be 6 per cent of port price of importable

Column (12) Refers to transportation cost (TC) from Bombay (Maharashtra) to Bhopal (Madhya Pradesh). Transportation charges for oil is assumed to be 125 per cent of those between Bombay to Bhopal for soybean (Source: column 12 of Table A-6.8)

Column (13) Refers to reference price under importable hypothesis

Table A-6.10: Comparison of world reference price and domestic price for sugar under importable hypothesis: 1981–2005

Year	World FoB Pr. Europe US$/MT	Freight Europe to India US$/MT	Border Price (CIF) US$/MT	Exchange Rate ₹/US$	Border Price (CIF) ₹/Qtl	Port Costs ₹/Qtl	Landed Price at Indian Port ₹/Qtl	UTTAR PRADESH			MAHARASHTRA			TAMIL NADU		
								Ex-Factory Price ₹/Qtl	Transport Costs ₹/Qtl	Reference Price ₹/Qtl	Ex-Factory Price ₹/Qtl	Transport Costs ₹/Qtl	Reference Price ₹/Qtl	Ex-Factory Price ₹/Qtl	Transport Costs ₹/Qtl	Reference Price ₹/Qtl
1	2	3	4 = 2+3	5	6 = 4×5/10	7	8 = 6+7	9	10	11 = 8-10	12	13	14 = 8-13	15	16	17 = 8-16
1981	579.66	38.7	618.34	8.3	514.67	8.39	523.06	396	15.2	507.8	379	NIL	524.5	398	NIL	524.5
1982	275.91	31.5	307.45	9.3	286.34	9.50	295.84	365	17.8	278.0	355	NIL	296.2	363	NIL	296.2
1983	238.65	33.7	272.38	9.9	270.63	10.62	281.25	331	20.7	260.6	332	NIL	281.7	342	NIL	281.7
1984	188.10	34.3	222.41	10.9	242.65	12.67	255.33	351	23.6	231.8	344	NIL	254.7	355	NIL	254.7
1985	142.00	33.1	175.13	12.4	216.92	14.31	231.23	416	25.7	205.5	391	NIL	231.4	390	NIL	231.4
1986	181.61	31.3	212.96	12.4	263.52	15.21	278.73	480	27.8	250.9	438	NIL	278.7	439	NIL	278.7
1987	184.71	34.5	219.23	13.0	284.36	16.95	301.32	475	29.6	271.7	460	NIL	301.4	409	NIL	301.4
1988	244.80	38.7	283.49	13.4	380.91	19.15	400.06	501	33.2	366.9	494	NIL	400.2	422	NIL	400.2
1989	345.08	48.0	393.08	15.7	618.21	23.22	641.44	567	36.6	604.8	555	NIL	638.4	443	NIL	638.4
1990	395.47	38.0	433.47	17.2	746.03	25.55	771.59	630	39.1	732.5	607	NIL	771.3	576	NIL	771.3
1991	295.65	44.4	340.10	20.8	707.20	28.09	735.29	667	46.1	689.2	619	NIL	737.4	641	NIL	737.4
1992	274.71	44.4	319.15	25.9	826.40	33.23	859.63	687	53.5	806.1	655	NIL	859.4	670	NIL	859.4
1993	271.16	42.3	313.43	29.1	913.53	38.21	951.74	801	60.3	891.5	802	NIL	948.3	830	NIL	948.3
1994	317.52	37.4	354.92	31.4	1,113.38	42.43	1,155.81	1,020	64.9	1,090.9	1,009	NIL	1,156.7	989	NIL	1,156.7
1995	390.19	42.3	432.47	31.6	1,365.91	48.12	1,414.03	1,011	70.1	1,344.0	1,002	NIL	1,414.4	925	NIL	1,414.4

Table A-6.10: (*Continued*)

Table A-6.10: (*Continued*)

Year	World FoB Pr. Europe US$/MT	Freight Europe to India US$/MT	Border Price (CIF) US$/MT	Exchange Rate ₹/US$	Border Price (CIF) ₹/Qtl	Port Costs ₹/Qtl	Landed Price at Indian Port ₹/Qtl	UTTAR PRADESH			MAHARASHTRA			TAMIL NADU		
								Ex-Factory Price ₹/Qtl	Transport Costs ₹/Qtl	Reference Price ₹/Qtl	Ex-Factory Price ₹/Qtl	Transport Costs ₹/Qtl	Reference Price ₹/Qtl	Ex-Factory Price ₹/Qtl	Transport Costs ₹/Qtl	Reference Price ₹/Qtl
1	2	3	4=2+3	5	6=4 5/10	7	8=6+7	9	10	11=8-10	12	13	14=8-13	15	16	17=8-16
1996	375.84	42.3	418.11	35.2	1,471.24	52.78	1,524.02	1,093	73.6	1,450.5	1,056	NIL	1,524.0	1,064	NIL	1,524.0
1997	316.17	42.3	358.45	35.9	1,285.57	57.67	1,343.24	1,162	82.1	1,261.2	1,139	NIL	1,343.2	1,151	NIL	1,343.2
1998	272.13	42.3	314.40	40.0	1,258.74	61.71	1,320.46	1,242	92.0	1,228.5	1,209	NIL	1,320.5	1,214	NIL	1,320.5
1999	213.29	42.3	255.57	42.8	1,093.88	69.81	1,163.69	1,259	102.1	1,061.6	1,211	NIL	1,163.7	1,183	NIL	1,163.7
2000	200.17	42.3	242.45	44.1	1,070.28	72.17	1,142.45	1,328	108.6	1,033.9	1,275	NIL	1,142.5	1,260	NIL	1,142.5
2001	249.99	42.3	292.27	46.9	1,369.28	74.87	1,444.15	1,349	113.1	1,331.0	1,292	NIL	1,444.2	1,287	NIL	1,444.2
2002	229.96	42.3	272.24	48.5	1,321.23	78.07	1,399.30	1,372	117.6	1,281.7	1,260	NIL	1,399.3	1,283	NIL	1,399.3
2003	220.26	42.3	262.54	47.3	1,241.35	81.27	1,322.63	1,187	122.3	1,200.4	1,137	NIL	1,322.6	1,153	NIL	1,322.6
2004	223.79	42.3	266.07	45.5	1,209.32	84.31	1,293.63	1,366	125.9	1,167.7	1,331	NIL	1,293.6	1,328	NIL	1,293.6
2005	273.65	42.3	315.93	44.0	1,389.82	87.68	1,477.51	1,617	131.8	1,345.7	1,597	NIL	1,477.5	1,540	NIL	1,477.5

Table A-6.10: (*Continued*)

Years	UTTAR PRADESH				MAHARASHTRA				TAMIL NADU				Average of	
	Reference Price ₹/Qtl	Ex-Factory Price ₹/Qtl	VOP ₹bln	Value Weight %	Reference Price ₹/Qtl	Ex-Factory Price ₹/Qtl	VOP ₹bln	Value Weight %	Reference Price ₹/Qtl	Ex-Factory Price ₹/Qtl	VOP ₹bln	Value Weight %	Reference Price ₹/Qtl	Ex-Factory Price ₹/Qtl
	18=11	19=9	20	21	22=14	23=12	24	25	26=17	27=15	28	29	30	31
1981	507.8	396	6.6	0.34	524.5	379	10.0	0.52	524.5	398.0	2.6	0.14	518.6	387.5
1982	278.0	365	5.8	0.34	296.2	355	8.9	0.52	296.2	363.2	2.4	0.14	289.8	359.9
1983	260.6	331	5.3	0.34	281.7	332	8.5	0.54	281.7	341.7	2.0	0.13	274.2	332.8
1984	231.8	351	4.0	0.40	254.7	344	5.1	0.50	254.7	354.7	1.0	0.10	245.1	348.0
1985	205.5	416	3.0	0.31	231.4	391	5.3	0.55	231.4	390.4	1.4	0.14	222.6	399.2
1986	250.9	480	4.1	0.32	278.7	438	6.7	0.51	278.7	439.1	2.2	0.17	269.2	452.3
1987	271.7	475	7.0	0.42	301.4	460	7.2	0.44	301.4	409.1	2.4	0.15	288.2	459.6
1988	366.9	501	9.8	0.40	400.2	494	11.2	0.46	400.2	422.2	3.2	0.13	386.0	487.8
1989	604.8	567	13.9	0.38	638.4	555	16.6	0.45	638.4	443.3	6.4	0.17	625.3	540.7
1990	732.5	630	22.0	0.37	771.3	607	30.1	0.51	771.3	576.4	6.9	0.12	756.3	612.4
1991	689.2	667	20.5	0.35	737.4	619	30.2	0.51	737.4	641.4	8.3	0.14	719.9	639.3
1992	806.1	687	29.4	0.38	859.4	655	36.1	0.47	859.4	669.7	11.4	0.15	838.2	669.9
1993	891.5	801	25.5	0.38	948.3	802	31.9	0.48	948.3	830.0	9.7	0.14	925.9	805.5
1994	1,090.9	1,020	29.7	0.40	1,156.7	1,009	31.8	0.43	1,156.7	988.9	13.0	0.17	1,129.6	1,010.0
1995	1,344.0	1,011	48.5	0.33	1,414.4	1,002	71.1	0.49	1,414.4	924.8	26.3	0.18	1,390.2	991.3
1996	1,450.5	1,093	63.5	0.37	1,524.0	1,056	82.2	0.48	1,524.0	1,063.8	24.6	0.14	1,495.7	1,071.4
1997	1,261.2	1,162	51.5	0.46	1,343.2	1,139	46.3	0.41	1,343.2	1,150.9	14.1	0.13	1,304.2	1,151.3
1998	1,228.5	1,242	48.2	0.42	1,320.5	1,209	50.8	0.44	1,320.5	1,213.5	16.7	0.14	1,280.5	1,223.8

Table A-6.10: (*Continued*)

Table A-6.10: (Continued)

Years	UTTAR PRADESH Reference Price ₹/Qtl	Ex-Factory Price ₹/Qtl	VOP ₹bln	Value Weight %	MAHARASHTRA Reference Price ₹/Qtl	Ex-Factory Price ₹/Qtl	VOP ₹bln	Value Weight %	TAMIL NADU Reference Price ₹/Qtl	Ex-Factory Price ₹/Qtl	VOP ₹bln	Value Weight %	Average of Reference Price ₹/Qtl	Ex-Factory Price ₹/Qtl
	18=11	19=9	20	21	22=14	23=12	24	25	26=17	27=15	28	29	30	31
1999	1,061.6	1,259	39.6	0.32	1,163.7	1,211	62.1	0.51	1,163.7	1,183.4	20.6	0.17	1,128.6	1,223.3
2000	1,033.9	1,328	47.1	0.33	1,142.5	1,275	74.3	0.52	1,142.5	1,259.9	20.2	0.14	1,103.9	1,291.9
2001	1,331.0	1,349	58.5	0.32	1,444.2	1,292	96.8	0.53	1,444.2	1,286.9	26.3	0.14	1,405.7	1,310.7
2002	1,281.7	1,372	67.4	0.39	1,399.3	1,260	78.5	0.46	1,399.3	1,283.4	26.3	0.15	1,350.8	1,309.8
2003	1,200.4	1,187	67.8	0.39	1,322.6	1,137	82.2	0.48	1,322.6	1,153.3	22.2	0.13	1,271.6	1,159.9
2004	1,167.7	1,366	53.1	0.50	1,293.6	1,331	41.1	0.39	1,293.6	1,328.1	12.2	0.11	1,227.5	1,349.1
2005	1,345.7	1,617	67.8	0.58	1,477.5	1,597	32.8	0.28	1,477.5	1,539.9	16.6	0.14	1,398.3	1,601.1

Notes and Basic Data Sources:

Indian state covered under importable hypothesis includes Uttar Pradesh, Maharashtra and Tamil Nadu

Column (1) Calendar year corresponds to Indian sugar year, i.e., October–September, October–September 1980/81 is under 1981

Column (2) The international price refers to the October–September price of raw sugar, FoB Caribbean ports and refined sugar prices, FoB European ports from FAS, ERS, USDA, Washington, DC, USA; The international price is converted into plantation white sugar by:

white plantation sugar = (white sugar − raw sugar) × 0.9 + raw sugar.

Column (3) Refers to freight charges from Europe to India and were taken from Pursell, Gulati and Gupta (2007)

Column (5) Refers to market exchange rate for period October–September; IMF, IFS data set, 2007

Column (7)	Port charges from Pursell, Gulati and Gupta (2007) data set
Columns (9), (12) and (15)	Refers to domestic price of sugar, i.e., ex-factory realisation price of sugar; The ex-factory realisation price was calculated by Ex-factory price = free sale ratio × (price of free sale sugar − excise and cess on free sale sugar − marketing and traders margin) + (1 − free sale ratio) × price of levy sugar. Data on free sale ratio, cess and excise on sugar are from Sugar Cooperative; Levy and free sale sugar prices are from Bulletin on Food Statistics; Marketing cost and traders' margin on free sale sugar is assumed to equal three percent of the free sale sugar price.
Columns (10), (13) and (16)	Refers to transportation cost (TC) and were calculated by constructing rail and road transport index by following the methodology developed by Pursell and Gupta (1998) (Source: CSO report, GoI)
Columns (20), (24) and (28)	Refers to value of production in reference price
Columns (21), (25) and (29)	Value weight = VOP/aggregate VOP of the states
Columns (30) and (31)	Aggregate price of the three states = sum (share in production × price in the state) for the three states

Table A-6.11: Comparison of world reference price and domestic price for sugar under exportable hypothesis: 1981–2005

										UTTAR PRADESH			MAHARASHTRA			TAMIL NADU	
Year	World Price Europe US\$/MT	Freight Europe to Egypt US\$/MT	CIF Egypt US\$/MT	Exchange Rate ₹/US\$	Indian Border Price ₹/Qtl	Port Costs ₹/Qtl	Price at Port Indian ₹/Qtl	Ex-Factory Price ₹/Qtl	Transport Costs ₹/Qtl	Reference Price ₹/Qtl	Ex-Factory Price ₹/Qtl	Transport Costs ₹/Qtl	Reference Price ₹/Qtl	Ex-Factory Price ₹/Qtl	Transport Costs ₹/Qtl	Reference Price ₹/Qtl
1	2	3	4 = 2+3	5	6 = (4–3)5/10	7	8 = 6–7	9	10	11 = 8–10	12	13	14 = 8–13	15	16	17 = 8–16
1981	579.66	14.2	593.86	8.3	482.47	8.4	474.1	396	15.2	458.8	379	NIL	475.5	398	NIL	475.5
1982	275.91	11.5	287.41	9.3	256.96	9.5	247.5	365	17.8	229.7	355	NIL	247.9	363	NIL	247.9
1983	238.65	12.3	250.95	9.9	237.12	10.6	226.5	331	20.7	205.8	332	NIL	226.9	342	NIL	226.9
1984	188.10	12.6	200.70	10.9	205.21	12.7	192.5	351	23.6	169.0	344	NIL	192.0	355	NIL	192.0
1985	142.00	10.7	152.70	12.4	175.89	14.3	161.6	416	25.7	135.8	391	NIL	161.7	390	NIL	161.7
1986	181.61	8.9	190.51	12.4	224.73	15.2	209.5	480	27.8	181.7	438	NIL	209.5	439	NIL	209.5
1987	184.71	12.0	196.71	13.0	239.59	17.0	222.6	475	29.6	193.0	460	NIL	222.8	409	NIL	222.8
1988	244.80	17.0	261.80	13.4	328.94	19.1	309.8	501	33.2	276.6	494	NIL	309.9	422	NIL	309.9
1989	345.08	16.2	361.28	15.7	542.72	23.2	519.5	567	36.6	482.9	555	NIL	516.5	443	NIL	516.5
1990	395.47	15.9	411.37	17.2	680.63	25.6	655.1	630	39.1	616.0	607	NIL	654.8	576	NIL	654.8
1991	295.65	15.9	311.55	20.8	614.78	28.1	586.7	667	46.1	540.6	619	NIL	588.8	641	NIL	588.8
1992	274.71	15.4	290.11	25.9	711.31	33.2	678.1	687	53.5	624.6	655	NIL	677.8	670	NIL	677.8
1993	271.16	17.9	289.06	29.1	790.31	38.2	752.1	801	60.3	691.8	802	NIL	748.7	830	NIL	748.7

1994	317.52	13.7	331.22	31.4	996.05	42.4	953.6	1,020	64.9	888.7	1,009	NIL	954.5	989	NIL	954.5
1995	390.19	15.5	405.69	31.6	1,232.37	48.1	1,184.3	1,011	70.1	1,114.2	1,002	NIL	1,184.6	925	NIL	1,184.6
1996	375.84	15.5	391.34	35.2	1,322.47	52.8	1,269.7	1,093	73.6	1,196.1	1,056	NIL	1,269.7	1,064	NIL	1,269.7
1997	316.17	15.5	331.67	35.9	1,133.94	57.7	1,076.3	1,162	82.1	994.2	1,139	NIL	1,076.3	1,151	NIL	1,076.3
1998	272.13	15.5	287.63	40.0	1,089.48	61.7	1,027.8	1,242	92.0	935.8	1,209	NIL	1,027.8	1,214	NIL	1,027.8
1999	213.29	15.5	228.79	42.8	912.93	69.8	843.1	1,259	102.1	741.0	1,211	NIL	843.1	1,183	NIL	843.1
2000	200.17	15.5	215.67	44.1	883.65	72.2	811.5	1,328	108.6	702.9	1,275	NIL	811.5	1,260	NIL	811.5
2001	249.99	15.5	265.49	46.9	1,171.21	74.9	1,096.3	1,349	113.1	983.2	1,292	NIL	1,096.3	1,287	NIL	1,096.3
2002	229.96	15.5	245.46	48.5	1,116.05	78.1	1,038.0	1,372	117.6	920.3	1,260	NIL	1,038.0	1,283	NIL	1,038.0
2003	220.26	15.5	235.76	47.3	1,041.45	81.3	960.2	1,187	122.3	837.9	1,137	NIL	960.2	1,153	NIL	960.2
2004	223.79	15.5	239.29	45.5	1,017.16	84.3	932.9	1,366	125.9	806.9	1,331	NIL	932.9	1,328	NIL	932.9
2005	273.65	15.5	289.15	44.0	1,203.83	87.7	1,116.2	1,617	131.8	984.4	1,597	NIL	1,116.2	1,540	NIL	1,116.2

Table A-6.11: (*Continued*)

Table A-6.11: (Continued)

Years	UTTAR PRADESH				MAHARASHTRA				TAMIL NADU				Average of	
	Reference Price ₹/Qtl	Ex-factory Price ₹/Qtl	VOP ₹bln	Value Weight %	Reference Price ₹/Qtl	Ex-Factory Price ₹/Qtl	VOP ₹bln	Value Weight %	Reference Price ₹/Qtl	Ex-Factory Price ₹/Qtl	VOP ₹bln	Value Weight %	Reference Price ₹/Qtl	Ex-Factory Price ₹/Qtl
	18=11	19=9	20	21	22=14	23=12	24	25	26=17	27=15	28	29	30	31
1981	458.8	396.0	6.0	0.34	475.5	379.0	9.0	0.52	475.5	398.0	2.4	0.14	469.6	387.5
1982	229.7	364.9	4.8	0.34	247.9	355.4	7.4	0.52	247.9	363.2	2.0	0.14	241.4	359.9
1983	205.8	331.3	4.2	0.33	226.9	331.7	6.8	0.54	226.9	341.7	1.6	0.13	219.4	332.8
1984	169.0	350.9	2.9	0.39	192.0	344.2	3.8	0.51	192.0	354.7	0.8	0.10	182.3	348.0
1985	135.8	415.5	2.0	0.30	161.7	391.0	3.7	0.56	161.7	390.4	1.0	0.14	153.0	399.2
1986	181.7	479.6	3.0	0.31	209.5	437.9	5.0	0.52	209.5	439.1	1.7	0.17	200.0	452.3
1987	193.0	475.2	4.9	0.41	222.8	459.7	5.3	0.44	222.8	409.1	1.8	0.15	209.5	459.6
1988	276.6	501.3	7.4	0.40	309.9	493.7	8.7	0.47	309.9	422.2	2.5	0.13	295.7	487.8
1989	482.9	567.4	11.1	0.37	516.5	554.5	13.4	0.45	516.5	443.3	5.2	0.17	503.4	540.7
1990	616.0	630.3	18.5	0.37	654.8	606.9	25.5	0.51	654.8	576.4	5.9	0.12	639.8	612.4
1991	540.6	666.7	16.1	0.34	588.8	618.7	24.1	0.51	588.8	641.4	6.7	0.14	571.3	639.3
1992	624.6	687.1	22.8	0.38	677.8	655.0	28.5	0.47	677.8	669.7	9.0	0.15	656.7	669.9
1993	691.8	801.3	19.8	0.38	748.7	801.6	25.2	0.48	748.7	830.0	7.6	0.15	726.2	805.5
1994	888.7	1,019.9	24.2	0.40	954.5	1,008.8	26.2	0.43	954.5	988.9	10.7	0.17	927.4	1,010.0
1995	1,114.2	1,010.8	40.2	0.33	1,184.6	1,001.9	59.5	0.49	1,184.6	924.8	22.0	0.18	1,160.4	991.3

Year													
1996	1,196.1	1,092.6	52.4	0.37	1,269.7	1,056.5	68.5	0.48	1,269.7	1,063.8	20.5	0.14	1,241.4	1,071.4
1997	994.2	1,161.8	40.6	0.46	1,076.3	1,139.1	37.1	0.42	1,076.3	1,150.9	11.3	0.13	1,037.2	1,151.3
1998	935.8	1,242.1	36.7	0.41	1,027.8	1,208.7	39.5	0.44	1,027.8	1,213.5	13.0	0.15	987.8	1,223.8
1999	741.0	1,259.4	27.6	0.32	843.1	1,211.3	45.0	0.51	843.1	1,183.4	15.0	0.17	808.0	1,223.3
2000	702.9	1,327.8	32.0	0.32	811.5	1,275.4	52.8	0.53	811.5	1,259.9	14.3	0.14	772.9	1,291.9
2001	983.2	1,348.9	43.2	0.32	1,096.3	1,292.1	73.5	0.54	1,096.3	1,286.9	19.9	0.15	1,057.9	1,310.7
2002	920.3	1,372.4	48.4	0.38	1,038.0	1,259.9	58.3	0.46	1,038.0	1,283.4	19.5	0.15	989.4	1,309.8
2003	837.9	1,186.8	47.4	0.38	960.2	1,137.1	59.7	0.48	960.2	1,153.3	16.1	0.13	909.2	1,159.9
2004	806.9	1,366.1	36.7	0.49	932.9	1,331.0	29.6	0.39	932.9	1,328.1	8.8	0.12	866.7	1,349.1
2005	984.4	1,616.8	49.6	0.57	1,116.2	1,596.5	24.7	0.28	1,116.2	1,539.9	12.6	0.14	1,036.9	1,601.1

Notes and Basic Data Sources:

Indian state covered under exportable hypothesis includes Uttar Pradesh, Maharashtra and Tamil Nadu;

Under the exportable hypothesis, Indian sugar is assumed to compete with sugar from other major exporters in Egypt

Column (1)   Calendar year corresponds to Indian sugar year, i.e., October–September; October–September 1980/81 is under 1981

Column (2)   The international price refers to the October–September price of raw sugar, FoB Caribbean ports and refined sugar prices FoB European ports from FAS, ERS, USDA, Washington, DC, USA; The international price is converted into plantation white sugar by:

white plantation sugar = (white sugar − raw sugar) × 0.9 + raw sugar.

Column (3)   Refers to freight charges from Europe to Egypt and assumed to be half the freight from Caribbean to Europe; Source: Pursell, Gulati and Gupta (2007) data set

Table A-6.11: (*Continued*)

Table A-6.11: (*Continued*)

Column (5)	Refers to market exchange rate for period Oct–Sept; IMF, IFS data set, 2007
Column (6)	FoB Indian prices = [CIF Egypt prices – freight from Egypt to India] × exchange rate / 10
	Freight from Egypt to India = freight from Europe to Egypt
Column (7)	Port charges from Pursell, Gulati and Gupta (2007) data set
Column (9),	Refers to domestic price of sugar, i.e., ex-factory realisation price of sugar; The ex-factory realisation price was calculated by
(12) and (15)	Ex factory price = free sale price ratio × (price of free sale sugar – excise & cess on free sale sugar – marketing & traders margin) + (1 – free sale ratio) × price of levy sugar.
	Data on free sale ratio, cess and excise on sugar are from Sugar Cooperative; Levy and free sale sugar prices are from Bulletin on Food Statistics; Marketing cost and traders' margin on free sale sugar is assumed to equal three per cent of the free sale sugar price.
Columns (10), (13) and (16)	Refers to transportation cost (TC) and were calculated by constructing rail and road transport index by following the methodology developed by Pursell and Gupta (1998); Source: CSO report, GoI
Columns (20), (24) and (28)	Refers to value of production in reference price
Columns (21), (25) and (29)	Value weight = VOP/aggregate VOP of the states
Columns (30) and (31)	Aggregate price of the three states = sum (share in production × price in the state) for the three states

Appendix IV

Figures

Figure A-4.1: Conditional standard deviation of wheat market price at:

(a) Karnal market

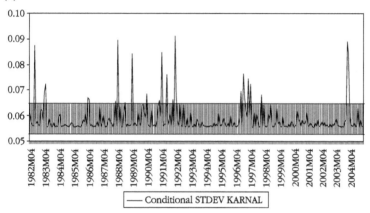

(b) Ludhiana market

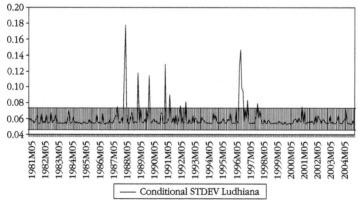

Source: All figures in this section have been computed by the author using E-Views.

Note: M = Month

Figure A-4.2: Conditional standard deviation of groundnut seed market price at:

(a) Madras market

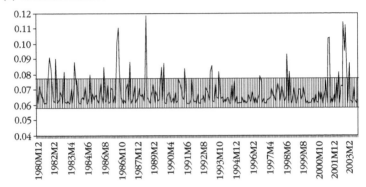

(b) Nandyal market

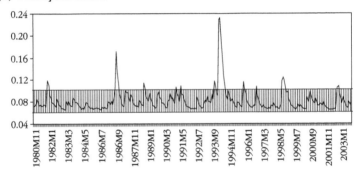

(c) Rotterdam market

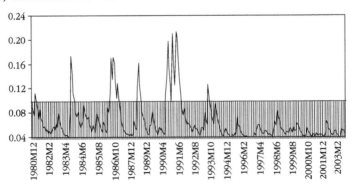

Figure A-4.3: Conditional standard deviation of groundnut oil market price at:

(a) Madras market

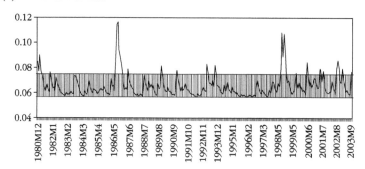

(b) Hyderabad market

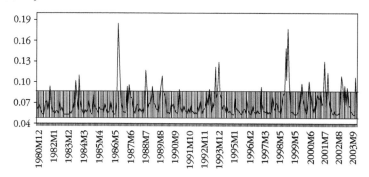

(c) Rotterdam market

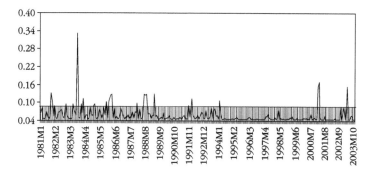

Figure A-4.4: Conditional standard deviation of rapeseed/mustard seed market price at:

(a) Calcutta market

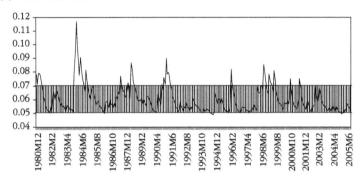

(b) Hapur market

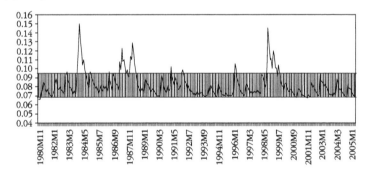

(c) Kanpur market

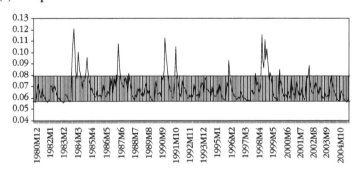

Figure A-4.5: Conditional standard deviation of rapeseed/mustard oil market price at:

(a) Calcutta market

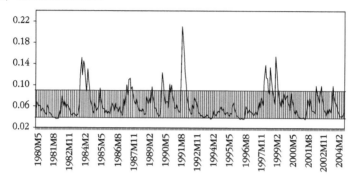

(b) Delhi market

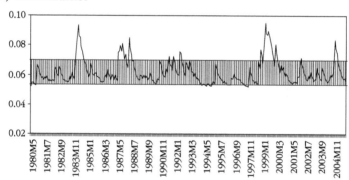

(c) Dutch market

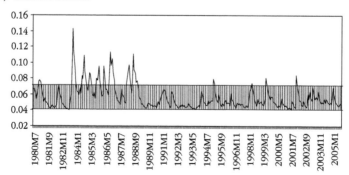

Figure A-4.6(a): Conditional standard deviation of soybean seed market price at Rotterdam

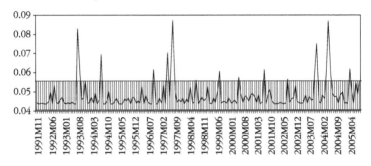

Figure A-4.6(b): Conditional standard deviation of soybean oil market price at the Netherlands

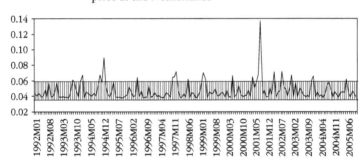

Figure A-4.7: Conditional standard deviation of sugar market price at:

(a) Bombay market

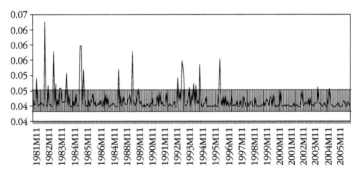

(b) Kanpur market

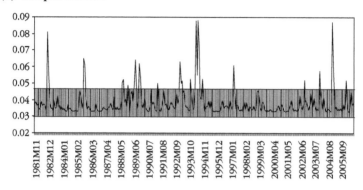

(c) Caribbean port (raw sugar)

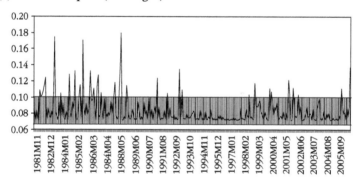

Bibliography

Acharya, S. S. 1997. 'Agricultural Price Policy and Development: Some Facts and Emerging Issues', Presidential address, *Indian Journal of Agricultural Economics*, 52(1): 1–47.

———. 2000. 'Subsidies in Indian Agriculture and Their Beneficiaries', *Agricultural Situation in India*, 47(5): 251–60.

———. 2001. 'Domestic Agricultural Marketing Policies, Incentives and Integration', in S. S. Acharya and D. P. Chaudhri (eds), *Indian Agricultural Policy at the Cross Roads: Priorities and Agenda*, pp. 129–212. Jaipur and Delhi: Rawat Publications.

Acharya, S. S. and R. L. Jogi. 2004. 'Farm Input Subsidies in Indian Agriculture', Working Paper No. 140, Institute of Development Studies, Jaipur.

Ahluwalia, Montek S. 1996. 'New Economic Policy and Agriculture: Some Reflections', *Indian Journal of Agricultural Economics*, 51(3): 412–26.

Anderson, K. and R. Tyres. 1990. 'How Developing Countries Could Gain from Agricultural Trade Liberalisation', in I. Goldin and O. Knudson (eds), *Uruguay Round in Agricultural Trade Liberalisation*. Paris and Washington: Organisation for Economic Cooperation and Development (OECD).

Anderson, K., W. Martin and D. van der Mensbrugghe. 2005. 'Market and Welfare Implications of Doha Reform Scenario', https://www.gtap.agecon.purdue.edu/resources/download/2241.pdf (accessed 18 October 2007).

———. 2006. 'Market and Welfare Implications of Doha Reform Scenarios', in K. Anderson and W. Martin (eds), *Agricultural Trade Reform and the Doha Development Agenda*. London: Palgrave Macmillan; and Washington, DC: World Bank. http://siteresources.worldbank.org/INTRANETTRADE/Resources/2390541109114763805/Ch12_AndersonMartinMensbrugghe.pdf (accessed 18 October 2007).

BAPPENAS/USAID/DAI FOOD POLICY ADVISORY TEAM REPORT. 1999. 'The Future of World Rice Market and Policy Options to Counter Rice Price Instability in Indonesia', Working Paper No. 03, USAID, Washington, DC.

Batley, R. 1994. 'The Consolidation of Adjustment: Implications for Public Administration', *Public Administration and Development*, 14(5): 489–505.

Bhagwati, J. and T. N. Srinivasan. 1993. 'India's Economic Reform: A Report', Ministry of Finance, Government of India.

Bhalla, G. S. 1995. 'Globalization and Agricultural Policy in India', *Indian Journal of Agricultural Economics*, 50(1): 7–26.

———. 2004. 'Globalisation and Indian Agriculture', *State of the Indian Farmer: A Millennium Study*, vol. 19. New Delhi: Academic Foundation.

Bhasin, V. K. 1996. 'Emerging Indian Rice Trade Scenario', in R. Chand and T. Haque (eds), *Vision of India's Rice Trade*. New Delhi: National Centre for Agricultural Economics and Policy Research (NCAP).

Bhatia, B. M. 1991. *Famines in India*. New Delhi: Konark Publishers.

Bhattacharya, B. B. and C. H. Hanumantha Rao. 1988. 'Agriculture–Industry Interaction: Issues of Relative Prices and Growth in the Context of Public Investment', Paper presented at the Eighth World Economic Congress, New Delhi, 1–5 December 1988.

Blandford, D. 1983. 'Instability in World Grain Markets', *Journal of Agricultural Economics*, 43(3): 379–95.

Bollerslev, T. 1986. 'Generalised Autoregressive Conditional Heteroscedasticity', *Journal of Econometrics*, 31: 307–27.

Box, G. E. P., and G. M. Jenkins. 1976. *Times Series Analysis: Forecasting and Control*. San Francisco: Holden-Day.

Chand, R. 1998. 'Removal of Import Restrictions and India's Agriculture: The Challenge and Strategy', *Economic and Political Weekly*, 33(15): 850–54.

———. 2000. 'Emerging Trends and Regional Variations in Agricultural Investments and Their Implications for Growth and Equity', Policy Paper 11, National Centre for Agricultural Economics and Policy Research (NCAP), New Delhi.

———. 2002. *Trade Liberalisation, WTO and Indian Agriculture: Experience and Prospects*. New Delhi: Mittal Publications.

———. 2004. 'Impact of Trade Liberalization and related Reforms on India's Agricultural Sector, Rural Food Security, Income and Poverty', Paper presented at the 5th Annual Global Development Conference, Global Development Network, New Delhi, 28–30 January.

———. 2005. 'Whither India's Food Policy? From Food Security to Food Deprivation', *Economic and Political Weekly*, 40(11): 1055–62.

———. 2007. 'Wheat Supply, Price Prospects and Food Security', *Economic and Political Weekly*, 42(19): 1659–63.

———. 2010. 'Understanding the Nature and Causes of Food Inflation', *Economic and Political Weekly*, 45(9): 10–13.

Chand, R. and D. Jha. 2001. 'Trade liberalization, Agricultural Prices and Net Social Welfare', in S. S. Acharya and D. P. Chaudhri (eds), *Indian Agricultural Policy at the Crossroads: Priorities and Agenda*, pp. 17–111. Jaipur: Rawat Publications.

Chand, R., D. Jha and S. Mittal. 2004. 'WTO and Oilseeds Sector: Challenges of Trade Liberalisation', *Economic and Political Weekly*, 39(6): 533–37.

Chand, R., S. S. Raju and L. M. Pandey. 2007. 'Growth Crisis in Agriculture: Severity and Options at National and State Levels', *Economic and Political Weekly*, 42(26): 2528–33.

Chavan, P. 2002. 'Some Features of Rural Credit in India: A Study after the Period of Bank Nationalisation', Unpublished M.Phil thesis, Indira Gandhi Institute of Development Research (IGIDR), Mumbai.

———. 2005. 'Banking Sector Liberalization and the Growth and Regional Distribution of Rural Banking', in V. K. Ramachandran, and M. Swaminathan (eds), *Financial Liberalization and Rural Credit in India*. New Delhi: Tulika Books.

Chopra, R. N. 1988. *Food Policy in India: A Survey*. New Delhi: Intellectual Publishing House.

Commission of Agricultural Cost and Prices (CACP). 1998. 'Report of the Commission for Agricultural Costs and Prices on Price Policy for Kharif Crops of 1998–99 Season', mimeo.

Commodity Online. 2009. 'India's Rice Export Ban to Help Global Competitors', *Commodity Online*, New Delhi, 16 July. http://www.commodityonline. com/news/indias-rice-export-ban-to-help-global-competitors-19641-3-19642.html (accessed 28 October 2013).

Datta, S. K. 1996. 'India's Trade Prospects for Rice', in R. Chand and T. Haque (eds), *Vision of India's Rice Trade*. New Delhi: National Centre for Agricultural Economics and Policy Research (NCAP).

Dedehouanou, H. and P. Q. van Ufford. 2000. 'Comparing Liberalisation in Agricultural Input and Draught Animal Markets in Benin', in Aad van Tilburg, Henk A. J. Moll and Arie Kuyvenhoven (eds), *Agricultural Markets Beyond Liberalization*, pp. 173–90. New York: Kluwer Academic Publishers.

Desai, B. M. 2002. 'Terms of Trade, Trade and Technical Change: Strategies for Agricultural Growth', *Economic and Political Weekly*, 37(8): 801–4.

Desai, B. M. and E. D'Souza. 1999. 'Economic Reforms, Terms of Trade, Aggregate Supply and Private Investment in Agriculture', *Economic and Political Weekly*, 34(20): 1220–24.

Dohlman, E., S. C. Persaud and R. Landes. 2003. 'India's Edible Oil Sector: Imports Fill Rising Demand', *Economic Research Service*. Washington, DC: USDA.

Engle, R. 1982. 'Autoregressive Conditional Heteroscedasticity with Estimates of the Variance of United Kingdom Inflation', *Econometrica*, 50(4): 987–1007.

Fackler, P. L. and B. K. Goodwin. 2001. 'Spatial Price Analysis', in B. L. Gardner and G. C. Rausser (eds), *Handbook of Agricultural Economics*, pp. 971–1024, Amsterdam: Elsevier.

Food and Agriculture Organization (FAO). 2002. *Commodity Market Review 2001–02*. Rome: Commodities and Trade Division, FAO.

Ghosh, J. 1992. 'Twelve Theses on Agricultural Prices', *Social Scientist*, 20(11): 20–25.

———. 2005. 'Trade Liberalisation in Agriculture: An Examination of Impact and Policy Strategies with Special Reference to India', Background Paper for Human Development Report 2005, New Delhi.

Goldar, B. and A. Gulati 1991. 'Effective Incentives for Sugarcane and Sugar', Working Paper, National Council for Applied Economic Research (NCAER), New Delhi.

Government of India (GoI). 1957. 'Report of the Foodgrains Enquiry Committee 1957', Ministry of Food and Agriculture (Department of Food), GoI, New Delhi.

———. 1965. 'Report of the Jha Committee on Foodgrain Prices for 1964–65', Department of Agriculture and Cooperation, GoI, New Delhi.

———. 1980. 'Report of the Special Expert Committee on Cost of Production Estimates', Ministry of Agriculture, Department of Agriculture and Cooperation, GoI, New Delhi.

———. 1986. 'Agricultural Price Policy: A Long Term Perspective', Ministry of Agriculture, GoI, New Delhi.

———. 2002. 'Report of the High Level Committee on Long Term Grain Policy', Department of Food and Public Distribution, Ministry of Consumer Affairs, Food and Public Distribution, GoI, New Delhi.

———. 2006. 'Approach Paper to 11th Five-Year Plan', Planning Commission, GoI, New Delhi.

Gulati, A. 1987. *Agricultural Price Policy in India: An Econometric Approach.* New Delhi: Concept Publishing Company.

———. 1989. 'Input Subsidies in Indian Agriculture: A State-wise Analysis', *Economic and Political Weekly*, 24(25): A57–A66.

———. 1998. 'Indian Agriculture in an Open Economy: Will it Prosper?', in Isher Judge Ahluwalia and I. M. D. Little (eds), *India's Economic Reforms and Development: Essays for Manmohan Singh.* New Delhi: Oxford University Press.

Gulati, A. and A. N. Sharma. 1992. 'Subsidising Agriculture: A Cross Country View', *Economic and Political Weekly*, 27(39): A106–A116.

———. 1994. 'Agriculture under GATT: What it Holds for India', *Economic and Political Weekly*, 29(29): 1857–63.

Gulati, A., A. Sharma and D. S. Kohli. 1996. 'Self-Sufficiency and Allocative Efficiency: Case of Oilseeds in India', National Council of Applied Economic Research (NCAER), New Delhi, mimeo.

Gulati, A., J. Hanson and G. Pursell. 1990. 'Effective Incentives in India's Agriculture', working paper no. 32, Policy, Planning and Research (Trade Policy), World Bank, Washington, DC.

Gulati, A. and P. K. Sharma. 1990. 'Prices, Procurement and Production: An Analysis of Wheat and Rice', *Economic and Political Weekly*, 25(13): A36–A47.

Gulati, A. and P. K. Sharma. 1991. 'Government Intervention in Agricultural Markets: Nature, Impact and Implications', *Journal of Indian School of Political Economy*, 3(2): 205–37.

Gulati, A. and S. Narayanan. 2003. *Subsidy Syndrome in Indian Agriculture*. New Delhi: Oxford University Press

Gulati, A. and T. Kelly. 1999. *Trade Liberalization and Indian Agriculture*. New Delhi: Oxford University Press.

Hanumantha Rao, C. H. 1994. *Agricultural Growth, Rural Poverty and Environmental Degradation in India*. New Delhi: Oxford University Press.

Hazell, P. B. R., V. N. Misra and B. Hojjati. 1995. 'Role of Terms of Trade in Indian Agricultural Growth: A National and State Level Analysis', EPTD discussion paper no. 15, International Food Policy Research Institute (IFPRI), Washington, DC.

Heifner, R. G. and R. Kinoshita. 1994. 'Differences among Commodities in Real Price Variability and Drift', *Journal of Agricultural Economics Research*, 45(3): 10–20.

Hoda, A. and A. Gulati. 2008. *WTO Negotiations on Agriculture and Developing Countries*. New Delhi: Oxford University Press/Johns Hopkins University Press.

Hueth, D. and A. Schmitz. 1972. 'International Trade in Intermediate and Final Goods: Some Welfare Implications of Destabilized Prices', *The Quarterly Journal of Economics*, 86(3): 351–65.

Jha, S. and P. V. Srinivasan. 1999. 'Grain Price Stabilization in India: Evaluation of Policy Alternatives', *Agricultural Economics*, 21(1): 93–108.

Krishna, R. and G. S. Raychaudhuri. 1980. 'Some Aspects of Wheat and Rice Price Policy in India', World Bank Staff Working Paper No. 381, World Bank, Washington, DC.

Krishnaji, N. 1990. 'Agricultural Price Policy: A Survey with Reference to Indian Foodgrain Economy', *Economic and Political Weekly*, 25(26): A54–A63.

Krishnamurty, K. 1985. 'Inflation and Growth: A Model for India', in K. Krishnamurty and V. N. Pandit (eds), *Macroeconomic Modelling of the Indian Economy: Studies in Inflation and Growth*, pp. 39–42. Delhi: Hindustan Publishing Corporation.

Lezin, Andzio-Bika H. W. and W. Long-bao. 2005. 'Agricultural Productivity Growth and Technology Progress in Developing Country Agriculture: Case Study in China', *Journal of Zhejiang University Science*, 6(1): 172–76.

Liefert, W. M. 2007. 'Decomposing Changes in Agricultural Producer Prices', Working Paper No. 07–01, International Agricultural Trade Research Consortium (IATRC).

Liefert, W. M. 2011. 'Decomposing Changes in Agricultural Producer Prices', *Journal of Agricultural Economics*, 62(1): 119–36.

Little, I., T. Scitovsky and M. Scott. 1970. *Industry and Trade in Some Developing Countries: A Comparative Study*. Paris: OECD.

Misra, V. N. 1998. 'Economic Reforms, Terms of Trade, Aggregate Supply, and Private Investment in Agriculture: Indian Experience', *Economic and Political Weekly*, 33(31): 2105–9.

Misra, V. N. and Peter B. R. Hazell. 1996. 'Terms of Trade, Rural Poverty, Technology and Investment: The Indian Experience, 1952–53 to 1990–91', *Economic and Political Weekly*, 31(13): A2–A13.

Mittal, A. 2005. 'Industrial Agriculture: Land Loss, Poverty and Hunger', International Forum on Globalization, San Francisco. http://www.ifg.org/pdf/hunger&pov-anuradha.pdf_1.pdf (accessed 18 January 2008).

Mody, A. 1981. 'Resource Flows between Agriculture and Non-Agriculture in India, 1950–1970', *Economic and Political Weekly*, 16(10–12): 425–40.

Moledina, A. A., T. L. Roe and M. Shane. 2003. 'Measurement of Commodity Price Volatility and the Welfare Consequences of Eliminating Volatility', Working Paper, Economic Development Centre, University of Minnesota, Minneapolis.

Myrdal, G. 1968. *Asian Drama*. New York: Pantheon.

Nair, K. N. and R. Ramakumar. 2007. 'Agrarian Distress and Rural Livelihoods: A Study in Upputhara Panchayat, Idukki District, Kerala', Working paper no. 392, Centre for Development Studies (CDS), Trivandrum.

Nayyar, D. and A. Sen. 1994. 'International Trade and the Agricultural Sector in India', *Economic and Political Weekly*, 29(20): 1187–203.

Nurkse, R. 1953. *Problems of Capital Formation in Underdeveloped Countries*. New York: Oxford University Press.

Odhiambo, W., H. O. Nyangito and J. Nzuma. 2004. 'Sources and Determinants of Agricultural Growth and Productivity in Kenya', KIPPRA Discussion Paper No. 34, Productive Sector Division, Kenya Institute of Public Policy Research and Analysis.

Organisation for Economic Co-operation and Development (OECD). 2002. 'Decomposition of Country-Specific Commodity Trees', OECD Internal Working Document, Paris.

Offutt, S. E. and D. Blandford. 1986. 'Commodity Market Instability: Empirical Techniques for Analysis', *Resources Policy*, 12(1): 62–72.

Pandit, V. 2000. 'Data Relating to Prices in India', *Indian Economic Review*, 35(1):77–96.

Parikh, K. 1997. 'Overview: Prospects and Retrospect', in Kirit Parikh (ed.), *India Development Report, 1997*. New Delhi and New York: Oxford University Press.

Parikh, K., P. V. Srinivasan and S. Jha. 1993. 'Economic Reforms and Agricultural Policy', *Economic and Political Weekly*, 28(29–30): 1497–1500.

Patnaik, P. 2003. 'Agricultural Production and Prices under Globalisation', in his *The Retreat to Unfreedom: Essays on the Emerging World Order*, pp. 198–210. New Delhi: Tulika Books.

Patnaik, U. 1996. 'Export Oriented Agriculture and Food Security in Developing Countries and India', *Economic and Political Weekly*, 31(35–37): 2429–50.

Pinstrup-Andersen, P., R. Pandya-Lorch and M. W. Rosegrant. 1997. 'The World Food Situation: Recent Developments, Emerging Issues, and Long-Term Prospects', 2020 Vision Paper. Washington, DC: International Food Policy Research Institute.

Pursell, G. 2007. 'Smuggling and the Economic Welfare Consequences of an FTA: A case study of India–Bangladesh Trade in Sugar', Working Paper No. 05, Australia South Asia Research Centre (ASARC), Australian National University.

Pursell, G. and A, Gupta. 1998. 'Trade Policies and Incentives in Indian Agriculture, Sugar and Sugarcane', Background Paper No. 01, World Bank, Washington, DC.

Pursell, G. and A. Gulati. 1993. 'Liberalizing Indian Agriculture: An Agenda for Reform', Working Paper WPS 1172, Policy Research Department, World Bank, Washington, DC.

Pursell, G., A. Gulati and K. Gupta. 2007. 'Distortions to Agricultural Incentives in India', Data Spreadsheet for Agricultural Distortions, Working Paper No. 34, World Bank. http://www.worldbank.org/agdistortions (accessed 23 October 2008).

Ramachandran, V. K. and M. Swaminathan. 2001. *Does Informal Credit Provide Security? Rural Banking Policy in India*. Geneva: International Labour Office.

———. 2005. *Financial Liberalisation and Rural Credit in India*. New Delhi: Tulika Books.

Rao, J. M. 1988. 'Agricultural Supply Response: A Survey', *Agricultural Economics*, 3(1): 1–22.

———. 1989. 'Getting Agricultural Prices Right', *Food Policy*, 14(1): 28–42.

Reserve Bank of India (RBI). 1991. 'Report of the Committee on Financial Systems', Mumbai: RBI.

Sathe, D. and S. Agarwal. 2004. 'Liberalisation of Pulses Sector: Production, Prices and Imports', *Economic and Political Weekly*, 39(30): 3391–97.

Schultz, T. W. 1964. *Transforming Traditional Agriculture*. New Haven: Yale University Press.

———. 1978. 'Constraints on Agricultural Production', in T. W. Schultz (ed.), *Distortions of Agricultural Incentives*, pp. 3–23. Bloomington: Indiana University Press.

Sekhar, C. S. C. 2004. 'Agricultural Price Volatility in International and Indian Markets', *Economic and Political Weekly*, 39(43): 4729–36.

———. 2008, 'Surge in World Wheat Prices: Learning from the Past', *Economic and Political Weekly*, 34(20): 12–14.

Sen, A. 1992. 'Economic Liberalisation and Agriculture in India', *Social Scientist*, 20(11): 4–19.

Sharma, P. K. 1991. 'Effective Incentives in Indian Agriculture: Role of Transport and Marketing Costs', Paper for World Bank research project RPO 675–50, 'Incentives and Resource Allocation in Indian Agriculture', World Bank, Policy Research Department, Washington, DC.

Shetty, S. L. 1990. 'Investment in Agriculture: Brief Review of Recent Trends', *Economic and Political Weekly*, 25(7–8): 389–98.

———. 1997. 'Financial Sector Reforms in India: An Evaluation, *Prajnan*, 25(3–4): 253–287.

Shonfield, A. 1960. *Attack on World Poverty*. New York: Random House.

Shukla, T. 1965. *Capital Formation in Indian Agriculture*. Bombay: Vora & Co.

Singh, M. 1995. 'Inaugural Address, Fifty-Fourth Annual Conference of the Indian Society of Agricultural Economics', Kolhapur, 26 November 1994, reprinted in *Indian Journal of Agricultural Economics*, 50(1): 1–6.

Smith, L. D. and A. M. Thomson. 1991. 'The Role of Public and Private Agents in Food and Agriculture Sectors of Developing Countries', Economic and Social Development Paper No. 105, FAO, Rome.

Srinivasan, T. N. 1993. 'The Uruguay Round and Asian Developing Economies', in Ian Goldin (ed.), *Economic Reform, Trade and Agricultural Development*, pp. 229–74. New York: St Martin's Press.

The Hindu Business Line. 2009. Delhi edition, *The Hindu*, 27 October.

Tyagi, D. S. 1993. 'Pricing of Fertilizers: Some Reflections on Subsidy Question', in Vidya Sagar (ed.), *Fertilizer Pricing Issues Related to Subsidies*, pp. 13–25. New Delhi: Classical Publishing Company.

Vaidyanathan, A. 2000. 'India's Agricultural Development Policy', *Economic and Political Weekly*, 35(20): 1735–41.

———. 2007. 'Water Policy in India: A Brief Overview', Occasional Paper No. 6, Centre for Public Policy, Indian Institute of Management, Bangalore.

van der Mensbrugghe, D. 2004. 'LINKAGE Technical Reference Document: Version 6.0', mimeo, World Bank, Washington, DC. http://siteresources. worldbank.org/INTPROSPECTS/Resources/334934-1100792545130/linkageTechNote.pdf (accessed 28 October 2013).

Velazco, J. 2001. 'Agricultural Production in Peru (1950–1995): Sources of Growth', in Lydia Zepeda (ed.), *Agricultural Investment and Productivity in Developing Countries*, Economic and Social Development Paper No. 148, FAO. http://www.fao.org/docrep/003/x9447e/x9447e00.htm (accessed 13 July 2007).

Vidya Sagar (ed.). 1993. *Fertilizer Pricing: Issues Related to Subsidies*. Jaipur: Classical Publishing House.

Vyas, V. S. 1994. 'Agricultural Policies for the Nineties: Issues and Approaches', *Economic and Political Weekly*, 29(26): A54–A63.

World Bank. 1997. 'The Indian Oilseed Complex: Capturing Market Opportunities', Report No. 15677-IN, Rural Development Sector Unit, South Asia Region, Washington, DC.

———. 1999a. '*India Foodgrain Marketing Policies: Reforming to Meet Food Security Needs*, Vol. I and II, Report No. 18329-IN, Rural Development Sector Unit, South Asia Region, Washington, DC.

———. 1999b. *World Development Indicators*. CD ROM.

About the Author

Ashutosh Kumar Tripathi is Assistant Professor at the Indian Institute of Management, Rohtak (IIM Rohtak). He was formerly based at the Institute of Rural Management Anand (IRMA) and has also worked in research organisations such as the Bankers Institute of Rural Development (BIRD) (an autonomous body of NABARD), Lucknow, Research and Information System for Developing Countries (RIS), New Delhi, Indian Council for Research on International Economic Relations (ICRIER), New Delhi, and Oxfam-India, in the areas of microfinance, agricultural development and trade policy. Tripathi has received many prestigious fellowships and awards including the Young Researcher Award Fellowship–2005 and the Junior Research Fellowship Award of the Indian Council of Agricultural Research (ICAR), New Delhi. The author holds a doctorate in Economics from Jawaharlal Nehru University, New Delhi. He was Fox International Fellow at Yale University, USA. Tripathi has also published several research articles in international and national journals on different aspects of agricultural development including price policy, trade and safeguard measures, along with other developmental aspects, such as food security and microfinance.

Index

ad valorem tariff 148, 209, 238
aggregate agricultural exports 157;
    subsidy policy effect 214–15,
    218, 221
aggregate agricultural output 58,
    113; decision-making and, 22;
    in developing countries 10–11;
    fertiliser consumption and, 36;
    public and private investment,
    effect of, 37–38; Terms of Trade
    (TOT) and, 36
aggregate capital formation 45–46
aggregate price effect 212, 214–15,
    217–18, 220–21
Agreement on Agriculture (AoA) 8
Agreement on the Application of
    Sanitary and Phytosanitary (SPS)
    Measures 8
Agricultural and Processed Food
    Products Export Development
    Authority (APEDA) 146, 152–54
agricultural credit 7, 49. *See also*
    credit support
agricultural growth: 1980s 9, 23, 25,
    29–32, 54, 225–26; cereals 25–26;
    estimates from regression analysis
    37–38; factors relating to, 32–38;
    fertiliser use 50, 53–54; GDP and,
    23–24; gross terms of trade 40–41,
    44; growth of agricultural output
    (last 25 years) 225–26; growth
    rates of yields 27–30; horticultural
    crops and fibres 25–26, 28; input–
    output price ratios 42–44; millets
    25–26; non-food grain crops 25;
    non-food grain crops, output of,

25–26; post-reform period 224–25,
    231. *See* post-reform period; post-
    WTO period 27, 229–30; price and
    non-price factors 38–54; price and
    non-price variables 39; proportion
    of area under food grains 30–32;
    pulses 25; slowdown in (decel-
    eration), 16–18, 22–23, 27, 29,
    47, 54, 57, 225–26; value of crop
    output 24–27
agricultural markets/marketing 2, 4,
    7, 20; competitive markets 5
agricultural policy. *See also* agri-
    cultural price policy; agricultural
    trade policy; critique of planning
    framework 4–5; domestic policies
    7–8; external trade policy 8; and
    growth performance, post-reform
    period (1990s), 9–18, 23; insula-
    tion of domestic markets 5; post-
    reform period 5–9; pre-reform era
    3–4; trade liberalisation measures
    8; World Trade Organization
    (WTO) agreements 8–9
agricultural price policy 100, 226–27;
    determination of procurement
    price 77–81; for food grains 58–69;
    mid-1960s 56; minimum support
    prices 63–67; non-price interven-
    tions 38–54, 226, 232; post-reform
    period 57; 1980s 56; short-term
    concern with demand manage-
    ment 58; trends in procurement
    prices 64–68
agricultural prices. *See also* agri-
    cultural price policy; Minimum

Support Prices (MSPs); analysis of variability in 121–38; decomposing variability in 208–23; divergence between domestic and world reference prices 198–206; excess supply, effect of, 3; inter-sectoral distribution of income and consumption, impact on, 1–2; long-run 103–13; procurement prices, determination of, 77–81; relationship between costs, prices realised and procurement prices 69–77; volatility 12–14, 114–38

Agricultural Prices Commission (APC) 60, 63

agricultural trade flow 142; and commodity composition 155–60; oilseed and edible oils 165–71; rice 163–65; sugar 171–74; wheat 161–63

agricultural trade intensity ratio 156

agricultural trade policy 19; commodity-specific external, 143–55; evolution of 141–43; and trade flow 155–74

agriculture, significance of 1; government influence in production and investment decisions 1; scale of operation 1

All-India Basic Plan 59

Approach Paper to the Eleventh Plan 22

area under agricultural crops 30–32

area under irrigation 47–48

ARIMA process 121, 123*n*6, 124, 133, 135, 234

artificial export surpluses 105

augmented Dicky–Fuller test 234

balance of payments (BoP) problems 8, 141–42

buffer stocking facilities 3, 62–64, 82, 85, 101

canalisation of exports and imports 8, 141, 144–46, 155

capital formation 44–46; aggregate 45–46; gross 37, 45, 47; gross fixed capital formation (GFCF) 37; public and private gross, 37

cereals 20; crop diversification 30–31; global production 104–5; growth pattern of, 25–26, 28; growth rates of yields 27

Cobb–Douglas production function 32, 35

coffee 13, 141*n*1, 142, 157

collective interest holder 2

Commission for Agricultural Costs and Prices (CACP) 62, 64, 68–70, 70*n*7, 79, 92, 180, 211

co-movement of procurement prices 79

competitive markets in India 5

competitiveness of commodities 12, 16, 19, 144, 178–80, 208–9, 238; comparison of price ratios of oilseeds with edible oils 192–94; divergence between domestic and world reference prices 198–206; groundnut seed and oil 185–87; rapeseed/mustard seed and oil 188–89; rice 164–65, 183–85; soybean seed and oil 170, 189–92; sugar 194–98; wheat 180–83

conditional standard deviation in prices 121, 123–24, 128, 132, 234–35; groundnut seed and oil 128–29, 288–89; mustard seed/oil 132, 290–91; rapeseed/rapeseed oil 132–33, 290–91; soybean

and soy oil 135, 292; sugar 137, 292–93; wheat 123, 287
consumer price index (CPI) 233
cost of cultivation (CoC) 58, 62, 70, 72
cost of production (CoP) 58, 64, 67, 70–74, 76–77, 79–81, 92, 95, 98, 227
cotton 13, 47, 157, 160, 175, 229
credit support 3–4, 7, 32, 38, 48–50, 224; direct 50; institutional 48–52; relative share of borrowing of cultivator households 49; size-wise distribution 50; trends 49
crop diversification 30–32, 54, 225; cereals 30–31; post-WTO period 32; pulses 30–31
crop output, level and growth rate of, 24–27. *See also* aggregate agricultural output

de-canalisation measures 7
decomposing variability in agricultural prices 208–23, 230–31, 236–38; edible oil price, changes in, 217–20; model used 209–10; Price Transmission Elasticity (PTE) 210; rice producer's price, changes in, 214–17; sugar 217–23; wheat producer's price, changes in, 211–14
developed countries 15, 104, 106, 111, 138, 142, 228; farm incomes 2; price support 2; tariffs 8; world market price structure and 11–13
Di-Ammonium Phosphate (DAP) 54
Dicky–Fuller test 234
direct price effect 210–16, 218–19, 221–22, 238
disaggregation of crop 24–25, 50

Dispute Settlement Body (DSB) of the WTO and India 8, 8n2
Doha Round negotiations 14
domestic food prices 16, 100–101, 228
domestic prices of essential commodities 4, 11–13, 85; gap between international prices and, 67, 95, 100, 119, 137; international prices influencing, 17, 162n16, 178; non-tariff barriers and, 148; timeframe for, 180; volatility 13, 16, 100, 119, 133, 140, 143–44
domestic price support policies 164, 173–75, 225, 227–28, 230–31. *See also* decomposing variability in agricultural prices; world reference prices, comparison with domestic prices

economic reforms, 1990s, 6
Essential Commodities Act (ECA): of 1955 7, 68; of 1965 152; of 1998 196; of 1999 153
export of selected agricultural commodities: 1991–2006 157–58; oil meal 157; oilseed cake meal (1979–2006) 169, 171; pulses 175; quantitative restrictions (QRs) on 7–8; reform period and growth in, 12, 21–22; rice (1980–81 to 2007–08) 146, 164–66; wheat (1980–81 to 2007–08) 162–63

farm income 2, 92–95, 101
fertiliser consumption/use 36, 50, 53–54; relative price shifts and, 53–54; in terms of per hectare gross cropped area 53
fisheries 24
food aid 3, 61

Food and Agricultural Organization (FAO) 104, 163, 168–73, 246
Food Corporation of India (FCI) 60, 64, 68–69, 82, 143, 145, 147, 164
food grain policy 61–62, 146–47; evolution of, 58–63; government intervention 4, 101, 113, 144, 162*n*15, 174, 231; procurement trends and determinants 82–92
Foodgrains Enquiry Committee, 1957 60
Foodgrains Prices Committee 60
food imports 3, 56, 61
food subsidies 2

GATT Article XXVIII 9
Generalised Autoregressive Conditional Heteroscedasticity (GARCH) approach 102–3, 121–38, 229, 234
government intervention in food grain market 4, 101, 113, 144, 162*n*15, 174, 231
Green Revolution 3, 224
gross capital formation 37, 45, 47
gross cultivated area (GCA), TE 1989–90 30
gross domestic product (GDP) 1, 7, 23–24, 35, 37, 42–44, 46–47, 155–57, 175, 226; agricultural trade and its share 156; of agriculture and allied sector 239; deflators 42; share of public capital formation 44–46
gross fixed capital formation (GFCF) 37
gross value of output (GVO) 92–96
groundnut seed and oil 262–68; conditional standard deviation in prices 128–29; inter-year variability of annual prices 118–19; price

volatility 124, 126–29; short-run volatility in prices 128; trade profitability/competitiveness 185–87; trend in nominal world price 107–9; world reference prices, comparison with domestic prices 202–3

Hindustan Vegetable Oils Corporation (HVOC) 148
horticultural crops and fibres 157, 160; in GCA 32; growth pattern of, 25–26, 28

import of selected agricultural commodities 100, 158–60, 178–79, 228; oilseed and edible oils 168; rice 164–66; volume of raw and refined sugar 172–73; wheat 162–63
Indian Sugar and General Industry Export Import Corporation (ISGIEIC) 153
Indian Sugar Exim Corporation Ltd. (ISEC) 153
input–output price ratios 40, 42–44
international market prices of agricultural commodities 102, 118, 120–21, 123–24, 128–29, 132–33, 135, 137–38, 228–29
inter-year variability of annual prices 113–14; in domestic market prices 139, 229; groundnut oil 119; groundnut seed 118–19; rape/mustard seeds 119; rapeseed/mustard oil 119; rice 118; soybean oil 120; soybean seed 119; sugar 120–21; wheat 114–18
inter-year volatility. *See* long-run volatility of price

investments in agricultural sector 6, 21, 32, 35–38, 44–47, 50, 63, 224, 226. *See also* capital formation
irrigation 46–47; coverage area 37, 47–48; expansion of 48; growth in area under 48; investment 36

Jha Committee 61–62

Levy Control Orders 64, 68
levy prices 64, 68–70, 90, 242
log linear regression equation 78–79; standard deviation of log (P_t/P_{t-1}) over a period 103
long-run agricultural prices, trends 103–13; oilseeds and edible oils 107–10; rapeseed/mustard oil 132; rice 105–7; soybean and soy oil 133; sugar 110–13; wheat 103–5
long-run volatility of price 121, 124, 132–33, 135, 235

macroeconomic policy 4–5, 15, 21–22, 224
market-based agricultural transformation 101
market-based reform project 5, 16–17, 19–20
market intervention policies 3; at government level 4, 101, 113, 144, 162n15, 174, 231
millets 9; growth pattern of, 25–26, 28
milling margins 68–70
Mineral and Metals Trading Corporation (MMTC) 162
Minimum Export Price (MEP) 8, 144
Minimum Support Prices (MSPs) 8, 62–69, 71, 74–75, 77, 95, 162,

227, 251–52, 256; prices realised and, 71, 74–76; in terms of rice equivalent and state levy prices in select states 69, 71; for wheat and paddy 65–67
Muriate of Potash (MOP) 54
mustard seed/oil 269–72; conditional standard deviation in prices 132–33; price volatility 129–33; quarantine restrictions 152; trade profitability/competitiveness 188–89; world reference prices, comparison with domestic prices 202

Narasimham Committee 7
National Dairy Development Board (NDDB) 148
neoclassical economics 2
net area sown 35–39. *See also* area under agricultural crops
nitrogen, phosphorous, and potassium (NPK) 36–37, 53–54
non-food grain crops 24, 27; growth pattern of, 25–26; output of 25–26, 28; yield growth rates 29–30

oilseed and edible oils 248. *See also* groundnut seed/oil; mustard seed/oil; rapeseed/rapeseed oil: agricultural trade flow 165–71; crop diversification 30–31; decomposing variability in prices 217–20; export of oilseed cake meal 169, 171; exports of oil meal 157; growth pattern, 1980s 25–26, 28; import policy for, 150–51; imports 160, 168; long-run price, trends 107–10; tariff regime 149, 152; trade policy regime for agriculture 147–52; world reference prices,

comparison with domestic prices 201–4;
Open General License (OGL) 148

peak marketing period 88
post-reform period 206, 224, 226, 231; agricultural growth 16, 18–19, 21–23, 25, 27–32, 54, 225; agricultural prices 63, 75; agriculture policy 5–9; agriculture's share in total GDP 23; capital formation 45; consumption of fertiliser 50–53; credit dispersal 51–52; edible oil production and consumption 167; expansion of irrigation 48; farm profitability/income 18; gross terms of trade 42; growth in imports and exports 155–65; strategies on subsidies 63; supportive mechanisms 9, 57; volatility analysis 140
price realised: and cost of production 76–77; to MSPs 71, 74–76
price stabilisation 59, 61, 101
Price Transmission Elasticity (PTE) 210, 212, 214–15, 218, 221, 237
private investment in agricultural sector 4, 21, 37–38, 44–46, 226
procurement price 7, 10, 43, 57–69, 77–81, 162n15, 181, 183, 211, 227, 231; determinants 88–92; government agencies, role of 85; regional concentration 86–88; relationship between costs, prices realised and, 69–77; trends 82–92
product price support 2
Project Equipment Corporation (PEC) 162
public distribution system (PDS) 62–63, 82, 148

public investment in agricultural sector 6, 37, 44–47, 63, 224
public procurement of rice 82
pulses 142, 157, 229–30; crop diversification 30–31; export 175; growth pattern of, 25–28; import 160

quantitative restrictions (QRs) 141, 144–45; on exports and imports 7–8
quota controls 13

rapeseed/rapeseed oil 269–72; conditional standard deviation in prices 132–33; long-run volatility of price 132; price volatility 129–33; quarantine restrictions 152; short-run volatility of price 132; trade profitability/competitiveness 188–89; trend in nominal world price 108–9; world reference prices, comparison with domestic prices 202, 204
reform period and agricultural policy 227–28. *See also* agricultural policy; agricultural price policy; post-reform period; export-led growth process 12, 21–22; implications 21–22; issues related to 9–17; pattern of growth 22–23; patterns of output and price interaction, 1990s 11; post-reform era 5–9, 16; pre-reform era 3–4, 15; procurement operations of the government 10; rationale for provision of input subsidies 9; slowdown in Indian agricultural growth 16; soybean and soy oil import policy 13; trade liberalisation policy 11–12, 15–17

Retention Pricing Scheme (RPS) 54
rice 245–47, 258–61; agricultural
trade flow 163–65; analysis of variability in market prices 123–25;
competitive advantages in exporting 200; cost and returns per
hectare 96–97; cost in production
71–74, 76; decomposing variability in prices 214–17; determination of procurement price
81; export and import volume
164–66; export restrictions 146;
global production 107; indices
of costs and prices 78; inter-year
variability of annual prices 118;
levy price and milling margins
68–70; long-run price, trends
105–7; market arrivals of, 87;
minimum support prices 63–67;
prices realised 71, 74–76; price
support operations 82; procurement of 82–92; production cost
80; production in Asia 106; profitability from cultivation in nominal
terms 92; quantities exported and
subsidy 147; trade policy regime
for agriculture 145–47; trade prof-
itability/competitiveness 183–85;
trend in nominal world price 106;
trends in procurement prices
64–67; USA production 106–7;
Wholesale Price Index (WPI) for
76–77; world reference prices,
comparison with domestic prices
200–201

Sen, S. R. 62
Sen Committee 62
soybean and soy oil 273–76; conditional standard deviation in
prices 135; imports 13; inter-year
variability of annual prices 120;
long-run volatility of price 133;
price volatility 133–35; short-run
volatility of price 133; trade prof-
itability/competitiveness 189–92;
trend in nominal world price
108–10; world reference prices,
comparison with domestic prices
202, 204
spices 13, 25, 27, 141n1, 142, 157
State Agricultural Produce Market
Act, 1966 7
State Trading Corporation (STC) 141,
146, 148, 162
subsidies 15, 42, 101, 104, 226; budgetary 144, 215; counter-cyclical
106, 113; critique of 5; export
3, 19, 144–45, 147, 154, 162,
164, 171, 173, 175, 178, 183–84,
198–201, 206, 211–12, 214, 217,
223, 230–31, 238; food 2; import
13; on input 5–7, 9–10, 57, 63,
95, 224, 227; by OECD countries
164; strategies, post-reform period
6, 63
sugar/sugarcane 249–50, 277–86;
agricultural trade flow 171–74;
conditional standard deviation in
prices 137; crop diversification
30–31; decomposing variability
in prices 217–23; de facto import
restriction 153; import volume of
raw and refined sugar 172–73;
inter-year variability of annual
prices 120–21; long-run price,
trends 110–13; long-run volatility of price 135; price volatility
135–38; short-run volatility of
price 135–38; tariffs and QR status
154; trade policy regime for agriculture 152–55; trade profitability/

competitiveness 194–98; world reference prices, comparison with domestic prices 203–5

tea 13, 141n1, 142, 157
Technology Mission for Oilseeds, 1986 25
Terms of Trade (TOT) 21–22, 37, 240–41; between agricultural and non-agricultural sectors 40–41; analytical basis of 22; estimates from regression analysis 37; gross 35–36, 40–41, 44; import substitution and 22
tobacco 141n1, 157, 175, 229
trade liberalisation in agricultural commodities 8, 11–12, 15–17, 44, 100, 145–47; commodity-specific external 143–55; of non-basmati rice in mid-1990s 157; and trade flow 155–74
trade policy regime for agriculture: channelling of trade 142; evolution 141–43; export–import policy 142–43; oilseeds and edible oils 147–52; rice 145–47; sugar 152–55; wheat 143–45; WTO Uruguay Round Agreements 142
trade profitability/competitiveness 12, 16, 19, 144, 178–80, 208–9, 230, 238; data sources and cost adjustments 180; groundnut seed and oil 185–87; measuring 178–80; movement of world and domestic agriculture commodity prices 177–78; mustard seed/oil 188–89; price ratio for oilseeds v/s edible oils 192–94; rapeseed/ rapeseed oil 188–89; reference prices, calculating, 179–80; rice 183–85; soybean and soy oil 189–92; sugar/sugarcane 194–98; wheat 180–83
trans-log production function 32

Urea 54
Uruguay Round Agreement on Agriculture (URAA) 8, 12–13, 227
US Public Law-480 (PL-480) 60, 61n4

vanilla crop 14n5
volatility of agricultural prices 12–14, 100–102, 228–29; connotations variability and uncertainty 102n1; intra-year variability 114; long-run volatility 121; methodology for measuring 102–3, 233–35; patterns 114–21; short-run volatility 121, 123

wheat 243–44; agricultural trade flow 161–63; analysis of variability in market prices 121–23; calculation of weighted reference price for 253–54; conditional standard deviation in prices 123; cost and returns per hectare 93–94; cost in production 71–74, 76; decomposing variability in prices 211–14; determination of procurement price 81; export and import volume 162–63; indices of costs and prices 78; intra-year variability in prices 114–18; long-run price, trends 103–5; market arrivals of, 87; minimum support prices 63–67; prices realised of, 71, 74–75, 77; price support operations 82; procurement of 82–92; production cost 80; profitability from cultivation in nominal terms

92; trade policy regime for agriculture 143–45; trade profitability/competitiveness 180–83; trends in procurement prices 64–67; world reference prices, comparison with domestic prices 199–200; zero customs duty on, 144–45

Wholesale Price Index (WPI) 76–77

world grain stocks 104–5

world reference prices, comparison with domestic prices 182–95, 198–206, 251–52, 256–86

World Trade Organization (WTO) agreements 8

yield growth rate 27–30, 95, 99, 227; post-WTO period 29; TE 1980–81 to TE 1989–90 27–29; TE 1990–91 to TE 1996–97 27–29

For Product Safety Concerns and Information please contact our EU
representative GPSR@taylorandfrancis.com
Taylor & Francis Verlag GmbH, Kaufingerstraße 24, 80331 München, Germany